The Ombudsma

The Ombudsman Handbook

Designing and Managing an Effective Problem-Solving Program

JAMES T. ZIEGENFUSS, JR., *and*
PATRICIA O'ROURKE

McFarland & Company, Inc., Publishers
Jefferson, North Carolina, and London

LIBRARY OF CONGRESS CATALOGUING-IN-PUBLICATION DATA

Ziegenfuss, James T.
    The ombudsman handbook : designing and managing an
effective problem-solving program / James T. Ziegenfuss, Jr.,
and Patricia O'Rourke.
        p.   cm.
    Includes bibliographical references and index.

    ISBN 978-0-7864-4896-8
    softcover : 50# alkaline paper

    1. Personnel management.   2. Problem solving —
Case studies.   3. Ombudspersons.   I. O'Rourke, Patricia,
1944–   II. Title.
    HF5549.Z54   2011
    658.3'15 — dc22   2010043952

British Library cataloguing data are available

Front cover image ©2011 Shutterstock.

Manufactured in the United States of America

*McFarland & Company, Inc., Publishers
    Box 611, Jefferson, North Carolina 28640
    www.mcfarlandpub.com*

Table of Contents

Acknowledgments

I HAVE BEEN THINKING about organizational problem solving for decades. Graduate training in psychology and management further underscored this perspective. This notion of communications and listening was deepened in my training in the doctoral program at the Wharton School of the University of Pennsylvania. My advisors, Eric Trist and Peter Davis, would see this as I do, as a social and a technical system intervention. Russell Ackoff has regarded ombudsmen as an innovative management communication tool and has advocated their use in major private corporations. At Pennsylvania State University, my late colleague Rupert Chisholm was also an advocate of this thinking for private corporations. With training in public administration my first real involvement was in the design of public programs.

I am especially indebted to two colleagues, Jan Charette and Monique Guenin, formerly with the Pennsylvania Department of Public Welfare's Office of Client Rights. The three of us worked hard to design and develop a health care ombudsman program for twelve hospitals over a six-year period. The effort has been most rewarding. During this time, we addressed all of the design and development processes in the book. The start-up was demanding, but certainly less so than the problem-solving client work.

I have balanced this public sector experience with private sector studies. In my early research I came to know Mary Rowe, ombudsman at MIT and co-founder of the Corporate Ombudsman Association. I have great admiration for her work and very much appreciate her collaboration and support in ombudsman research. I also thank the Corporate Ombudsman Association for its research support some years ago. I learned much from visits to corporate ombudsmen: Beth Lewis, Clair Balfour, Richard Daignault, Jeanne Scott, Tony Perneski, Donna Simpson, and Kathleen Zicat.

In recent years I have been focused on strategy and quality improvement/customer service. I see the ombudsman as one tool for executing a strategy of close employee and customer contact. Ombudsmen are also one means for identifying problems and for addressing conflict between organizations and their employees and customers.

Over the years many graduate students have worked on pieces of this research, for which I am grateful. At Penn State University, Glenn McGuigan, research librarian, has contributed reference searching and Steve Dahm helped in manuscript preparation. I have most enjoyed continuing to work with Patricia O'Rourke, one of the first ombudsmen I met and recognized as an outstanding expert in this field. The benefits to individuals and to their organizations make our investment in design and problem-solving work well worth the effort.—James T. Ziegenfuss, Jr.

PEOPLE OFTEN ASK ME, "Where did you learn to be an ombudsman and do you have to have a degree in it?" Like many ombudsmen, I came to the work as a generalist. In my early career I worked in the public relations and communications departments of large organizations, and they required that I communicate with people at all organizational levels — from senior vice presidents to sales staff, technical staff and unionized workers, as well as customers. I began to understand how the interrelated structures of all organizations could become undone if people were unable to understand one another and communicate effectively. After this early experience in the transport, chemical and insurance industries, I moved into community-based health and social services and then into a large university teaching hospital where I have worked as an ombudsman (under various titles) for many years. My earlier experience served me well as I worked with professionals and managers who wanted to communicate effectively with patients and helped patients and families obtain the information and services they needed from doctors and other clinical staff. I feel privileged that so many had confidence in my skills. An ombudsman cannot work alone but relies on the expertise of others so I am particularly grateful for the many dedicated doctors, nurses, managers, and technical and support staff who gave hours of their time to ensure that dissatisfied patients received satisfactory and compassionate answers to their questions, complaints and needs.

Work as an ombudsman led to a focus on the protection of patients as research subjects and to membership of many research ethics committees. Truth telling in medicine was the focus of my master's research followed by a Ph.D. on the history and ethical implications of alternative medical systems. For several years, I worked every spring with a team presenting ethics courses to medical students. A diploma in human relations enhanced skills so necessary to ombudsman work. Over the past ten years I have taught courses in ethics to education students and in religion and alternative healing to undergraduates from many university departments. My students have broadened my understanding of the needs of patients, often unarticulated in the clinical setting.

I particularly want to thank my colleagues, whose legal, nursing and medical training I value and who have been a constant source of encouragement and support: Lynne Casgrain, complaints and quality commissioner for all the hospitals of the McGill University Health Centre, ombuds colleagues, Danièle Thibodeau and Patricia Boyer, ombuds colleagues, and Dr. Jean E. Morin, MD, medical examiner responsible for complaints about medical acts. In addition, I am grateful for the helpful advice and editing skills of Dr. Mary Mooney, Ph.D., McGill Sports Medicine Clinic, the library sleuthing of Giovanna Badia of the Medical Library of the Royal Victoria Hospital of the MUHC and the support and encouragement of Suzanne Belson, longtime ombudsperson at Concordia University, Montreal, and a senior investigator at the Department of National Defence (Canada). Working with James Ziegenfuss has been an enjoyable and intellectually stimulating experience, and his extensive knowledge of the importance of ombudsmen to organizations has inspired me over the years. We both strongly believe that every organization can benefit from ombudsmen and hope that this book will serve as a manual for those establishing the position.— Patricia O'Rourke

Preface

Who are the organization's problem solvers and how do they work? This book considers the purposes, activities, and benefits of ombudsmen as problem solvers.

Ombudsmen are important because of their potential impact on three key areas in companies and other institutions: quality of working life, productivity, and organizational development. They could be said to be an organizational development tool, since they contribute to the quality of working life and simultaneously provide a means for removing barriers to productivity. The existence of troubleshooting ombudsmen also suggests that management understands that all organizations have problems and that some attempt must be made to assist members in resolving them. In this respect, organizations with ombudsmen programs have been on the cutting edge of innovative management strategies for some years.

Some decades ago organizations began to hire people to deal with customer complaints. Governments, hospitals, educational institutions, large corporations, banks, and other business establishments set up departments to address complaints from clients, customers, employees and members of the public. Individuals have grown accustomed to internal grievance mechanisms. Although some managers may feel that the recent recession, like the depression of the '30s, will lead clients and employees to "put up and shut up," the people struggling in the wake of today's economic crash grew up with a strong belief that governments, universities, banks, schools and hospitals are there to serve them. They are unlikely to resign themselves to indifferent teaching, inadequate management, or poor service.

Handling complaints is good public relations but it is not a public relations exercise. It might once have been easy to mollify the customer or client by giving her something extra, such as complimentary airline tickets, a free hotel room or a month's free cable service. Such exercises were presumptuous.

They expected the customer to use the airline, stay in the hotel or continue to consume the service that made her so unhappy. Now, however, customers receiving cheap "gifts" feel that they are being "bought" and that problems are being papered over. Twenty years ago, the World Wide Web was in its infancy. With the Web, dissatisfied customers or employees can trash a company's reputation by writing a series of inflammatory blogs, satirizing the service on a social networking site, posting videos of employee malfeasance on YouTube. Some individuals have designed websites with one goal: to help customers quickly find a site to express their anger and disappointment. A Canadian site, Penciltrick, makes it easy for people to complain about any institution or service. Anyone can comment but perusal of the comments sections leaves the impression that few businesses actually read these sites. Only a handful reached out to the embittered writers with an offer of help.

This is one of the challenges of the wired world. An irate patient told one of the authors: "just read my blog." The blog named and shamed the hospital and service. Only because the author found the ombudsman on the hospital website was she able to get an answer and a promise that the ombudsman would launch an investigation into a situation, now resolved. Sometimes, even complaining is not enough and it takes widespread mockery to make changes. The now famous YouTube song "United Breaks Guitars" was written by musician Dave Carroll after United Airlines did not respond to his claim for the $3,500 Taylor guitar that the airline damaged. Satire is an effective way to complain but not everyone has the talent, or persistence.

Other challenges include a growing empowerment of citizens to demand their rights, increasing cultural diversity and a concomitant empowerment. Cultural groups, rightly, refuse to accept prejudicial behavior, no matter how subtle, and are willing to act on perceived infringements of the rights they share with their fellow citizens. Other changes over the past decades include an awareness of the destructive nature of workplace or classroom bullying and harassment.

Over the past 25 years, ombudsmen have flourished in a diversity of organizations. They go by many titles (patient advocate, complaints officer, customer satisfaction manager) but they all function in similar ways: they receive and investigate complaints from clients or employees or both, resolve them and make recommendations. Never has it been more important for private and public organizations to be instantly responsive to complaints.

An organization that welcomes complaints signals openness to customer-driven and employee-initiated change, honors public promises of transparency and helps organizations avoid litigation and negative media coverage. In more and more organizations ombudsmen are now handling complaints from customers and employees. Our book *Organizational Troubleshooters* (McFarland, 1988) ended with a confident call for expansion of ombudsman programs. This has indeed happened. Over the past 20 years, many more organizations have employed ombudsmen. Even the numbers of government ombudsmen have grown. They were used in 21 countries in 1983, and now total five times that number in 2004 (International Ombudsman Institute website). Thousands of ombudsmen work in American hospitals and long-term care facilities.

The past 20 years have seen an enormous expansion in the numbers of ombudsman offices worldwide. John McMillan, Commonwealth Ombudsman of Australia, noted at least 30 new proposals for ombudsman offices over a few years (McMillan, 2008, 2 of 8). Official figures, based on membership in ombudsman associations, likely represent only a small percentage of the total number of ombudsmen worldwide. Based on membership and other lists for the major associations in the United States and Canada, at least 2,000 to 3,000 ombudsmen work in the public and private sectors in those two countries alone. These ombudsmen are interacting with multiple departments and units throughout their host organizations and widely demonstrating the use of the ombudsman concept.

This book addresses the needs of executives and managers, practitioners, professors and students of human resources, marketing and other business and public administration programs. It is designed to help those establishing ombudsman programs as well as practicing and aspiring ombudsmen.

We should begin with a word on terminology. We have used the classical term "ombudsman" or "ombudsmen" throughout the book, aware that many individuals and organizations, objecting to the gender bias, refer to "ombuds" offices. In fact, the English name of the Forum of Canadian Ombudsmen (Forum Canadien des Ombudsmans) is not a grammatical error but the result of a decision to preserve the original Swedish usage.

The book is designed to extend and integrate professional understanding of problem solving ombudsmen. It describes how client and employee ombudsmen, in government, education, health care and business, contribute to their organizations by helping to boost productivity, prevent lawsuits and avoid bad publicity. The book includes cases and methods of resolution, and offers guidelines for implementing an ombudsman program.

The book is designed for:

- Managers and executives, especially human resource leaders.
- University professors and students in business and public administration programs especially management, human resources, and marketing.
- Practicing or aspiring ombudsmen.

The disciplines represented include a diversity of management fields from public and private sectors including human resources management, government, education, health care, and the military.

We hope that this book will help the reader to learn how to improve customer service and employee relations programs, understand the organizational value of complaint systems and know how to design effective ombudsman programs.

The number of universities and colleges in North America discussing ombudsmen concepts in courses in human resources, marketing, public relations and other business or health care management programs are significant. Human resource, risk management, quality departments and public relations services in every corporation, healthcare, education or government office are all potential readers.

The book is designed to take the reader from the need for ombudsmen through to an understanding of their usefulness to an organization. We include fictional case histories and information on how to design, establish and maintain an effective ombudsman program. We are greatly committed to this activity, have been involved in its development for decades, and believe that ombudsmen contribute simultaneously to improving both organizational productivity and the quality of organizational life for employees and customers.

Chapter 1

Human Resources Problems and the Need for Ombudsmen

Are there any organizations without employee or customer problems? Every organization, large or small, public or private, experiences problems between management and employees. And in real life, consumers of the organization's goods and services complain about them. Often the problems entail questions of individual interest versus organizational interest, including whether there is equity in treatment. Is an employee's layoff fair or is it not? Does the corporation respond to customer complaints? Can a patient get detailed information about the bill? Can she challenge the doctor's treatment plan? These stories should sound familiar:

> COLLEAGUE 1: I just paid $525 for a lawn mower. I used it six times, and the engine blew up. When I called to complain, no one would listen. They said to stick it in my car and drive it in myself if I wanted it fixed. It doesn't even fit and I won't do it anyway.
>
> COLLEAGUE 2: You think that's bad. Boy, did I get bad news in one hell of a way. My division manager said I was being transferred to St. Louis in three weeks. He said no discussion and walked out. I don't even know what my new status will be.

There is a long history of attempts to solve "people problems" which are present in all organizations. During the early years of our industrial and management history, problem resolution was generally in favor of the organization.

"Let the buyer beware" was the message for the customer. Most employees were glad to have jobs. They were not inclined to make their complaints public. With the emergence of unions, formalized processes to address complaints were developed. These internal grievance mechanisms were thought to increase fairness and to improve conflict resolution. And they did!

In recent years, however, the approach to problem solving has increasingly involved the courts — for both employees and consumers. It is hardly news that litigation in almost every area of life has risen dramatically, and litigation in employee and consumer relations in particular has experienced a dramatic increase. Labor relations and labor conflict law practice is certainly a growth industry, but one with very high human and financial costs. This is encouraging a search for alternative mechanisms for dispute resolution. Public and private organizations are simply finding that it is far too expensive to have in-house and private firm attorneys solve organization/employee and organization/consumer problems.

Simultaneously, consumers and employees are discovering that using the courts is not a quick and inexpensive path to complaint resolution. Cases often take several years or more to resolve and involve thousands of dollars in expenses. This does not begin to account for human time and energy diverted from other tasks and interests (Binham, 2005).

This litigation situation raises an obvious question: If we do not use the courts to solve problems, just who and what can we use? One of the most exciting developments in this area has been the appearance and growing acceptance of ombudsmen, or employee and customer relations representatives, over the past 20 or so years. Complaints handlers, either formally or informally defined, exist in many organizations. They have various titles: manager of employee relations, patient relations representative, student relations coordinator, customer representative, executive assistant. Some are officially appointed ombudsmen; others do the job under another title.

The formal notion of ombudsman has a long history, first appearing in Swedish government circles in 1809. Ombudsmen have gained wide acceptance in public administration in this century but have been neglected by the private sector with only brief mention of their potential usefulness appearing in the 1960s (Silver, 1967). Corporate troubleshooters are pervasive but are not identified by any particular title and are only lightly visible in the private sector literature under the title of ombudsman. The use of ombudsmen in organizations generally, and especially in private sector organizations, is a fairly recent development, particularly when the job is labeled and identified as a formal position (Rowe, 1987; Robbins and Deane, 1986; Ziegenfuss and O'Rourke, 1995; Ziegenfuss, 1995, 1998, 1999, 2007). This is underscored by the fact that there are few publications on corporate ombudsmen; the literature in professional business journals only began to emerge in the 1980s . Even so, by now there are many formal ombudsmen at work in the three service fields of government, health, and education. Together, these formally recognized ombudsmen are a large group, though they constitute only a small part of all problem solvers at work in organizations across the country.

The problem is how to develop greater awareness of the concept of problem solving ombudsman work, which is part of the reason we have written this book. There are barriers to this awareness. For example, both public and private organizations are very concerned about their image. They are wary about letting the public hear of their organizational problems. This means that corporations that have begun to use troubleshooting ombudsmen may be reluctant to talk about it, even when they have found them to be very effective. This reticence and fear is hampering the diffusion of an innovative, exciting concept. At this point ombudsman efforts are recognized as one of the most productive dispute resolution mechanisms. Dispute resolution programs and methods are increasingly needed for a wide range of reasons both internal and external to nonprofits, government agencies and corporations (Colvin, 2004; Brewer, 2007; Dyer, 2009; Gilad, 2009). That is, there are external pressures *pushing* as well as internal pressures *pulling* organizations toward ombudsman program development. A review of some illustrative pressures will demonstrate the intensity of this push and pull.

External Pressures — The Push from Without

Organizations are increasingly being pressured to confront and resolve problems that have only in part been created within the boundaries of the organization. Both public and private organizations exist in a complex organizational environment that includes social, political, and economic influences. A review of some eight environmental areas will begin to map the diversity and depth of this push toward the establishment of ombudsman programs. These eight external pressure areas are law, economics, culture, technology, education, politics, sociology, and demography (Kast and Rosenzweig, 1985; Ziegenfuss, 2002, 2007).

A first area of concern for private employers and increasingly for public ones is the threat and the actuality of increased *litigation* from employees. The movement for employees' rights has been gaining greater strength for many years. Clearly the time when corporations could have it entirely their own way is past. The costs of litigation over wrongful termination, sexual harassment, racial discrimination, and frivolous management actions are higher each year. This employee activism is a good example of the current concern for the costs of litigation and the changing nature of the organizational response to employee demands.

A second area that frequently leads to conflict with employees is *economic* pressure. Cost control has been a particularly high priority, as American corporations have been streamlined to compete successfully with foreign companies in the midst of a declining economy. Disputes over layoffs, plant closings and relocations, the virtual collapse of the automotive industry, the sub-prime mortgage crisis, and the subsequent economic turmoil, as well as general concern for productivity have all laid the groundwork for significant conflict between labor and management. Add to this legislation and self-imposed controls prompted by concerns about climate change. Public sector organizations have also been experiencing similar conflict, in some cases for the first time. Economic pressure due to governmental budget cutbacks and general retrenchment is real and significant. This economic pressure will continue to be present, and as long as it exists, mechanisms for solving organizational conflict will need to be developed.

The third external pressure area is *culture,* the goals, values, and other characteristics of the society in which the organizations exist. We have been seeing a general tendency toward assertiveness, toward democratization in the workplace, and toward demands for participation in management and organizational decision-making. The expectations of the work force are increasing rapidly. Current commentators identify changes that have taken place in the values of the people in the labor pool from which the work force is drawn (e.g., a younger generation with an interest in work/family life balance, an entitled youth culture of people with high expectations of advancement and rewards, and the move towards flex-time and tele-commuting). These changes are setting up conflicts between the newer assertiveness and participative values of the work force on the one hand and the top-down, command and control manner in which companies have traditionally been organized and managed on the other.

A fourth external pressure area is *technology.* It is news to no one that technological development is proceeding at a rapid pace in practically every field. This has led to both real and hypothesized nightmares about work dislocation and replacement by automation. Workers often experience conflict over the perceived advantages of the new technology and the threat of job change. Workers feel pressured by never ending technological developments. The outsourcing of many goods and services, with help desks located as far away as Bangladesh, and the digital revolution, which has affected the newspaper, publishing, film camera and video rental industries, only add to the realization that all society faces major social and economic change.

A fifth major external pressure that is providing momentum for troubleshooter programs is *education.* The work force in nearly all industries is better educated, and has a different set of interests and values than in earlier years. Employees are able to identify their own needs and interests and are increasingly demanding that they be met. Additionally, an educated work force means fewer employees who are willing to "do it the organization's way" without some opportunity to create new and innovative solutions. In short, higher levels of education lead to conflict between a paternalistic industrial or government culture and a work force that is sophisticated, assertive, and ready to use a variety of skills and abilities.

Sixth, with regard to *politics,* federal, state, and local government is increasingly looking to corporations to provide equity, both in their dealings with employees and as members of the community. That is, government is putting more and more pressure on companies to manage their labor/management relations fairly. The goal is to ensure that both private corporations and government agencies deal responsibly and honestly with employees. For this reason government is increasingly willing to get involved in labor/management disputes and to actively assist in resolving conflicts. A solution would be for corporations to create their own conflict resolution mechanisms that would obviate the necessity for this interference.

There are also *sociological* changes — changes in the way the work force and individual segments of it are organized — that create pressure for ombudsman programs. For example, employees are increasingly refusing to relocate as quickly as corporations would like them to. Additionally, there is family/corporation conflict as a result of two-wage earner families attempting to balance the responsibilities of job and home and quality of life. There are also changing patterns of career development. Recent university graduates have higher expectations of advancement than did their parents. People who continue to work beyond age sixty-five are seen by the young as blocking their career advancement and conflict between older and younger employees may become more pronounced. Women increasingly occupy the professions (law, medicine) and the senior ranks of corporations. Increased numbers give them the power to confront the "old boy network" that has restricted their advancement in the past. These and other sociological shifts are creating more conflicts between workers and employers. These conflicts can either be resolved by mechanisms within the organization, or they will be made public in the courts.

Finally, there are *demographic* changes that lay the groundwork for increasing stress and conflict in organizations. The most obvious of these is the aging of the work force. As more and more people arrive at age sixty-five able and willing to continue working, how will retirement issues be dealt with and how will job performance issues be managed in a way that is fair from the standpoint of both individual and company? Many North American and Western European countries face a steadily declining birth rate and need highly skilled older workers to stay on the job. How can this be managed? Progressive retirement? Part-time or flex-time management and professional jobs? Job sharing? Restructured government and private pension plans and health benefits? So far, these problems have not been handled very effectively.

There are also concerns about the relocation of the work force. For example, if the labor pool declines or if a company desires another location, how can worker/organization relations be maintained? What happens when corporate functions are outsourced to countries like China, India and Bangladesh? And what if the complaint function itself is assigned to an offshore worker?

On a more fundamental level, we might point to developments that cut across all the categories mentioned above. For example, the many contextual changes in the greater work environment are contributors to the ferment that produces both complaints and an external push for conflict resolution. Here are some illustrative trends affecting the depth and pace of change in society through recent decades. The list is a lesson in context, the world "out there" to which managers frequently do not relate. These trends are seen as potential pressures for ombudsman programs. As a world society we are moving:

1. From an industrial society to a services and information dominated society in place of agricultural/manufacturing.

2. To socio-technical thinking, balancing social/psychological needs with the technological imperative.

3. From a national interest and an inward focus to a global focus in a world connected economy.

4. From short term attention to profits and crises to long term proactive management, e.g., environment and climate.

5. From hierarchy and control to decentralization and mass customization.

6. From protective governments to self-help and self survival.

7. To open communication and free flowing information networks.

8. From top down directives to flatter organizations closely networked.

9. From European attention to a focus on Asia, especially China and India.

10. To international strife driven by terrorism and uneven development.

How do these trends lead to conflict and a need for ombudsmen? In general, the trends reflect increasing change within organizations as well as in society as a whole. We are moving from an industrial culture to an information-dominated one. At the same time, we are shifting from a technological imperative to more humanized technology that attends to social needs. We are facing the dislocation and competition of a world economy, whereas we had only a national economy in the past. We are forcing people to think about long-term as opposed to short-term commitments, and we are increasingly moving toward decentralization in an attempt to recognize individual autonomy and freedom for personal development. We are learning that governmental and institutional help will not solve everything, and that we must solve our own problems; we are also moving from representative democracy to individual involvement at all levels aided by technology. Information flow hierarchies are no longer as important as they were, since we are increasingly interested in networking. Our orientation is shifting from north to south, and we are looking for multiple options on practically everything. And we expect instant information and answers to problems because knowledge (either online news or information) is only a keystroke or thumbstroke away. We want our complaints settled instantly, too.

This tremendous upheaval in society at large exerts considerable pressure on corporations and public agencies to adapt. In the process of adaptation, conflicts between organizations and employees arise on a continual basis. This creates a tremendous need for troubleshooter programs that facilitate individual and organization-wide change.

Internal Pressures: The Pull from Within

Organizations can and must respond to external pressures for change and development. But rarely are these pressures entirely external. The emerging interest in the redesign of public and private organizations means that there are significant internal pressures for change as well. They are derived from beliefs about the nature of organizations themselves as well as from more specific assumptions about the characteristics of public and private organizations.

Do employees complain? Do consumers complain? The answer is obviously yes to both questions. Employee complaints are commonplace in all organizations, both public and private. That fact is a well-known observation about the nature of the organizational world! Some employees change jobs because of an inability to tolerate general corporate or specific management conditions, only to find that similar problems exist in the new organization. The search for a complaint-free organization is futile one. The real question is, how does your organization handle complaints? Are they ignored, or are they acknowledged and responded to? The second alternative, acknowledgment and resolution by the ombudsman, is the result of a *pull from within* organizations, a pull that involves a convergence of different trends.

First, it is rapidly becoming known that "good" organizations (that is, those with high productivity *and* positive working conditions) devote a large amount of time and energy to listening to their employees and customers. Productive service organizations like hospitals and highly regarded corporations such as IBM use listening as a way to learn about organizational successes *and* failures — what they are doing well and what needs to be improved. Without actual data, they feel they are not well enough informed to take appropriate actions. The move toward total quality management in the last two decades has underscored this emphasis on customers.

Second, part of this rationale for listening is the realization that it has payoffs for the bottom line. Quite simply, organizations want to do more of what they do well and eliminate what they are not doing well, since the latter results in lost time, energy, and money, regardless of whether they are manufacturing toasters or are providing patient care. In short, if management listens well, an organization will perform better.

Third, listening is a part of a more general movement toward participative management. This management approach is based on the belief that the more employees participate, the stronger the organization will be. With greater participation, management is better able to respond to the complexity of the world and to the demands of the employees, customers, and suppliers who have a stake in the organization. Complaining is one way that these individuals can participate. Management responses tell them whether their participation is effective in generating action — in other words, whether their views and needs "count for anything."

The participative movement is also derived in part from a more negative trend. The fourth trend is the continuing increase in litigation by employees. This was cited as an external pressure, but it is reiterated here as internally derived as well. Both private corporations and public agencies are increasingly being sued for a wide variety of reasons ranging from unjust firing to discrimination. In many cases, these are unresolved complaints, many of which could have been addressed without the use of the courts (for example, through the redesign of internal dispute resolution policies and procedures). Because organizations are often not responsive or at least do not seem to be responsive, both customers and employees sue. Actual litigation, the threat of litigation, and a desire for prevention therefore constitute a powerful "internal pull."

Litigation and media exposure is also part of a fifth and larger trend, the employee rights movement. Labor unions protect the constitutional rights of workers in large organizations. In smaller and non union organizations there are wide variations with regard to privacy, dissent, and due process in work-related issues. Considerations relating to the quality of working life dictate that the protection of constitutional rights is essential to worker satisfaction. Employees are increasingly demanding fair treatment. Complaints are often just the start of this process, which ends in litigation or denunciation to the media or government rights commissions when the complaints are ignored.

So far, the trends cited have been employee-oriented. But customers complain as well. The sixth trend is the renewed attention to customer relations. A somewhat novel idea — that customers *should* complain and that the organization *should* listen — is now recognized as critical to productivity and to the maintenance of quality. This is because customer complaints increase productivity by bringing problems to light that are indicators of quality gaps. In other words, they enhance quality by flagging deficient goods and services for attention by management and technical personnel.

The seventh trend involves the development and testing of alternative dispute resolution methods. Alternatives to the human and financial costs of litigation (including lowered profits and poor quality of working life) are in great demand. The problems are not new ones, but to a great extent the solutions are still not apparent. Some newer methods — town hall meetings, online forums, focus groups — however, are recognized for their successes. This book is of course devoted to highlighting one response to this search for faster and more effective means of dispute resolution.

The eighth trend that is part of the internal pull toward troubleshooter programs is the desire to create open communication. Many of those who find fault with management focus on communication problems as a key source of difficulty in troubled organizations. Therefore, an interest in developing more open communication between employees and management is leading the list of development tasks for contemporary managers. A completely open communication system is one that includes opportunities for employees and customers to complain freely and responsibly about difficulties in the workplace or with the goods and services provided by the company. An ombudsman is one more means by which employees and consumers can exercise this communication function. Some critics suggest that ombudsmen are actually interfering with the process of communication by allowing employees or customers to circumvent division directors or vice presidents. However, this reflects views about the way the world should be, not how it actually is! We all know of managers who are difficult to talk to. The fact that an alternative communication channel exists is a positive force in a complex organization and can prevent unhappy employees from blowing the whistle publicly.

The ninth trend is a desire to reduce turnover, for example, in many hi-tech industries and in specific job classes where turnover is high, such as in nursing positions in hospitals. As an illustration, in several major Fortune 500 companies, ombudsmen consider one of their most significant benefits to be the reduction of turnover among highly paid scientists and technical personnel. The problem is, of course, that employees with complaints usually make a few attempts to have them addressed, and when this does not happen, they begin to look for other jobs.

The tenth trend is somewhat philosophical, and involves efforts to create justice and equity within organizations (Kirkham, 2008). Does a sense of fairness prevail? Has the corporation or public agency done all it can to promote justice among both employees and consumers? Ethical problems and the lack of fair treatment at the hands of managers and employees have caused much grief to workers and customers alike. As we will see, ombudsman programs are one of the more important methods by which justice and fairness can be promoted within organizations.

The eleventh trend is an overall interest in humanizing the organization. We have been trying to humanize modern technology, by reducing its more impersonal or destructive aspects. The continuing development of technology is not rejected; it is only tempered by a concern for social and psychological needs. One way to do this is to create positions with the responsibility to address human concerns — both the actual wrongs experienced by workers and consumers and the perceived ones (which are frequently as damaging).

The twelfth trend is an interest in developing a corporate culture that represents values and goals that are attractive to both managers and employees. These values and goals include an emphasis on openness and participation and on a problem-solving approach ·that says that the complaints of all employees and customers are valued, whether the setting is a university, a major corporation, a hospital, or a prison. The presence of an ombudsman is both a symbolic and an actual reflection of a cultural value of openness and a willingness to listen. Not only is this is a very powerful symbol but a potent reality that exerts its influence as more recognition is given to the contribution of distinct organizational cultures.

The final trend that contributes to an internal pull is the success of ombudsman programs in those organizations that have tried them. Typically, these programs have initially met with some resistance; once underway, though, they tend to be highly valued by managers and employees as well as by customers. Moreover, the solution of problem after problem by expert troubleshooters is a strong recommendation for the development of ombudsman programs in other companies in the same industries and for an expansion across fields. This is in part why more and more programs are being established in industry, education, health care, corrections, and elsewhere. It is obvious, in short, that the idea is not gaining acceptance because of failure, but instead because of success.

Summary

This first chapter has attempted to identify some of the pressures that are leading to the development of ombudsman programs in various industries. We have not made an attempt here to systematically track the history and development of ombudsman programs in business, education, health care, corrections, and other fields, since this is covered in Chapter 3. However, illuminating the overall trends that are leading corporate executives in the ombudsman direction is important.

Most managers will recognize the trends outlined above. They were described as creating either a *push* or a *pull,* the push being external pressures coming primarily from outside the organization and the pull, forces within the organization that are providing momentum for ombudsman programs. The external pressures were categorized in terms of law, economics, culture, technology, education, politics, sociology, and demography; the internal pressures were identified as a desire for excellence and productivity as well as for more organizational learning, more participative management, less employee litigation, more secure employee rights, better customer relations, dispute resolution methods that improve the quality of working life, open communication, reduced employee turnover, greater justice and equity, more humane organizations, a more democratic corporate culture, and the recognition of the successes of early ombudsman programs. These trends are now spreading to many new industries, both here and abroad, and so it is not surprising that more and more ombudsman programs are appearing. In the next chapter, the ombudsman concept is introduced in greater detail.

Chapter 2

Methods for Solving
Organizational Problems

Complaint programs, including those using ombudsmen, are designed to promote excellence, to increase organizational learning, to increase participation, to decrease litigation, to avoid bad publicity, to promote positive customer and employee relations.

Productive, quality-oriented organizations *listen* to employees and customers using complaints to help change (that is, improve) the organization. This statement holds for both private and public organizations, including industries as diverse as manufacturing and health care. For example, in the early days of ombudsman office creation, Rowe (1987, p. 133) noted that CEOs who have added an ombuds office usually justify its creation by one or more of these three statements: the office more than pays for itself— it is cost-effective; the rights and responsibilities of employees and of the company are well supported by such an office; it is a humane and caring human resource policy to have such an office. Ombudsmen in corporations exist because CEOs see cost benefits, believe in employee rights and responsibilities, and feel that the program is part of a good human resources policy. Similar concerns apply in the area of health care, where patient representatives or ombudsmen handle complaints that target staff behavior, medical communication and nursing care, environmental comfort, admissions, bills, and follow-up care — a full range of "customer" concerns. Hospital and nursing home ombudsmen help to ensure that quality is maintained and that problems are quickly and effectively addressed (Keith, 2000, 2001; Netting, et al., 2002). The presence of an ombudsman gives comfort to friends and relatives of patients and to patients themselves because "someone" has the responsibility for handling problems.

The Columbia Encyclopedia (online edition, 2008), describes the work of the ombudsman in the following way: "As a government agent serving as an intermediary between citizens and the government bureaucracy, the ombudsman is usually independent, impartial, universally accessible, and empowered only to recommend. In the United States the term ombudsman has been used more widely to describe any machinery adopted by private organizations (e.g., large business corporations and universities) as well as by government to investigate complaints of administrative abuses."

Today these individuals provide general problem solving for both employees and customers. The problems they handle for fellow employees range from hiring, firing, and promotion conflicts to sexual harassment cases. Ombudsmen serving customers (such as hospital patient representatives or patient ombudsmen, student ombudsmen in colleges and universities, customer relations representatives, consumer advocates) address a wide range of issues, such as product quality and product deficiency, support/repair service needs, billing and payment, organizational responsiveness, poor treatment by professional and support staff, professional mistakes. Other concerns that receive their attention can be inferred from the fact that there are currently troubleshooters (who have many different job titles) in the following organizations: hospitals; nursing homes; the military; defense contractors; manufacturing companies; educational institutions, including both colleges and school districts; correctional institutions; federal, state, and local government; public utilities; banks; churches (the Roman Catholic Archdiocese of Vienna, Austria, has had a child abuse ombudsman since 1996) and the media. To give a sense of how long they have been recognized, according to early articles in *Time* (December 7, 1981, p. 62) and *Business Week* (February 12, 1979, p. 117), specific corporations that had complaint-processing mechanisms include IBM, American Express, TWA, Tektronix, Chemical Bank, McDonald's, Northrop (now Northrop Grumman), and others. Their programs differ significantly, of course, and range from a "people-intensive personal problem-solving system" to correspondence and telephone-based systems. Some are formally recognized programs with staff and support services, while others involve only a single individual handling complaints. Ombudsmen may have a wide range of job titles; the following list is certainly not exhaustive: employee relations manager, counselor, corporate ombudsman, equal employment opportunity specialist, human relations specialist, employee representative. One of the earliest surveys of members of the Corporate Ombudsman Association revealed that specific titles included alternative communications channel; assistant to secretary for citizen affairs; corporate ombudsman; employee problem resolution officer; exempt compensation program manager; franchise liaison manager; manager, employee relations; manager, human resources; manager, work problems counseling; ombuds assistant; principal staff engineer-ombudsman; special assistant to CEO; vice president; vice president ombudsman; ombudsman and ombudsperson (Ziegenfuss, Robbins, and Rowe, 1987, p. 38). In 2010, the ombudsman is more likely to occupy a stand-alone role because independence is the cornerstone of the work. A corporate vice-president is unlikely to function as an ombudsman, attempting to act in a dual role as line executive and impartial problem solver. The characteristics of ombudsman can be summarized as follows. Ombudsmen focus on communication and active listening, use a wide variety of techniques from coaching to intervention, serve in virtually all industries and professions, distribute their work time among complaint handling, education, and consultation activities, rely on personal charisma as well as organizational position, come from a wide variety of educational backgrounds are paid from $50,000 U.S. for a long-term care ombudsman to $100,000+ and more for a corporate ombudsman.

Formal and Informal Ombudsmen

Organizations typically have two types of ombudsmen: formal ones and informal ones. The second group vastly outnumbers the first. Almost all organizations employ people to whom employees turn when they don't know how to handle a problem. This "go-to person" may be a middle manager, a foreman, a head nurse or teacher. He or she is relied upon for wise advice and discretion. Formal ombudsmen are also expected to be "wise and discreet" as they are also recognized and responsible for resolving complaints brought to their attention. To think of ombudsmen in formal versus informal terms is to think of them as branches of a tree. Both formal and informal ombudsmen types belong to the same family, though clearly to separate branches. The first group is formally recognized and funded and may have authority based in law. The informal branch just carries out these functions without official authority and in addition to other duties. It is important to note that the two models can coexist in the same organization, so that for instance a hospital can have both a formal patient ombudsman and an informal employee ombudsmen (such as an employee relations manager who defines his or her job in this way). The point is that there are more similarities than differences in the family. But in order to understand this, however, we need to have a more complete understanding of who ombudsmen are and what they do. Formal troubleshooters are called ombudsmen in the professional and academic literature. The term *ombudsman* has a long and rich history, much of which is associated with the public sector. An early edition of the *International Handbook of the Ombudsman: Evolution and Present Function*, says the following:

> The ombudsman is not a term coined by modern technological society for some new invention like radar, microwave, and transistor. It is an old

Swedish word that has been used for centuries to describe a person who represents or protects the interests of another. It gained a more specific meaning in 1809 when the Swedish government appointed a public official to investigate public complaints against public administration. As the word became more frequently used, especially outside Sweden, it was misused and corrupted, and it is now often used loosely for any public complaints officer, that is, for any officer or office of any organization that receives public complaints about the way it conducts its business or how others conduct their business. Thus, radio stations, newspapers, churches, businesses, and other nongovernmental bodies have their own ombudsman offices, and it is difficult for people to distinguish the more specific use of the term to refer to government ombudsman offices established to receive complaints from the public about the administrative actions of public authorities [Caiden, MacDermot, and Sandler, 1983, p.3, and see Hyson, 2009, p. 304].

In the private sector there has been a lag in catching on to the concept. One of the earliest mentions of the notion of *corporate* ombudsman comes from Silver in a 1967 *Harvard Business Review* article. Silver (1967, p. 77) saw the derivation of the ombudsman concept as based on the notion of corporate social responsibility and fair play. In his view, the ombudsman would be an investigator, a policy interpreter, a decision recommender, and a complaint denier (for inappropriate complaints). Only two groups would be excluded from using the ombudsman — top management and unionized personnel.

How can we describe the commonalities among the purposes and work of ombudsmen? As they moved to embrace the concept, the organizers of the first Corporate Ombudsman Conference were faced with exactly this task, and decided on a definition of ombudsman that would include a wider range of organizational problem solvers than it excluded: "Ombudsman — one skilled in dealing with reported complaints to help achieve equitable settlements" (Corporate Ombudsman Association, 1984). In other words, their job is to take complaints, investigate conflicts, and help to create solutions to problems. This succinct job description still stands though it has been greatly elaborated upon in recent years. Ombudsmen now have codes of ethics and codes of practice (see International Ombudsman Association website). Some examples may help to make this clear. A newspaper report provided the following account of an early corporate ombudsman program: "United Technologies Corporation (UTC) established a corporate ombudsman program last summer. It went into effect in August. Overseeing the program is Walter F. Eells, vice president and ombudsman. The program is designed to enable confidential communication in writing or through a toll-free phone service between employees and top officials of the corporation and its operating units. Eells, who joined the company in 1956, most recently was vice president for management development and salaried personnel relations at UTC. He previously served in a variety of personnel assignments at other company units including Pratt & Whitney, Hamilton Standard, Norden Systems and Essex.... Q. How did the program come about? A. Back in early April we decided we wanted to have a two-way employee communication system of the broadest possible kind. So top management asked the corporate human resource staff to look at what's being done around the country and make a recommendation on what action UTC might take. I was assigned the responsibility to do that study. We implemented the written, confidential two-way communication program (DIALOG) on August 1" (Ross, 1986, p. 6). The purpose here was to encourage and provide the means for employee communication. Employees are just one ombudsmen client group, however. A patient ombudsman in a hospital has a formal role that involves listening to patients' complaints about treatment and support services as the following case history will illustrate:

In tears, the young woman entered the hospital ombudsman's office. The ombudsman's job is to sort out the problems and complaints of the hospital's patients and their families, and she encouraged her visitor to unburden herself. "She was from a rural community and had just been told by her surgeon that she required an operation that was not lifesaving, but ultimately necessary," the ombudsman said. "The surgeon saw no reason to wait and had already booked the operating room for two days later. He urged her to make a decision that day." But the patient was feeling pressured and upset. She told the ombudsman she didn't understand what the operation really involved and she wanted to go home and discuss it with her family. "That seemed quite reasonable to me," the ombudsman said. "But she was worried that she would offend the surgeon if she refused her immediate consent. I told her it was her body and her hesitation was quite normal." The ombudsman immediately arranged for a nurse to outline the operation to the patient. Then she put in a call to the surgeon to explain the woman's hesitation and to make sure the operation could be safely delayed, which he confirmed. "The upshot was the patient went home, discussed the operation with her family and returned confidently for the operation three months later" (Carson, 1986, F1).

This story illustrates both the purpose and a possible outcome of ombudsman programs in hospitals — greater peace of mind for the patient. On the informal side, some clients of agencies become ombudsmen for colleagues. The following account identifies an informal but highly visible ombudsman for a county welfare agency. Every prison has its jailhouse lawyer. The Dauphin County (Pennsylvania) Assistance Office has Robert Richardson. Richardson, 57, of Hall Manor is a welfare recipient. Yet, every weekday from 9 A.M. to 2 P.M., he is at the welfare office at 124 Pine St., giving advice. Often clad in a suit, tie and tennis shoes, Richardson sits at a table in a corner with his briefcase. Near him is a handmade sign taped to the wall, which says, "Contact Mr. Richardson for your welfare problems." He said he is there because of "a dedication to help the ones who need help." He also says: "I'm like an advocate who represents all clients from Dauphin County. I'm kind of a troubleshooter. I try to straighten out problems." Unlike some welfare advocates, Richardson gets along with the assistance office management. "He has been a great help to us. I think people feel more free to talk to him because he has no ax to grind," said James Hindinger, executive director of the local office. "I have a rapport with Mr. Hindinger and the workers," Richardson said. "He appreciates the work I am doing as a liaison between the caseworker and the recipient" *(Harrisburg Patriot News,* 1986). As we have seen, the welfare ombudsman is at the informal end of the continuum, a continuum that includes everything from volunteers to those with fully recognized authority. Despite this diversity, though, ombudsmen tend to deal with certain basic kinds of problems.

Types of Complaints Handled

The extent of ombudsman activity in a wide variety of industries from manufacturing to health care suggests that complaint topics are almost limitless. Examples drawn from the business sphere include personnel policies, physical conditions, recreational activities, sexual harassment, discrimination, supervisory conflict, interdepartmental conflict, production processes, personality conflict, personal problems, and general dispute resolution. A formal ombudsman could cite the following cases from a typical month of employee complaints:

- A manager asked the ombudsman confidentially to find out where he stands. Through an organizational change, he had lost some of his responsibilities. Finding: He was still very highly regarded. The change was made to prepare for an anticipated work load increase in the area he retained.
- A complaint about "forced" overtime among engineers. Finding: The company policy was fair and correct, but some managers were operating by their own interpretations, which were not always correct. A frank letter from the vice president helped, but it did not entirely eliminate these abuses.
- The denial of medical insurance payments to an employee for reasons unclear to him. Finding: The claim was payable and the man received his reimbursement.
- A patient ombudsman in a hospital had these sample patient (customer) complaints:
  - Inadequate information from a physician about an upcoming surgical procedure.

- An incorrect bill that was seemingly inexplicable.
- "Missing civility" towards an elderly grandmother from the floor's night nursing team.
- Missing watch and ring from the bedside.

In each of these instances, the ombudsman's action involved investigation, communication with the involved parties, and follow-up. These may not be the types of complaints handled in all systems, but they are representative. For customers, the complaints are very wide ranging, involving such items as product quality and service, sales practices, return policy, and billing. In spite of this obvious diversity, though, the complaints tend to share some common features. More specifically, they are of an interpersonal rather than a technical nature for the most part, or at least involve personal judgments. As an illustration, consider the following two cases.

Data Fudging. Deborah Thornton was a young and dedicated scientist in an industrial research and development laboratory. She was working as a part of a new-product team that was developing a new artificial sweetener. One afternoon, she noticed a discrepancy in one senior scientist's reports and checked it. It appeared he was "fudging" the data but she was not sure. He was an irascible guy. Since he would be responsible for her promotions and her continued work on the project, she was afraid to ask him about it. She did not want to embarrass or anger him and had no idea what to do, so she just watched and worried, becoming more and more distracted.

Privacy Violation. Walter Matthews was a senior engineer in a major paper company. At age forty-seven, he had spent twenty-seven years working at that company. He contracted cancer and needed treatment, but he was determined to carry on as before. He was shocked to find an announcement of his medical condition posted on the bulletin board as both a note of concern and notice of his expected sick leave. Tearing it down, he went to the department supervisor to complain and to request privacy. The supervisor was unsympathetic and refused to have his name removed from the illness list. Though most programs consider *no* complaints to be insignificant, there is some natural sorting out as larger problems displace smaller ones in priority. For example, a complaint about inadequate lighting is important but is less immediately demanding of attention than potential sabotage, suicide, or sexual harassment. The next question that will concern us is what do ombudsmen do with these complaints when they get them.

Primary Ombudsman Activities

In our own research (see, e.g., Ziegenfuss, Charette, and Guenin, 1984; Ziegenfuss, 1985c; Ziegenfuss and O'Rourke, 1995; Ziegenfuss, 2007), on ombudsman programs, one author has helped to design and develop while the other author investigated and resolved many situations. We have come to the conclusion that ombudsmen work involves three primary activities: complaint processing, education and training, and consultation. This is not a perfect classification since the categories overlap, but the commonly accepted definitions of these activities describe reasonably well what ombudsmen do. Complaint processing includes fact finding through inquiries, investigation, feedback of the data to the participants, and problem/conflict resolution. Education involves teaching organizational members about company or agency policies, procedures, and the rationale for decisions; conducting workshops in client communication or conflict prevention; addressing community and professional groups on rights. Consultation is advisory work with senior and middle management regarding both problems and proposed actions for resolution and for prevention. In an early description of ombudsman activities, which is still valid today, Mary Rowe (1987, pp. 130–131) identified eight principal functions pertaining to corporate ombudsmen but certainly relevant to problem solvers and ombudsmen in general. These functions amount to a definition of ombudsmen activities:

1. *Dealing with Feelings.* On occasion, living and working bring rage, grief and bewilderment to everyone. Managers and employees often feel there has been "no one to listen." Possibly the most important function of a complaint handler (or complaint system) is to deal with feelings. If this function is not otherwise provided by line and staff managers, it will fall to the ombudsman.

2. *Giving and Receiving Information on a One-to-One Basis.* Many employees do not even know the name of their CEO, much less how the company determines promotions, transfers, or benefits, or how it deals with problems in the work place like harassment. It is therefore very important that line and staff managers be prepared to give out information, and make referrals to helping resources, on a one-to-one basis, at the time and in the fashion needed by an individual with a problem. This may again be all that is needed. If appropriate information and referrals are not made available by other managers, this function may fall to the ombudsman.

3. *Counseling and Problem-Solving to Help the Manager* or *Employee Help Himself* or *Herself.* Many employees and managers face tenacious problems with only three alternatives in mind: to quit, to put up with their problem, or to start some formal process of complaint, or suit or investigation. These are not the only alternatives, nor are they always the best available. The skilled ombudsman will help a visitor develop and explore and role-play new options, then help the visitor choose an option, then follow-up to see that it worked.

And in many cases, the best option may be for the person with a problem to seek to deal with it effectively on his or her own.

4. Shuttle Diplomacy. Sometimes a visitor will opt for a go-between. This is especially true where one or more parties need to save face or deal with emotions before a good solution can be found. This is much the most common type of intervention reported by ombuds practitioners, especially if the company is quite hierarchical in style and organization. In some companies, this function may also be pursued by the ombudsman — during or between the steps of a formal, complaint-and-appeal grievance process — as an option for settling outside any adjudicatory process.

5. Mediation. At other times, a visitor will choose the option of meeting *with* others, together with the ombudsman. Like shuttle diplomacy, this usually happens on an informal basis. However, the "settlements" of shuttle diplomacy and mediation may be made formal by the parties involved.

6. Investigation. Investigation of a problem or a complaint can be formal or informal, with or without recommendations to an adjudicator — for example, to a grievance committee or to a line or senior manager. All four of these investigatory options are reported by ombuds practitioners, and are more or less common depending on the company and the ombudsman.

7. Adjudication or *Arbitration.* This function is very rare for the ombudsman. Here, the classic phrase about ombuds practitioners is likely to obtain: "They may not make or change or set aside a management rule or decision: theirs is the power of reason and persuasion."

8. Upward Feedback. Possibly the most important function of the ombudsman is to receive, perhaps analyze, then pass along information that will foster timely change in a company. Where policies are outdated or unintelligible, or new problems have arisen, or a new diversity appears in the employee pool, an ombudsman may be a low-key, steady-state change agent at very low cost to the employer. This function also provides a mechanism for dealing with some very difficult confidentiality problems. An ombudsman can, for example, suggest that a department head instigate an apparently "routine" department-wide discussion about safety or harassment or waste-management or theft, in response to an individual concern, at no cost to anyone's privacy or rights, in such a way as to eliminate an individual problem (if not necessarily the perpetrator) (Rowe, 1987, pp. 130–131).

Individually and collectively, these activities are the ones that lead to the realization of the goals of the ombudsman program presented at the outset of Chapter One. To shed further light on ombudsman work, we must explore the primary activity of complaint processing. The individual methods of complaint taking used by ombudsmen vary, but there seem to be five steps that are central to this process. These are distilled from a review of work in the many industries in which ombudsmen work, from health care to transportation to banking to government services. Though not all ombudsmen follow these steps in each case, they are generally representative of the nature of complaint-handling work.

Step 1: Identify the Complaint. This initial step involves reviewing the general problem as to facts and context, then reducing the complaint to a specific one-sentence problem (often not as easy as it would appear). Once the primary problem is identified, ombudsmen define the secondary problems if any.

Step 2: Investigate the Complaint. The ombudsman outlines a procedure for investigation and further clarifies the problem, if necessary. He or she then follows the usual procedure for investigation and discusses the facts and context of the case and creates relevant and specific recommendations. Recommendations for action are then identified.

Step 3: Report the Investigation Results. In step 3, the ombudsman examines the participants' responses for agreement, disagreement, apathy or withdrawal, tailoring actions to participants' positions. Typically, they will write a report (although some do not), write a letter to the client and/or hold a face-to-face review. In some cases the ombudsman may arrange a meeting between the client and a senior member of staff (vice-president, physician, university departmental chair, functional specialist, director or manager).

Step 4: Develop Responses to the Problems. Ombudsmen create and spur responses by listening and reflecting, collaborating on the creation of solutions, and independently suggesting alternatives.

Step 5: Monitor the Response Plans to Ensure Follow Through. Ombudsmen examine multiple systems changes according to their proposed time schedule, monitoring solutions for their effect at both the individual case level (treating problems) and throughout the organization (taking preventive actions). These steps are generally the same for all types of complaints. Not all steps are taken in each complaint case, though, since the work is actually very fluid and some problems are solved quickly, almost on the spot. For example, many ombudsmen refer complainants with an alcohol or drug problem to an employee assistance program. These cases require little in the way of monitoring for follow-through (step 5); it is only necessary to ensure that contact was made. Other problems call for managers and/or employees to make major changes in personal or organizational behavior that (1) they do not want to make, and/or that (2) require rather extensive periods to complete, such as cases of interpersonal conflict between managers in one department. In other cases, troubleshooters may invest much time in helping the participants create solutions to the problem. All other steps would be minimized in relation to this undertaking. Obviously some investigations uncover problems that are clear and easily solved, and others yield ambiguity, policy conflict, and much uncertainty about the correct response. Two examples will illustrate this point. The first case exhibits a set of ombudsman actions drawn from an early but very strong national survey of corporate ombudsmen (Ziegenfuss, Robbins, and Rowe, 1987). The survey asked ombudsmen to identify which of the following approaches and techniques were used and how often: dealing with feelings, active listening, describing options, giving advice, referral, coaching, shuttle diplomacy, mediation, investigation, making recommendations, turning the case over, arbitration/adjudication, generic intervention, and upward feedback. The first case shows how one ombudsman employed the various techniques.

Case 1: Personal and Organizational Danger

In a relatively small percentage of cases, ombudsmen confront problems that present the potential for serious personal and organizational consequences. Case 1 illustrates this potential impact.

The complaint: The employee presenting the complaint was an engineer in a research and development unit of a major defense contractor. Age forty-eight, he had worked for the company for some nineteen years as a loyal and solid performer. For the last two years, he had been technical engineering chief on a weapons system research and development project. His project involved competing with another project group to complete a design task increasing traction on a new-model army tank. The competition was intense and involved major bonuses and promotions. Both project groups depended on a joint supply stream for materials for their prototypes. Unfortunately, the engineer's project manager and the supply manager were fighting through an intense personality conflict. When supplies became limited, the supply chief directed the scarce supplies to the other project team (partly in spite). When the engineer confronted the supply chief, his own project director would not back him up. Since this would mean they would lose the competition (started thirty-six months ago), he was outraged. After two sleepless nights, he went to the corporate ombudsman.

Ombudsman Activities: The engineer appeared obviously distraught and looked like he had not been sleeping. He told his story with clear and significant anger. The ombudsman began with *active listening,* helping him to specify the problem as completely as he could. Along with listening, the ombudsman expressed sympathy and extended understanding of his concern and disappointment (*dealing with feelings*). He asked the engineer what action he was contemplating. The engineer suggested only half-jokingly that he would kill himself or wipe out the project (sabotage?). He told the engineer that he would *investigate* the situation and asked permission to contact the principals. This was approved by the engineer. They agreed to meet again the next day. The ombudsman *investigated,* finding the situation to be true, but that there was a possibility of additional supplies if the engineer's manager and the supply chief could come to terms. The ombudsman met again with the engineer, who was still very upset. The ombudsman *described the options*— to move on to a new project or to try to negotiate a treaty. The engineer only reluctantly agreed and was still obviously angry and upset. The ombudsman suggested he meet with a counselor friend to deal with his feelings about the conflict *(referral).* The next day, the ombudsman initiated *shuttle diplomacy* between the project manager and the supply chief to get them to agree to a meeting and a compromise. Eventually (after two individual visits each), they did meet. Agreement to provide supplies was secured but the conflict was far from over. The engineer was informed of the resolution but both he and the ombudsman agreed to meet again. The ombudsman also met with the Division General Manager to inform him of some of the problems emerging in the push for product innovation *(upward feedback).* The ombudsman recommended initiating a series of meet-and-discuss conferences to review the stress and performance situation *(recommendation).* He offered to facilitate if needed. In this case, the ombudsman employed a variety of approaches and techniques. The use of many tools in a single case is typical, particularly when outcomes are potentially very severe — suicide and sabotage. This is an apparently serious case. Other cases are serious but do not always appear to be so. A second case indicates "hidden significance" in a seemingly trivial case involving corporate sports (as adapted from Ziegenfuss, 1985c).

Case 2: The Company Softball Game

The Complaint: In one mid-size manufacturing corporation, several employees were heard to complain that the softball umpires had been asked to favor one division's team over the others. Divisional business competition was at a high level and it carried over into sports activities. The corporation's official troubleshooter (called a corporate ombudsman in this private company) was presented with the complaint after two employees decided it was too "risky" to bring the problem up directly with their divisional boss.

Ombudsman Actions: The ombudsman began by collecting specifics about the complaint. How was the one team favored by the umpires — calling strikes and balls, close calls on the baselines, and so on? Which umpires were involved? What were the days and specific examples? Who could corroborate the statements? A secondary problem was identified relating to the negative aspects of the intensity of the competition. This was noted but was not the specific subject of the complaint. The facts were gathered by talking to the umpires, players, and divisional managers. The allegation was found to be true, but it applied only to the last game played. The ombudsman asked for suggestions on how to resolve it. There was rather quick agreement on a replay of the game with a consensus that the reasons should be deemphasized. The ombudsman suggested a meeting of the two teams to clarify the problem and to diminish the emotional level, particularly the most heated aspects of the competition. The question of whether this was a common problem in other sports activities was raised. The recreation department decided to address the "level of competition" problem in a series of light memos and team discussions. Subsequent softball games and other activities were monitored over the next three months. Although there are complaints that are more serious than this — sabotage, discrimination, and dangerous physical conditions — sports activities are an important part of the corporate culture that must be maintained effectively, without destructive levels of competition.

Summary

We have just considered why complaints are taken seriously by the organization, who is working on complaint processing, and how these individuals work. In bringing this chapter to a close, we should reiterate what the presence of ombudsman-led complaint processing means for public and private corporate cultures, a topic that is currently of great interest as a part of broad organization design thinking (Morgan 2006; Tosi 2009). With an ombudsman program in existence, the organizational culture (whether of a manufacturing firm or government agency) has evidence that the welfare of employees and customers is taken seriously, and that sincere efforts will be made to redress any problems that might arise. For this and other reasons, there is a clear rationale for an expectation that more private corporations and public agencies will vigorously embrace the ombudsman concept.

Chapter 3

Ombudsmen in Diverse Settings: Distinctions and Similarities

From the statutory ombudsmen of early 19th century Sweden to 21st century North America, the role of ombudsman has evolved to address issues in such diverse sectors as health care, banks, schools and universities, the armed forces, retail establishments and other private sector organizations. In any of these institutions the ombudsman occupies a singular position. She or he is the "go-to" person for staff or clients: the fixer, problem-solver, and "shuttle diplomat" (Ziegenfuss, 1988). In many cases, the ombudsman is part of the organization she serves but, in the most effective systems, he or she works at arm's length from the management of the establishment. Effective ombudsmen are able to maneuver amidst the often warring or competing interests of individuals and departments. He or she is impartial and non-partisan, rising above the politics, bids for power and petty self-aggrandizement that may exist in the organization. Good ombudsmen recognize power plays but do not get caught up in the game. In some cases, they are actively involved in changing systems to reduce the dysfunctional politics that lead to complaints. This chapter, firstly, reviews the growth and diversification of the ombudsman in Western societies; secondly, examines the organizational structure of ombudsman offices; thirdly, describes four types of ombudsman practice, with illustrative case histories; and fourthly, the chapter will conclude with a discussion of some still unresolved issues concerning the ombudsman's independence, neutrality, confidentiality and the power to investigate.

Growth and Diversity of the Ombudsman

Ombudsman, customer service manager, patient representative and client service agent — what do these names mean, and does a difference in title mean a difference in the way a complaint is handled? When the first edition of this book came out, government ombudsmen were common. However, the presence of ombudsmen in hospitals, schools and in the private sector was still somewhat rare. For example, hospitals employed people called patient representatives but, in many institutions, their role was to protect the hospital from lawsuits or bad publicity, or to make sure patients were happy and comfortable. Patient representatives were often obliged to reflect and support management's interests. The title ombudsman was once the exclusive preserve of those appointed by a government to act independently in hearing the complaints of citizens. This type of legislative ombudsman is usually referred to as a "classical ombudsman." It had its origins in Sweden in 1809, but since the 1960s expanded to include many other types of government ombudsmen. The proliferation of ombudsman offices outside government since the 1960s led New Zealand, in 1991, to reserve the title of "ombudsman" to the Chief Ombudsman "unless statute permits or with prior written consent of the Chief Ombudsman" (Rief, 2004, p. 53). In fact, some, such as Gregory Levine, believe that using the term ombudsman for those outside the parliamentary structure may create expectations that cannot be met (Levine in Hyson, ed., 2009b, p. 304).

Government ombudsmen are usually established by the legislative branch of government and receive and investigate complaints from the public. They may have considerable power: to initiate investigations without a complaint and to compel and even to subpoena evidence (Rief, 2004, pp. 3–4). The kind of complaints brought by the public usually concern lack of fairness on the part of government administration (Rief, p. 3). Government ombudsmen are complementary, or supplementary, to the court system. A hallmark of good ombudsman offices is that they do not impose bureaucratic layers between client and ombudsman. Ombudsmen can often resolve issues quickly and informally. Some websites, for example, promise that someone in the ombudsman office will answer the phone in three rings (Crean, 2009, p. 8).

In 1967, legislatures in the United States and Canada began to create "independent ombudsman offices to handle complaints from citizens against bureaucratic actions" (Rowat, 2007, p. 43). By 2003, one hundred and ten countries, according to Rief, had both national classical and hybrid ombudsmen (Rief, 2004, 11). Hybrid ombudsman systems (including those that function as ombudsman offices without the title) include ombudsmen for human rights and for children (Rief, pp. 7–8). Hybrid public/private sector ombudsmen positions have also been legislatively created to resolve consumer complaints (Rief, p. 43). Publicly appointed hybrid ombudsmen may take complaints involving the private as well as the public sector. One example is the human rights commission that might receive a complaint about an allegedly racist landlord or homophobic employer. Some countries with a national ombudsman also have ombudsmen in each region, state or province; others, like Canada, have only regional, provincial or state ombudsmen (Rief, 2004, p. 11). Government ombudsmen might have responsibility for child protection, the school system, hospitals, long-term care institutions, municipalities (local government), police and correctional facilities. Government ombudsmen may be internal (dealing with workplace issues) or external, receiving complaints about government institutions, such as prisons, customs and immigration, the postal service. Many high-level government ombudsman offices serve as an appeal system, to be resorted to when attempts to resolve a complaint at a lower level have failed. At the local level, municipal ombudsmen are usually appointed by, and report to, City Council. The newly established City of Toronto ombudsman and her team, according to her annual report for April 2009 to December 2009, processed and closed 958 complaints and were working on 99 more, for a total of 1,057 in that period. She and her team dealt with a broad range of issues ranging from parking tickets issued in error to threatened housing evictions and paramedic delays (Crean, 2009, p. 8).

Typical Organizational Structure of an Ombudsman's Office

A variety of structures is possible. Below are some of the most typical ombudsman situations according to several factors.

Independence: The ombudsman position is independent of the line management organization, or reports to the board, or reports to an outside agency or government body.

The ombudsman is not part of another department (such as public relations, or quality assurance) and does not usually combine the ombudsman function with any other. However, the ombudsman may engage in employee training as part of the ombudsman function

Clientele: The ombudsman serves clients or employees but not usually both (except in some universities).

Some ombudsmen work at the appeals level only, dealing with complaints once individuals have tried to resolve them at the local level (a local ombudsman, a bank branch manager, a school principal). Appeals ombudsmen are often legislative ombudsmen.

Term of Office: The ombudsman's appointment may be for a fixed term with one renewal possible.

Powers: Ombudsmen do not have the power to conduct formal investigations unless mandated by law. The office may have the power to set its own hiring standards, independent of the organization.

Accessibility: The ombudsman is either highly accessible to clientele (universities, hospitals) or is discreetly tucked away, much like a therapist's office (employee ombudsman).

Some work from home, meeting clients by appointment.

Some may work largely by phone, email or mail. Alternatively, the ombudsman may accept drop-in complaints or visits by appointment.

Confidentiality: Some ombudsmen may shred all files; others are obliged to keep detailed records. Both usually provide anonymous statistics.

As you can see, at this point there is no "one best way" to structure the function — each ombudsman is uniquely fitted to their sponsoring organization.

Private Sector Organizational Ombudsmen

Much has been written about legislative ombudsmen. Many if not most are lawyers and various texts are available for those with this specialist interest. The rest of this chapter will therefore focus largely, though not entirely, on ombudsmen in the private and non-profit sectors, often called "corporate ombudsmen." Corporate ombudsmen usually report to the senior executive officer of their organization, or to the board. They may serve either clients or employees. Some are part of a risk management effort (Redmond and Williams, 2004 pp. 48–54). This section will examine, in some detail, the role and function of the private sector ombudsman.

It is important to note at the outset that not everyone applauds the proliferation of private sector ombudsmen. Chief among the critics was the late Donald C. Rowat (died 2008). Rowat was a Canadian professor of political science who called the development of corporate ombudsmen "the greatest distortion of the classical model in the United States" (Rowat, 2007, p. 45). His argument is that the dispute resolution movement "hijacked the word ombudsman" and "developed its own ombudsman jargon" (Rowat, p.46) which was then applied to internal dispute resolution processes rather than the system that dealt with complaints from the public (Rowat, p. 46). This, he believed, led to an attenuation of the codes of ethics and standards of practice promulgated by The Ombudsman Association. The Ombudsman Association (TOA) and the University and College Ombuds Association (UCOA) were merged and incorporated into the International Ombudsman Association (IOA) in 2005. Neutrality, one of the ombudsman standards set forth by the IOA, is essential for legislative ombudsmen because states have "the power of life or death" (p. 46) over their citizens, Rowat said. It is not at all clear, he continued, how neutrality can be achieved without "legislative protection"

(Rowat, p. 46). University ombudsmen were among the first private sector ombudsmen and they flourished in universities, which, in the 1960s, were widely seen to be hotbeds of radicalism and unrest. Other well-known types of early private sector ombudsmen represent readers, viewers and listeners of media, bank ombudsmen (at the branch level), hospital ombudsmen or patient representatives and ombudsmen found in private corporations. Some are workplace ombudsmen while others work exclusively with clients, patients or students. The types of organizations to be examined below are: universities, health care facilities, private enterprise (including single-sector ombudsmen and private ombudsmen) and media. Descriptions are accompanied by case histories to demonstrate the way in which the office functions.

Four Types of Organization

Universities

University ombudsmen were among the first on the scene. Academia, as Carolyn Stieber points out, "provided a particularly fertile environment for [their] acceptance" (Steiber, 2000, p. 50). Although the first was established at Eastern Montana College, 1966, the first major university to establish an ombudsman office was Michigan State University in 1967. There were 150 ombudsman offices in universities and colleges in the U.S. and Canada by 2000 (Stieber, p. 51) and that number has grown since. University and college ombudsmen also exist in many European universities. First created during the militant campus activity of the 1960s, the university ombudsman is now taken for granted on most North American campuses. He or she is the person to whom students can bring complaints about low grades, favoritism, unfair research practices and other concerns. While some university ombudsmen handle complaints from faculty and employees (Harvard, York University in Toronto), and other universities appoint a faculty ombudsman to handle faculty grievances (Baylor University; Northwestern; University of Michigan-Dearborn) the university ombudsman is, first and foremost, there for the client, who is the student.

CASE: UNIVERSITY OMBUDSMAN FOR STUDENTS

A 3rd year general arts undergraduate visited the ombudsman with the following story: Her philosophy class was heavily focused on group discussion and one person not only dominated but criticized and demeaned other students. The students at first tried to discuss his views with him but were met with derision. Then they tried to freeze him out. This was unsuccessful. The lecturer, a young part-timer, seemed unable to control the flow of discussion and seemed frequently at a loss. The dominating student, with no limits set, verged on actually bullying specific individuals.

The student was thinking of dropping the course. The ombudsman, realizing that this was a serious classroom management problem, received permission from the student to call in the lecturer who seemed relieved to have someone to talk to.

Discussion led the ombudsman to believe that the aggressive student probably felt emboldened because the authority figure, the lecturer, did not stop him and seemed not to be in control of her classroom. The ombudsman (who was a retired professor) asked the lecturer how she conducted class discussions. Discussions were free form, not planned small group discussions, and often occurred spontaneously. Little attempt was made to ensure that everyone was included and students often spoke over one another. The ombudsman recommended that the lecturer take some of the free courses offered by the university's teaching center to faculty to help them become effective teachers and classroom managers. One course focused on the difficult student and classroom management skills. Another course trained professors to lead effective classroom discussions and debates.

The ombudsman also recommended that the lecturer immediately contact one of the university teaching centre counselors so as to rehearse her next classroom discussion session. She also told her that counselors were available to sit in on classroom sessions. The counselor would not know the name of the student; she would be there merely to be able to analyze the situation and offer advice afterwards.

Meanwhile, the ombudsman recommended that the lecturer consider several strategies. She could speak to the student privately or address the issue in the classroom itself. The ombudsmen recommended that in her next class, two days hence, she could respond to the student's verbal attacks on others by saying that she would like to hear from others. She should also lay down some discussion ground rules, preferably on the course website. In future, this would be included in the classroom syllabus.

The ombudsman then returned to the student and told her what she had done. She suggested that she wait at least two more classes to see if the situation had improved. She asked the professor and the student to contact her in a week. If the situation worsened, the professor and student both had recourse to the university office that dealt specifically with workplace and classroom verbal and physical violence.

This case is a good example of how an ombudsman can work with a complainant, rehearse strategies and prevent future problems. Similar skills may be brought to bear on employee/manager issues in the corporate setting.

Health Care Facilities

Health care ombudsmen come in many varieties. They may serve hospitals, long-term care institutions, and mental health organizations. Unlike ombudsmen in many private organizations, health care ombudsmen usually deal exclusively with clients, not employees. However, health care institutions may provide employees with their own ombudsman. Many ombudsman offices began in the 1960s as the office of the patient representative. According to the Society for Health Care Consumer Advocacy of the American Hospital Association, most patient representatives now call themselves patient advocates (personal communication, email, SHCA, Feb. 24, 2010). Other institutions describe the person as the in-house patient ombudsman. The title "patient representative" is still in use (see Ontario Hospital Patient Representatives' Association). In some cases (long-term care facilities) health care ombudsmen come under the mandate of the county or state. In Canada, the province of Quebec is a pioneer in its extensive network of local complaints and quality commissioners, mandated by law to function in every health care institution and governed by provincial legislation with the goal of improving services.

In every case, whether governed by legislation or by their own board, the health care ombudsman is responsible for protecting the rights of the most vulnerable, as we can see from the following case history.

CASE: HOSPITAL OMBUDSMAN

Quietly drinking coffee in a corner of the hospital coffee shop, the ombudsman was joined by a nurse who breathlessly said, "Thank heavens I found you. I just heard something terrible happened in ward A." The ombudsman suggested they go to her office to discuss the issue further. The two, left, coffees in hand, to speak privately. Ward A was in the psychiatric wing so the ombudsman was prepared to hear a tale of patient aggression against staff. Instead, the nurse told her of an elderly woman with a psychiatric illness who was resident on the ward, mainly because she had no family and no other social supports. She was waiting for placement in a specialized psycho-geriatric long-term care home. The patient was usually cared for by a team who specialized in geriatric psychiatry but nighttime care was entrusted to an agency nurse. All the agency nurses were trained in psycho-geriatric care, and there had never been any problems. This particular morning, however, the nursing shift that arrived at 7 A.M. observed bruising on the patient's face and a cut on her lip. One front tooth was chipped. When the nurses on the night shift met with the day shift for report, they actually discussed whether or not they should call the ombudsman but decided it was not necessary as the injuries were not serious and the woman was not going to complain. "After all," they were reported to have said, "Mrs. X isn't going to be phoning anyone and she probably doesn't even understand what happened to her." The nurses notified the doctor who examined the patient, ordered an x-ray and asked the ward clerk to make a dental department appointment. Meanwhile, the nurses tended to her injuries, arranged for an orderly to accompany the patient, and waited for the nurse manager before going any further. They weren't sure if they were correct in not reporting this incident. They did, however, suggest that Risk Management be informed.

This particular ombudsman had a mandate to investigate problems, even in the absence of a complaint. However, she exercised this power judiciously, lest she be perceived as a meddler. She decided that this might be a situation in which she ought to become involved, complaint or no complaint.

After finishing her coffee, the ombudsman phoned the nurse manager, with whom she had an excellent relationship, and said she had heard, via the grapevine, that one of their patients had been mysteriously injured the night before. The nurse manager had only just received this information herself, so she was somewhat taken aback. The ombudsman asked to receive a copy of the incident report and asked if the team would be conducting an internal investigation. The nurse manager agreed with the ombudsman that this was a serious incident that needed to be to be properly documented and investigated. She invited the ombudsman to be a type of external examiner to get at the facts of the case. The investigation determined that it was the agency nurse, and not another patient, who caused the injuries. She had impatiently pushed the patient, who had fallen, face-forward, on the floor. The agency nurse was reported to the private company that employed her and the nurses discussed with the legal department whether or not they ought to lay charges with the police. The management team recommended that any nurse new to the service be monitored by staff nurses and also receive special training if required.

This case is a good example of how an ombudsman can be helpful when she is known to and has a good relationship with all types of employees. In this case she did not think that the team would ignore either the patient or the seriousness of the incident. But she was concerned about a patient who had no family to defend her and no ability to speak. These are the patients who are most vulnerable to abuse.

Private Corporations

Early private corporations to hire ombudsmen included newspapers, General Electric, McDonnell Douglas, Bell Laboratories and Anheuser-Busch (Stieber, 2000, p. 53). The numbers have since grown to include banks, airlines, hotels, transport companies and many other types of organizations which employ ombudsmen to serve clients or employees.

Below is an example of how a workplace ombudsman might function in a manufacturing setting.

CASE: CHEMICAL COMPANY EMPLOYEE OMBUDSMAN

A Health and Safety supervisor was asked by the department manager to find a way to reduce the numbers of incidents recorded in the annual statistical report. The manager suggested that minor incidents not be recorded.

The supervisor was responsible for a plant that had, in the past year, more than the usual number of accidents. He did not want to fudge the statistics, even if 20 percent of the incidents were extremely minor, because he was concerned about the rising number of major incidents in that area (hand crushed in machinery; concussion from slipping in spilled oil). Overall, the increased numbers of serious incidents, combined with a more than usual number of minor incidents, indicated a serious area of concern. The supervisor felt his manager did not want to be singled out as heading the "worst" plant but, equally, he also wondered if his manager grasped the gravity of what appeared to be a worsening situation. He wanted to suggest ways to improve workplace safety habits and morale, not fudge numbers.

Troubled, the supervisor went to the ombudsman who suggested various courses of action. The ombudsman also offered to meet, off-the-record, with the company's in-house legal staff to discuss, anonymously, the ramifications of what appeared to him to be a dishonest and illegal act. The ombudsman was able to return to the supervisor within 24 hours with information to help him put his case to the manager. The two rehearsed the actual meeting. The supervisor then met with the manager who agreed to use this plant as a pilot for a new health and safety campaign, thus saving face all around. The issue of ignoring minor incidents did not come up again.

As we can see from the case above, workplace ombudsmen not only serve as sounding boards, but can positively influence a work setting through their powers of persuasion. Had this ombudsman cried in alarm "But this is illegal! You must refuse!" the supervisor would have been left with a gut-grinding dilemma and no way to resolve it peacefully. Because he had informal relationships with in-house counsel, the ombudsman was able to obtain helpful information to confidentially convey to the supervisor, thus giving him the tools to solve his own problem.

Workplace ombudsmen usually advertise themselves as independent neutrals who provide employees with a safe place to discuss workplace issues without the fear that management will be informed, except in cases of threats of imminent harm. Confidentiality is underlined and supported by the promise of informality. Often, a promise is made that no permanent records, except statistics, will be kept, and the ombudsman will not provide notice to the company about claims. Frequently, the office may offer additional assurances of fairness and integrity by printing, on the leaflet, all or part of the Code of Ethics of the International Ombudsman Association (see Coca-Cola Bottling Company, 2007; American Express Company, 2007–2008, 2008–2009; Société des alcools du Québec, 2008).

Single Sector, Industry-Wide/Association Ombudsman Schemes

Industry-wide ombudsmen share with classical ombudsmen independence and neutrality. Usually, they offer a person who is dissatisfied with an internal complaints process another, independent, appeal process, similar to services offered by associations of lawyers and physicians. Appeals ombudsmen may serve the banking, investment or insurance industries or newspapers (Press Council). In the United States, the National Association of Securities Dealers included an ombudsman in 1996 (Rowat, 2003, p. 48).

A variation of the association ombudsman is the private-sector complaints commission (Netherlands), which includes utilities, travel agencies and garages. In the Commonwealth, according to Rowat, the United Kingdom leads with the greatest number of association ombudsman schemes, even including the removals (moving companies) industry (Rowat, 2003, p. 48).

Examples of Appeals Ombudsmen in Private Industry

The U.K. Removals Ombudsman program "is unique within the BIOA (British and Irish Ombudsman Association) because it's the only wholly voluntary private sector scheme that isn't underpinned by specific legislation" (Alderson, December 2009, p. 9). Founded in 2001 by the National Guild of Removers and Storers, it deals with complaints at an appeals level (Alderson, p. 9). The very existence of such an organization is reassuring to consumers. In fact, a former Removals Industry Ombudsman points to the position as an effective marketing device. Homeowners are likely to check if their chosen moving company is part of the scheme before signing a contract. This can be a deciding factor more important than cost (Radice, 2008, p.7).

The banking sector was the first in Canada to introduce a sector-wide ombudsman, in 1996. It was founded first to resolve complaints from small business then later expanded to include consumers (Ombudsman for Banking Services and Investments website, 2008). The second industry-wide scheme, created by legislation in the next year, was Ontario's Insurance Ombudsman (Rowat, 2003, 47). Others, such as the Franchise Ombudsman Program (created in Canada to help franchisees or franchisors contact an ombudsman to discuss issues relating to a franchise relationship), have sprung up. Like many other ombudsman programs, the files of the Franchise Ombudsman are protected from inspection by others and the ombudsman may not conduct formal investigations (which they refer to as "formal or indepth processes"). The office holder reports to a standing committee representing the Franchise community (Canadian Franchise Association website, 2010).

Private Ombudsmen

Private ombudsmen are a relatively new development. Companies without ombudsmen might find themselves subject to investigations from private organizations like *Complaints Are Us!*, founded in Toronto by Jane Steele Moore in 2000. She and her team of researchers, calling themselves Complaint Concierges, charge $50 for the first hour, $25 for each subsequent hour and more for rush jobs. They are available not only to individuals but to small organizations that need a contract ombudsman (Complaints Are Us! website, 2010).

Media

Newspapers were the first media outlets to employ ombudsmen. The *Courier Journal* and the *Louisville Times* appointed the first U.S. news ombudsman in June 1967. The *Toronto Star*, in Canada, appointed its first ombudsman in 1972. But, as the ONO website points out, the Tokyo *Asahi Shimbun* established a committee for reader complaints as far back as 1922. News ombudsmen go under such titles as "readers' advocate," "readers' representative" or "public editor." Some assistant managing editors or senior editors act as ombudsmen (Organization of News Ombudsmen website, 2010). Major television networks employ ombudsmen, particularly national networks (CBC/Radio–Canada) and public television networks, such as PBS in the United States, to ensure strict adherence to journalistic ethics (see LeBaron, 2008, 10).

Some news ombudsmen have become well known because they write about their work or publish their ombudsman columns (see Daniel Okrent, *Public Editor # 1: The Collected Columns: With Reflections, Reconsiderations and Even a Few Retractions of the First Ombudsmen of The New York Times*, 2006). According to Andrew R. Cline, Okrent, who was Public Editor of *The New York Times* from 2003 to 2005, and Michael Getler, who was ombudsman at the *Washington Post* from 2000 to 2005, were "two of the most independent of the 39 ombudsmen represented by the Organization of News Ombudsmen" (Cline, 2008, p.82).

Michael Getler went on to become the first ombudsman in the history of the U.S, Public Broadcasting Service and, according to the website, the "first for any major American general-interest television network or service" (Carnegie Council website, last updated April 11, 2008).

When people complain about the media, the issues may range from invasion of privacy, insensitive film or photographs, distortion of the facts to support a point of view, inaccuracy, and unfair comment. Press ombudsmen frequently operate according to a specific code of practice. For example, the Office of the Press Ombudsman of Ireland examines complaints about breaches of the Code of Practice for Newspapers and Periodicals (Press Council of Ireland and Office of the Press Ombudsman website, 2010). The CBC-/Radio–Canada ombudsman is independent of the program staff and management and reports to the president and the board. The ombudsman is an appeal authority. CBC/RDI governs itself by the code of ethics of the Journalistic Standards and Practices, which serves as a framework for complainants (CBC/Radio–Canada website on Media Accountability, 2010).

Most codes of practice have clear rules governing privacy rights as the following two cases demonstrate:

CASE: NEWS MEDIA OMBUDSMAN

With mounting alarm, Carlos read front-page coverage of a gangland slaying that seemed, at least to him, to implicate his son Eduardo, a straight-arrow honors student and president of his university's Hispanic association. "Here we go again," thought Carlos, "another ethnic 'guilt-by-association' slur." Eduardo's name did not appear in the story but he was clearly visible, standing in a crowd of young men, watching police arrest members of a local gang outside a bar featuring popular Latino acts. Carlos was not only greatly surprised to see his son in that neighborhood but he feared that his son's reputation would suffer by association.

The feature was an objective report of a serious crime and the street a public location. The ombudsman did not uphold the complaint.

A similar complaint had a different outcome. A newspaper published a front-page story about a child molester, recently discharged from prison. A large photograph of the building in which it was rumored he lived appeared above the fold. Two unidentified small boys were sitting on the front steps and the building's number was clearly visible. The article named the street. The parents complained that, given the nature of the offence, the photograph implied that the sons might be victims, or soon would be if the molester remained at large. They charged the newspaper with invasion of privacy and the complaint was upheld on the grounds that special care should be taken when publishing photographs of minors, especially when a photograph might endanger them. Furthermore, the location of the molester was unproven and the apartment was private property.

Newspapers and broadcast media provide their own forums for comment that range from the traditional letters-to-the-editor to the space provided for comment in online editions. In fact, the authors wonder whether the growth of online forums in general may reduce, though not eliminate, the need for ombudsmen because they offer readers the opportunity to comment instantly on what they have read. Often, people go to ombudsmen to let off steam; it be will be interesting to see if on-line forums reduce these types of ombudsman-public interaction.

Common Issues

Although ombudsmen in the banking sector may say they have nothing in common with ombudsmen in universities, and university ombudsmen might find themselves at sea working in health care, their *ways* of working might be remarkably similar. The sharpest practice differences are usually found between corporate and legislative ombudsmen.

However, all ombudsman offices state they are committed to: (1) independence, (2) impartiality and neutrality and (3) confidentiality. How independent, impartial and neutral can a corporate ombudsman be? Is the promise made by some corporate ombudsman offices to destroy written records reasonable, and is the destruction of documents essential to maintain confidentiality or does it, in fact, make it more difficult to keep track of what may be an on-going problem? These are issues, along with the power to investigate, that are viewed by some scholars as deeply problematic. We will conclude by discussing why these issues are still so hotly debated, so many years after the first corporate ombudsman arrived on the scene.

What Is a "Real" Ombudsman?

Some classical, government and other legislative ombudsmen believe that the corporate use of the title has debased the original concept and is used more as media branding for a customer service office than as an accurate description of what a corporate ombudsman does according to Stewart Hyson (Hyson, 2009a, p. 6). They argue that an ombudsman cannot be independent if she is paid by her own organization or is part of the management structure and reports to the board. Therefore, they say, she cannot be neutral. They ask whether any employee can impartially investigate departments in the organization for which she works. The issue of maintaining or destroying documents is also contentious. Over the years, professional associations reserved exclusively for legislative or classical ombudsmen have broadened their membership base to include others by offering associate membership. While some might argue against "allowing" customer service staff to think of themselves as ombudsmen, one could equally argue that the meeting attendance and the training offered by large ombudsman associations, as well as the exchange of ideas, has helped corporate ombudsmen define their roles more clearly and has raised the standards and profile of corporate ombudsman offices. Such expansion, far from being a debasement, could be seen as a "creative adaptation" (Gadlin, 2000, p. 41).

INDEPENDENCE

The first question a client often asks an ombudsman is "who do you work for?" or, even more bluntly, "who pays your salary?" This question, originally raised by Donald Rowat, goes "to the heart of ombudsmanship" according to Stewart Hyson (Hyson, 2009a, p. 6). Hyson refers to situations in which management has created what he calls a "grievance-handling or customer service desk" (Hyson, p. 6). Use of the term ombudsman, in these situations, he says, is "cosmetics" and "'packaging.'" In fact, the ombudsman as customer service agent is "part of the managerial chain of command and is beholden to the manager" (Hyson, p. 6). Hyson describes this type of ombudsman structure as one that limits what the ombudsman can investigate and denudes the position of public accountability (Hyson, p. 6).

Some believe that the ombudsman cannot really do her job unless she is totally independent of her institution. On the other hand, people who are a part of their organizations are often privy to useful background information gleaned from informal coffee meetings or hallway conversations (as we saw in the hospital case history). The ombudsman needs to win the trust of doctors, professors, managers or whoever may be complained about. Managers and professionals, just as much as the clients, need to know that the ombudsman will be impartial, scrupulously fair, knowledgeable and will respect their professional integrity and reputation. The way the department is structured will make clear to potential ombudsman clients where the real power lies. A client wants to know if the person handling his or her complaint will be fair and objective, or whether he or she is serving the interests of a doctor, a professor, or other authority figure within the organization. Ombudsmen who report to a government body independent of their organization may appear to have more freedom to act and recommend than one reporting to the HR director, the CEO or the chairman of the board. Clients may view them more favorably because they have both power and apparent objectivity. On the other hand, in spite off this ostensible advantage, organizational outsiders might not understand the industry or service about which they receive complaints and may not be trusted by employees, professionals and managers, and may actually be feared by them. This ombudsman will probably receive very limited information. Thus an ombudsman who is employed by the organization but sits outside the line management function is often best placed to see problems in context and have an almost panoptic view of the many forces at work that militate against good service. Who the ombudsman reports to is a vexed topic. Ideally, the disgruntled employee should be able to meet discreetly with someone who is totally independent of the organization and of the union. The sick patient should not fear that the health care ombudsman is afraid of offending a powerful surgeon or putting his job at risk if he fights the system. The ability to negotiate various worldviews is crucial to effective ombudsman investigations.

What most people accept, however, is that one cannot investigate one's own department. In fact, some would say one cannot investigate members of one's own profession (doctors, police or army officers). Set against this is the fact that members of highly specialized professions have highly specialized knowledge. The ability to effectively investigate a complaint about, for example, suspected medical malpractice relies, to a great extent, on a medical education. There are two aspects of this concern: The first is that medical technical knowledge may be needed to determine the nature and depth of the complaint. An ombudsman without medical expertise would not be able to address this issue. The second concern is the way in which a patient's problem is addressed — rudely, without sensitivity, with no information given — or as a transparent, apologetic demonstration of interest with full investigation. This last is within the ombudsman's purview and does not require an extensive knowledge of medicine.

IMPARTIALITY AND NEUTRALITY

While many businesses say they welcome complaints as a source of customer feedback, the reality is that complainers are often as unpopular as whistle blowers. That is why it is crucial for the ombudsman office to be strictly impartial. They may have empathy for the complainant's problem, but they need to analyze it dispassionately.

Many brochures advertising the ombudsman office to employees or clients state that the ombudsman is an independent neutral. What does that mean in practice? How neutral can an ombudsman be? In the face of attack, members of an institution have a tendency to close ranks and protect their own. We have seen police departments do this when accused of brutality and observed high-ranking Catholic churchmen react defensively in the face of multiple accusations of pedophilia in the priesthood. It can be enormously difficult for members of a group to admit that their own representatives have flagrantly fallen short of the high standards to which they are called. The initial tendency is to blame the complainer.

The ombudsman is in the privileged position of standing outside this self-protective cocoon. The ombudsman fights for "fair process" but he or she is not advocating for one side or the other (Redmond and Williams, 2004 p. 50). Distraught clients might frequently demand that the ombudsman represent them and managers might appeal to the ombudsman's loyalty with veiled threats of contract termination, in dysfunctional organizations. An essential ombudsman characteristic is fearlessness, the ability to handle the stress of competing interests, and a strong personality.

The dilemma for corporate ombudsmen arises because they lack legislative protection and may be seen as "difficult" if they insist on bringing forward serious allegations against their organization's management. The temptation to become corporate "lapdogs" to use Ontario Ombudsman André Marin's phrase (Marin, 2008, point 3) can be great. Some believe that corporate ombudsmen can never be truly neutral or impartial because they lack independence and legal protection. The goal, for the corporate ombudsman, is to adhere to the IOA ethical requirement that they remain scrupulously neutral in the face of pressure from management and clients. Managers who wish to establish an effective ombudsman program will create structures that will make this possible.

CONFIDENTIALITY AND THE DESTRUCTION OF DOCUMENTS

Confidentiality is emphasized in all literature promoting the ombudsman position. Most people are extremely reluctant to complain and only do so when they feel driven by extraordinarily bad behavior or when they feel their interests (a bank balance, a university grade, health) are at risk. They often approach the ombudsman tentatively and want to be able to control the progress of the complaint. The last thing they want is to be labeled "complainers." Ombudsmen who honor the rule of confidentiality speak of cases only with those in a position to help and only with the permission of the client. Even if the ombudsman must report to someone in the organization, she must not disclose the names of clients even to the CEO or members of the board. To further reinforce the obligation of confidentiality, many organizations state that the ombudsman will either take no notes of encounters or destroy them as quickly as possible. This type of promise and practice by organizational ombudsmen is problematic because it poses practical difficulties in ensuring effective follow-up. One of the writers has been a hospital ombudsman for many years, making careful notes and keeping them, under lock and key, for the legally required number of years. Quebec provincial law requires hospital complaints and quality commissioners to keep a client file. The client has access to this file, as does the government if the client permits. Many complainants revisit their concerns several years after the fact. The ability to keep files makes investigation easier. This leads to the last contentious issue, the power, or not, to investigate.

THE POWER (OR NOT) TO INVESTIGATE

Carolyn Stieber describes investigation as "a bedrock of work by classical ombudsmen, enabling them to discover the facts of a given matter, to sort just actions from unjust, and to separate normal administrative practice from maladministration" (Stieber, 2000, p. 53). They may investigate impartially but, based on their findings, Stieber says, classical ombudsmen, under legislative protection, may take a position that favors one side when they make recommendations (Stieber, 2000, p. 53), a decidedly non-neutral stance not usually permitted to the corporate ombudsman. In the corporate model, the ombudsman frequently is described as engaging in informal problem-solving, offering the client space to express feelings. Many scrupulously avoid the term "investigation." Howard Gadlin states that the different ways in which classical and organizational/corporate ombudsmen perceive their roles is highlighted by the "controversy about the centrality of investigations" (Gadlin, 2000, p. 44). Classically oriented ombudsmen investigate to "discover the facts and render a judgment" (Gadlin, p. 44). The "organizational orientation," he says, "may be more about uncovering the dynamics of a dispute or in locating a grievance in terms of the dynamics of conflict between the grievant and the person or office about whom they are complaining" (Gadlin, p. 44). He describes organizational ombudsman investigations as possibly "relational rather than inquisitive" which is why, he suggests, that organizational ombudsmen use the term "intervention" (Gadlin, p. 44).

As Stieber points out, when an ombudsman says she will "look into the matter" (see Stieber, p. 54), this could be construed as "a form of investigation, using different words" (Stieber, p. 54). One of the authors, with 30 years experience as an ombudsman, many before she enjoyed legislative protection, considered that much of her work did, in fact, involve a type of investigation: consulting patient charts, interviewing all sides in a dispute to ascertain the facts, reviewing policies and legal documents. The goal was to discover the facts so that she could interpret the situation to the patient and make any necessary recommendations to management. Canadian lawyer Gregory J. Levine points to the attenuation of the concept of ombudsman investigation and the development, in government offices, of what he calls "call centre governance" (Levine in Hyson, ed., 2009b, p. 297). The advent of faxes, toll-free numbers and emails has certainly made it possible for ombudsmen to speed up the gathering of information and for ombudsman offices to reduce their staff. This has sometimes come at the expense of losing "on the ground" investigations (Levine in Hyson, ed., p. 299). According to Levine, "If an investigation simply involves asking a bureaucrat for his or her 'side' of the story and then assessing that story on the basis of intuition, an office can do thousands of investigations at very little cost" (Levine in Hyson, ed., p. 300). In this way complaints may be dealt with rapidly but is this truly an investigation?

"Ombudsman investigation is about seeking out information, about knowing the facts that underlie the complaint," says Levine (in Hyson, ed., 2009b, p. 297). All of this requires training and the ability to think analytically and critically not only about the complaint but about the system for and in which one works. Levine says that little has been written on the topic of ombudsman investigation, in spite of ombudsman organizations' training programs (Levine, p. 298, and footnote 20, p. 306).

Summary

This chapter has reviewed the evolution of the ombudsman role from its origins in early 19th century Sweden, through its application in government to its widespread popularity in universities, colleges and schools, health care facilities, corporations both public and private, industry associations and independents well as the media. It has discussed the varieties of structures and their common elements, presented case histories and concluded with an overview of some of the controversies that still divide classical from corporate ombudsmen.

Chapter 4

Problem-Solving

We now have a view of ombudsman work as a whole, but we need to know more about the specifics of the job. This is a harder task than it may appear, since it can be approached in various ways. One alternative is to describe in formal terms what the rules and functions of the job are. Another possibility is to sketch what happens in practical terms — that is, to present an average "day in the life" of a troubleshooter. Both approaches have their advantages, and so we will utilize both of them, beginning with a relatively formal description of ombudsman activities.

We begin our discussion of ombudsman functions with the following case study:

Fired for Refusing Unethical Practice: An electronics store clerk was told by her supervisor to inform customers that there were only six of the special sale iPods at $69.00. A similar model was available for $99.95 of which plenty were on hand. When a customer came in after the last of the six $69.00 iPods were sold asking for one, the clerk checked the inventory. She found there were plenty of less expensive iPods and other MP3 players and informed her supervisor that she would not lie to customers. He told her that there were great financial rewards involved in staying with current sales policy and that he was offered these rewards. They were attractive to him — he said he was "on board." She refused and was promptly fired for insubordination. If the clerk wanted to complain about being fired, who would she talk to and what would happen? A complaint to the supervisor who fired her would not accomplish much. Personnel could listen, but the complainant would fear bias. A complaint — to an ombudsman, the employee relations manager, an executive assistant friend, or a formal corporate ombudsman, would generate a fair hearing and relevant action. The question, of course, is what exactly would an ombudsman do?

We saw in the previous chapter that ombudsman work involves three primary activities (complaint processing, education and training, and consultation) and that complaint processing is the most important of these. This central function in turn involves taking complaints, gathering the facts through investigation, reporting on their conclusions, suggesting follow-up actions, monitoring to see that those actions are taking place. With regard to our opening case, an ombudsman would process the clerk's complaint by gathering the facts, reporting to management, and helping to identify a solution(s). Second, ombudsmen are educators and trainers for the corporation or public agency. Policies, procedures, and other organizational rules and regulations need to be transmitted to employees. Ombudsman programs provide one way of educating and training employees regarding the full range of organizational purposes, policies, and rules. This education occurs in both formal and informal sessions, and for example may include small workshops and informal employee visits. The department store clerk's supervisor attempted to "educate" the clerk about the degree of fit between her view and his view of the corporation's policies. The ombudsman and other corporate executives may need to reeducate the supervisor about corporate values and sales policies. Last, ombudsmen act as consultants to management, employees, and customers, helping them solve a wide range of problems. Public agencies are quite accustomed to the idea that independent troubleshooters such as ombudsmen can be helpful to government by diagnosing and presenting problems (see Gellhorn, 1966; Caiden, 1983; Ziegenfuss, 2007). Private corporations are increasingly recognizing the usefulness of ombudsmen as internal consultants for developmental help and for impartial refereeing (Rowe, 1987; Robbins and Deane, 1986; Ziegenfuss and O'Rourke, 1995).

Someone will need to referee the conflict between the supervisor and the clerk. If clear policies are violated by the firing, other action will need to be taken. If this is "accepted organizational behavior," some feedback to management about potential negative consequences is warranted. An ombudsman as consultant can provide this feedback to the CEO in a way that maximizes the chance of constructive use of the information. This is a good starting description of the ombudsman's job. In the following pages, we elaborate on this description, and also discuss a few other issues related to troubleshooting activities.

Complaint Processing

We now need to consider the more specific actions involved in complaint processing. What steps should the ombudsman take when the department store clerk presents her complaint? The actions that we will discuss are not limited to the department store situation, but apply to ombudsmen as they process a wide range of other complaints — for example, from patients in hospitals, employees in scientific labs, and students and faculty in colleges and universities. One view of the functions of an ombudsman comes from an article by Rowe and Baker (1984) which is still pertinent. They identify interrelated functions that they feel the ombudsman provides: personal communication, confidential advice and counseling, investigation, conciliation, mediation, adjudication and upward feedback

Most of what Rowe and Baker say has stood the test of time. However, nowadays, most corporate ombudsmen consider themselves to be an informal resource, and so the investigative and adjudicative function has been downplayed, eliminated or presented in another guise (the ombudsman "inquires" and "recommends"). The International Ombudsman Association Standards of Practice (2009) clearly states, "The Ombudsman does not participate in any formal investigative or adjudicative procedures." Many have taken this to mean that the ombudsman does not investigate or adjudicate. In reality, many ombudsmen do both, in an informal way. After all, it would be difficult to solve a problem without asking questions or checking relevant documents. And, although they do not adjudicate legally, as a judge might, ombudsmen usually come to conclusions after the inquiry is complete.

Surveying all of these functions and providing examples will extend our definition of the ombudsman's job. Each function is a contributor to the whole and each interacts with the other functions. For example, inquiry into the store clerk's problem is not just an independent part of the ombudsman's job, but an interconnected part that will also involve personal communication and upward feedback to the CEO about corporate values and professional ethics. Each function relates to all of the others and to the whole task of complaint handling. This somewhat abstract idea will be evident in the descriptions of the various functions.

Communication

Many corporations, public bureaucracies, universities, and hospitals are large and impersonal. In private corporations, managers and employees are competitively oriented, and are often viewed as more concerned about their own careers than about the problems of colleagues and customers. Not only hospitals, but other types of organizations, too often focus on the technical and bureaucratic aspects of work, forgetting the importance of ordinary human connection. One essential goal of ombudsman programs is therefore to increase the level of communication within organizations. Ombudsmen practitioners will usually confirm that the greatest source of complaints is poor communication: the doctor did an excellent job but neglected to explain it to the patient and family; a manager in one department, jealous of another, accidentally "on purpose" neglects to send him copies of important memos. An employee, hearing rumors of layoffs, discusses his fears with a friend in a rival firm. An ombudsman can provide a friendly ear in all these situations and can direct employees to reliable sources of information.

The need for information is illustrated by our case study. In this example, what would happen when other store clerks learn that the woman was fired? To whom would they go to ask for clarification if they were troubled about the ethics of the sales policy? And, most important, to whom would the fired clerk turn for information about response options — an attorney? The point is that problems generate a need for additional information. Information is needed by the sales clerk about company policy and about options, by her sales colleagues, and (although he may not know it) by the supervisor, who may have been wrong in his assumptions about the level of support for unethical practices. This is why ombudsmen emphasize communication — for the employee's sake, for the sake of the organization's productivity, and for customer satisfaction. Conflict and anxiety are productivity barriers that can sometimes be removed by simple personal communication. For other problems, anger and anxiety are the results of wrongs that require both redress and advice. The refusal of a secretary or sales representative to cheat, leading to their inappropriate termination, cannot be solved with simple information.

Counseling

An individual in great demand is a confidant to talk to for both personal reasons and/or with respect to organizational politics. Most people use work "buddies" or friends in other units as counselors regarding their daily work problems, their career aspirations, and the constant juggling required to balance individual goals and objectives with those of the organization. Employees have personal problems they do not want to share with colleagues, but that are bothersome. They may need nothing more than a good ear with commonsense advice, or they may need a referral for more professional and prolonged assistance. This kind of activity is a key one for ombudsmen. Rowe and Baker (1984, p. 133) long ago described it as follows: "Counseling can help address employees' lack of skill and lack of faith in responsible dispute resolution. One of the least dramatic but most effective things that employee counselors accomplish is to help both managers and employees see a problem in perspective, to frame and present it effectively, and to show them what options they have within the organization for resolving it. Most frequently the confidential counselor succeeds by helping a visitor resolve a problem on his or her own. Companies that take an innovative approach to complaint handling for nonunion employees are beginning to allow or encourage some confidential discussion of employee problems by supervisors as well as by personnel staff." The key point here is that counseling is of two different types. The ombudsman is on a personal level. The ombudsman acts as "friendly advisor" to clients requiring career guidance. The ombudsman also acts in the role of professional referral agent and diagnostician and resource person who matches client needs with internal and external resources such as EAP and private counseling. For example, what does the fired store clerk do? Does she fight to change the system or just move on? Does she live in a jurisdiction where she can appeal to an outside employment rights agency? There are pros and cons to these actions. Personal counseling and/or referral to a lawyer may be needed, although legal referrals are not made until all internal remedies are exhausted. Customers use both formal and informal means to evaluate their options. Informally, they consult friends and co-workers at their place of business. What should they do with a defective product — a lemon automobile? What should they do about a physician error coupled with arrogance? Friends join them in their anger and say "sue." A customer relations ombudsman can offer personal guidance on how to solve the problem in the most effective manner, often meaning without the expense and time delay of litigation. However, in order to offer advice and counseling, the ombudsman must have an understanding of the nature of the problem.

Investigation and Conflict Resolution

As noted in the opening chapters, *all* organizations have employee and customer complaints. Contrary to a belief that a lack of complaints is evidence of management skill, an organization without complaints is probably an organization that does not listen. The inclusion of problem investigation, conciliation, and mediation activity is a statement about the organization and what it feels is appropriate (its core values). Ombudsman programs are one means by which employees and consumers can present their complaints to have them confronted by the organization. Their existence attests to management's recognition of the true reality of organizations: that all organizations have employees and customers who from time to time have complaints! The mature organization is one that is willing to admit to a reality with complaints, acting both to listen and to respond to voiced concerns. This reflects core values concern for employee and customer problems — and organizational security in a psychological sense, since senior executives are mature enough to admit that they are not perfect (nor are others). A mature and sophisticated organizational culture constantly identifies and attempts to correct problems.

Fact-finding and conciliation are intimately linked with this activity, as we will see. Rowe and Baker (1984, p. 133), have characterized the ideal process of investigation and mediation as follows: "A modern and creative approach to handling employee complaints stresses dispute resolution rather than adjudication. Many companies have procedures to investigate and mediate employee complaints in a far less polarized and formal manner than companies usually follow in unionized settings or when outside agencies are involved. The employee has to give permission for the investigation, which should be conducted on a low-key basis to protect everyone's privacy as well as the company's image." Many corporations, especially those with unions, already have formal grievance procedures, but these are often unsatisfactory. For example, they may be too formalized, adversarial in nature, time-consuming, bureaucratic, or quasi-legal; they may also involve labor contracts or promote win/lose outcomes. These characteristics contribute to the significant difficulty grievance systems experience in solving problems in a quick and effective fashion. There is a need for a less formal, less legalistic effort designed to solve problems through the use of negotiation and compromise. The informal ombudsmen and the more formal corporate or patient ombudsmen can cut through bureaucratic red tape, using much less formality in handling complaints. When a representative of a formal grievance system enters a unit or department, you know automatically that it is likely to be a time-consuming, step-by-step process to resolution, with the outcome defined in terms of who is right and who is wrong. The emphasis of the ombudsman is on problem solving and problem dissolving (Ackoff, 1981; Ackoff, Magidson, Addison, 2006). The conditions for the problem are made to disappear. The investigation is not focused on the assignment of blame and the determination of right and wrong. In the case of the sales clerk, is there not a possibility that the supervisor is completely mistaken in his view of the corporate sales policy? Is the problem simple-rehire the clerk, retrain, transfer, or fire the supervisor — or is there a more complex solution that requires personal and organizational responses such as open discussion of policy and ethics and training to more positively treat the problem and prevent a recurrence? Grievance systems make a formal determination of right and wrong. Ombudsmen do not. Ombudsmen do offer — however covert — a sense of whose position appears to be the more appropriate in this particular situation. This parallels but does not become adjudication.

Adjudication

Adjudicate means to judge and decide. If someone in the organization does not handle complaints, they will be taken outside to a court where a judge will make a decision, to the media or disseminated on the internet.

Rowe and Baker (1984, p. 134) noted the following corporate concerns about adjudication in general: "Many companies have designed formal complaint and appeal channels for adjudication of complaints. Some are multi-step systems designed to serve nonunion employees in unionized environments. As a result, they resemble traditional grievance systems in the scope and structure of their operations. A few such systems involve some form of binding arbitration that includes a neutral party from outside the company as a last step. This feature is said to be a critical aspect of the credibility and effectiveness of employee complaint procedures at companies such as American Electric Power, American Airlines, and TWA." Most ombudsmen reject adjudication, viewing it as an inappropriate ombudsman function. This is backed up by ombudsman codes of ethics and practice, particularly those in the corporate world. Ombudsmen do not feel that they should be responsible for deciding who is right and who is wrong. For example, most would refuse to serve as a "hearings judge" for the sales clerk/supervisor conflict. Instead, they regard themselves as facilitators of a problem resolution process whose success would depend in part on *not* assigning blame. In cases where ombudsmen do adjudicate disputes, the question of their fairness arises. Since ombudsmen are generally outside the line of supervision in organizations, there is the possibility that they could be biased against the individual's interests. However, there is a check to this bias. In practice, a constant tilting in favor of the organization would quickly dry up the stream of complaints. The employee grapevine is particularly efficient with regard to fairness. Employee and consumer perceptions that ombudsmen are biased would quickly kill the program. Regardless of whether ombudsmen adjudicate disputes, a critical task is passing on information derived from the complaints of employees and consumers.

Feedback

One problem managers face is how to find out what's going on in their organizations. While managers have a general "interest" in getting the feel of the organization, the good ones also recognize that they really need to know what employees and consumers think in order to know how they are doing from the standpoint of management effectiveness, productivity, and the quality of working life. A complaint program that systematically processes employee and consumer complaints is one way to find out just what employees are thinking. This occurs through "upward feedback." Ombudsmen pass information to executives at the top levels of the organization, who become aware of what employees and consumers complain about and can use that data to help judge the successes and failures of the work system and products. Ombudsmen are in fact part of a whole set of strategies for this purpose.

1984, p. 134) described the variety of programs used to
follows: "Companies use employee surveys, advisory coun-
l informal employee audits to stay alert to emerging prob-
structures can also contribute data. Quality circles can
oyee relations issues that are often at the core of 'technical'
problems. Health and safety committees (developed voluntarily or by federal
law — that is, Washington) can identify supervisors or employees whose behavior poses a special risk. Mentoring arrangements provide a good ear and savvy
advice on how the union employee should approach a problem encountered
on the job; a summary of these problems is useful to management. Employee
networks can help management understand the problems of special groups."
To this list of programs that help managers stay alert to emerging problems
we can add online surveys and questionnaires, feedback via social networking
sites, internal and external groups such as risk management or health and
safety committees that can identify potentially harmful situations.

The upward feedback of complaints about production processes, quality
of working life issues, or productivity barriers means that the organization at
least has an opportunity to address these problems, since of course the first
step in solving any problem, whether personal or organizational, is knowing
that the problem exists. Upward feedback provides the necessary data and
sheds light on any patterns in existing problems. This helps executives assess
whether there are differences between the organization's view of how it thinks
it treats employees and customers and how it actually treats them (the "theories
of action, theories in use" distinction of Argyris and Schon, 1975). Upward
feedback is one way to facilitate the organizational learning process. In summary, complaint processing — the ombudsman's primary activity — involves
personal communication; confidential advice and counseling; investigation,
conciliation, and mediation; adjudication; and upward feedback. As we have
observed, all of these functions are interrelated.

Education and Training

The second major component of the ombudsman's job is education and
training. Education is defined as instruction given to individuals or groups
to prepare and/or update them for work — the work of production or the
"work" of consuming goods and services. Ombudsmen provide preparatory
and/or continuing education to employees or consumers in both formal and
informal ways. They help to educate employees early in their career, and they
can also provide seasoned employees with additional training. More specifically, ombudsmen educate four groups: (1) employees who complain, (2) employees and others who are the subjects of those complaints, (3) upper management

and professional staff and (4) colleagues in the human problem response group — employee assistance staff, customer relations representatives, and others.

Continuing Education

Ombudsmen provide continuing education because managers, employees, and customers already have knowledge and experience about the company. This represents a base on which the educational efforts of ombudsmen can build. Ombudsmen provide continuing education and training on an almost unlimited number of topics. The list is defined by the subject of the complaints. The job and work experience of the sales clerk are just one of the topics. The involvement of ombudsmen in the sales clerk's problem produces continuing education for both the clerk and the supervisor, for example regarding policy acceptance and review of termination. It may also educate a few upper managers about the "trickle down" of corporate goals and values (hopefully a negative aspect uncovered). Each educational initiative is most significant for the individual and simultaneously has benefits for the organization as a whole. The clerk will be educated about her conflict. The supervisor may get "educated" about his interpretation of corporate sales policy. And some senior managers may get an education about what is happening in the trenches. Some of this education can be converted to training that works to prevent future occurrence of these problems. Along with continuing education, then, some ombudsmen provide preparatory education.

Preparatory Education

Ombudsmen also provide preparatory education, both in the intellectual sense and with respect to individual skills. For example, they may become involved in providing basic job readiness training for new managers. At this stage of their careers, these managers need to learn about work attitudes, conflict resolution, and productivity requirements. They must also acquire basic skills in customer and employee relations. Ombudsmen have considerable experience and skill in these areas, and so are in an excellent position to provide preparatory training. Educating senior management is often not labeled education but consultation, the final core activity of troubleshooters.

Consultation

Ombudsmen are consultants to senior management and to the participants in the conflicts they are called on to help resolve. In our view, ombudsmen are internal consultants. The designation *internal consultant* includes a wide range of consulting activities and consultant definitions. The following was offered by Meyers, Alpert, and Fleisher (1983): "There seems to be agreement that consultation is a joint effort at problem solving and that consultation involves indirect assistance of a third party. While there is agreement around these general issues, the models differ with respect to such issues as the role of the consultant, the problems to be addressed in consultation, and the means to go about helping. The theoretical framework and assumptions underlying each particular type of consultation naturally lead to these differences." There is no convenient classification system for the varieties of consultation models in ombudsman work, but all approaches and models involve some form of joint problem solving and process consultation (Schein, 1969). The approaches taken by consultants — and, by implication, ombudsmen — differ: "While other models are content-oriented, organization development is form-oriented. Thus, its goal is not content specific; rather, it is ... to help train members of organizations to be able to make the changes they democratically see fit to make on a system, not individual, level. Through fostering increased understanding of interpersonal communication, the uncovering of conflicts and interdependence, the increase in the desire and the ability to establish collective goals and make decisions, the OD consultant facilitates the development of a self-renewing system" (Meyers, Alpert, and Fleisher, 1983, p. 7).

In practical terms, a number of consultant types were defined by the Organization Development Institute, distinctions that also describe the ombudsman's consulting options. Ombudsmen can act as *purchase of service consultants,* as *expert advice consultants,* and/or as *process consultants.* The first of these are the consultants who provide a set of "packages" that can be applied in general fashion to a wide group of organizational problems. Examples of problems or needs that can often use set programs are time management or team building. Or an ombudsman involved with a whole series of cases relating to the ethics of sales policy (such as the clerk's dilemma) may decide to offer a half-day workshop to supervisors and managers. This might be designed and developed as a one-time effort or repeated throughout the organization. The ombudsman may be a consultant to the designers of the workshop and/or a member of the team using the case experience for training. While there are ombudsmen that could easily offer this service, particularly after years on the job — few spend much time providing standard packages of education and training. Since ombudsmen nearly always confront unique problems in new situations, prepackaged solution programs would rarely if ever work.

Ombudsmen also offer expert advice based on intimate knowledge of the organization and of problem solving and conflict resolution. The expert consultant is called in to diagnose a problem and to provide knowledgeable advice on how to respond. Data gathering and a report are key. The report makes direct suggestions and recommendations for action based on the expert's specialist knowledge of the problem and subject area. Ombudsmen "visit" many parts of the organization during their complaint handling. They observe and interview and report not only on the specific case but on the issues of concern, the patterns of problems that seem to be emerging. They are experts on problem pattern analysis and data feedback and on problem resolution. Delivering expert assessments and providing packaged training or services are both very different from process consulting, which we feel is the key consulting role for ombudsmen. This is the third type of ombudsman consultant work and in our view the preferred consulting approach: "The third consultant type, the *Process Consultant,* is again a professional group or individual who focuses attention on how work is accomplished. This is the usual model espoused by the Organization Development professional. In this consultant model, an organization diagnosis is made, the results of the diagnosis are shared with staff and management, and the needs of the organization are iden-tified, clarified, and put in perspective. Next, the consultant determines, in collaboration with the organization, which problems are most immediate and what has to be learned or done in order to correct these. The consultant, again in concert with staff, will create an intensive learning program especially designed to meet the individual organization's needs. After the program is planned, conducted and evaluated, new learning programs are created and the cycle begins anew" (Organization Development Institute, 1981). The ombudsman as process consultant is the organizational development consult-ant referred to by Meyers, Alpert, and Fleisher (1983), defined in detail by Schein (1969), and illustrated by Hirschhorn and Krantz (1982). While some ombudsmen may offer prepackaged programs, most act as process consultants in their ombudsman role. Some ombudsmen have expert knowledge, for example on conflict resolution, dealing with difficult clients; de-escalating the angry employee or client, workplace bullying and sexual harassment, work-place violence, but they are not used as often in their organizations for their technical expertise as for their abilities in helping others solve problems. The ombudsman assists in creating a process that will (1) resolve individual client complaints and problems (employee and/or customer), and (2) initiate diag-nostic assessment that will help to create learning and response actions for the organization as a whole. Ombudsmen work *with* employees and managers to continue the organization's development. They are not assigned responsi-bility for action; that remains with line and staff personnel. For the sales clerk problem, the question is whether the organization will investigate further to determine how widespread the problem is. How will the need for this process be promoted and sold? Ombudsmen act as consultants to management, offering ideas and facilitating the process of problem confrontation and resolution.

Neutrality

When ombudsmen work at complaint processing, education, and consultation, are they neutral or are they agents of the corporation or agents (advocates) of the client? This is a significant question. Rowe wrote about the issue in 1987 but what she said is not only still relevant but has become an essential part of an ombudsman's self understanding. Neutrality is enshrined in the IOA Code of Ethics and Standards of Practice (2007, 2009a) and is the bedrock of ombudsman practice. While some ombudsmen assume the title advocate, in general, ombudsmen do not advocate, either for employees or clients.

Mary Rowe said:

> An ombudsman clearly is *not* an ordinary kind of advocate: this practitioner specifically is not a conventional "employee advocate." But the definitions of 'neutrality' and 'impartiality' adopted by practitioners vary from company to company.
>
> About half the organizations with ombudsman offices have designated their practitioners as neutrals. Nearly all expect the practitioner to be at least impartial in all interpersonal interactions, including those with senior managers. (All expect the practitioner to uphold relevant laws, statutes and company policies; one is, in other words, not "neutral" with regard to the law or company policy.)
>
> Practitioners tend to talk about these matters in company-specific terms, such as: "I am an advocate for fair *process*, not for any specific person or position." "I am impartial and neutral up to the point that I find a law or company policy being flouted." "My company believes the long-range interests of the company lie with anyone who has been unfairly treated. If two people have each treated the other unfairly, the company may have an interest on both sides." Most practitioners simply say, "I have to find solutions that meet many sets of rights and interests," or "The ombudsman will take into account the rights of all employees and managers and the obligations of the company ... and also the rights of the company and the obligations of employees and managers." In technical terminology, the ombudsman is committed to integrative solutions, and avoids distributive solutions both by the design of the office (an informal non adjudicatory structure) and by personal commitment [Rowe, 1987, p.128].

Acting neutral in order that clients perceive the ombudsman to be fair and impartial is critical to the job. Whether the work of an informal or formal ombudsman is officially designated as a "neutral" is almost irrelevant. Perceived and real neutrality is essential to the successful carrying out of the job.

Ombudsman Job Characteristics

A few more brief comments on the characteristics of the ombudsman's job are warranted. A desirable job design has seven characteristics (Umstot, Mitchell, and Bell, 1978; Kast and Rosenzweig, 1985; Hellriegel and Slocum, 2010) that can be cited for review purposes: there is very high *skill variety*, with ombudsmen using a wide range of skills and talents in almost every case. Ombudsmen have responsibility for the case from start to finish. They assume responsibility for problem resolution *(task identity)*. The job itself has great meaning for both the individual with the problem and the organization *(task significance)*. Both suffer from the conflict. Ombudsmen have considerable *autonomy*, since they need freedom and discretion in order to get the job done. *Feedback* from clients and superiors is both clear and direct. Conflicts are resolved or they escalate. Ombudsmen goals are clear *(goal clarity)*. They must resolve conflicts for personal and organizational benefits. But *goal difficulty* is high, meaning that there is constant challenge in the job. These seven characteristics describe why the ombudsman's job is both highly stimulating and enticing. It is meaningful, important, and highly challenging, the kind of job in which one gets deeply involved.

The Flow of Work Activity

What is the flow of these ombudsman actions? An executive might ask whether ombudsmen provide each of these services to all employees and customers in some sort of flow sequence. In fact, they do not. The work in each case is most often unique, although there are repetitions of problem-solving paths. For organizations that are collecting complaints from both employees and customers or clients, the ombudsman's activities can be thought of as a two-track process. On the one hand, complaints from employees and/or customers are taken in. The transformation process (in systems terms) involves the primary work activities of complaint processing (personal communication; confidential advice and counseling; investigation, conciliation, and mediation; adjudication; and upward feedback), education and training (continuing, preparatory), and consultation (service, expert, process). The outputs include information that is passed on to executives regarding the nature of structure and process difficulties in the organization.

Summary

This chapter defined the ombudsman's job as consisting of three core activities: complaint processing, education and training, and consultation. Complaint processing involves personal communication; confidential advice and counseling; investigation, conciliation, and mediation; adjudication; and upward feedback. Ombudsman educational activity involves providing both continuing and preparatory education to employees and customers. Ombudsmen inform employees about the nature of conditions, policies, and rules in the organization and about the effects of their own behavior. Upward feedback is used for educating top management about the status of the organization's employees and customers (that is, whether they are satisfied or not) and about the organization's production performance. Finally, consultation is provided, with process work being the dominant consulting role.

Chapter 5

Designing and Implementing an Ombudsman Program

How do we begin? We use another example to illustrate.

Susan Davidson was a professional secretary with ambition and determination. She had top flight skills and was finishing a bachelor's degree in business at night. She wanted a promotion to an administrative position. When her boss's administrative officer announced she was leaving in two months, Susan informed Mr. Thompson she was interested. He said she was qualified and a hard worker and suggested a meeting to review the job and her other qualifications. He suggested dinner, which she politely declined, preferring instead to talk in the office. One week later he suggested dinner again, getting the same response from her. When all the candidates were selected for interviews, she was not in the group. When she inquired why, Mr. Thompson said she "did not measure up." She sued.

How does an employee solve this kind of problem? Davidson solved it by suing the company — and winning. When she started, she had no "hate" for the company, only anger about the way she was treated. However, when her company refused to address her problem, her anger about unfair treatment led her to the courts. This is one way the need for an ombudsman program is identified.

This chapter deals with the creation of ombudsman programs. Since formal types are most complex, it focuses on formal programs; a few brief remarks are also devoted to informal programs. We turn first to the formal start-up process, which is initially discussed as if we were walking through a program planning team's analysis.

A Formal Ombudsman Program's Beginning

How ombudsman programs get started is an interesting story with many variations. One corporation ignored complaints from employees and customers

61

that resulted in lawsuits ultimately costing several million dollars. In any severe case — from denial of promotion to sabotage and harassment — the costs eventually include aggravation for executives, the loss of one or two persons fired, heavy emotional stress, and unproductive work time with resulting dollar losses from senior executives' involvement in the case.

Organizations also have a long-term fear that bigger complaints will eventually surface. For example, company managers with several divisions developing chemicals used in fertilizers worried that some employees in the plant would feel that their concerns about job safety were not being heard. Employees might go to the courts with the problem, generating a lawsuit like the ones involving asbestos. The managers thought that if they could respond to and correct individual safety complaints, they could avoid major conflicts by resolving individual disputes at an early stage.

Program start-up is also stimulated when executives are astonished to find that they could lose so much money on "small matters" such as sexual harassment. Their surprise leads to an attitude of, "What if we had a real problem here?" This is a fairly common position, not particular to any executive group. As the financial and personal costs of settlements rise, this position is changing and so are large corporations' responses to complaints.

A question leading to program discussions is therefore how to reduce future litigation, both from employees and from dissatisfied or wronged customers. A wrongful termination case is an example. Management debate about options in one case usually leads to the need to explore alternative ways of resolving disputes within the corporation and between the corporation and outside parties. This prompts discussion of dispute resolution techniques and of the ongoing national search for alternatives to litigation.

Although it is an interesting subject for executives, perhaps only a few have information on the nature and development of new approaches to conflict resolution. Those with some experience in public affairs may know of the ombudsman role in government agencies. There is often no immediate direction to proceed, however. The executive taking a formal approach to development might appoint a program planning team to proceed through a series of development steps. While each process is unique, five typical steps are as follows:

> Step 1: Conduct environmental analysis: the external view.
> Step 2: Assess fit with corporate culture: the organization's internal status.
> Step 3: Design the ombudsman program.
> Step 4: Start up and operate.
> Step 5: Periodically evaluate progress.

These steps are similar to the program planning used for any new product or service (for example, see Scheirer, 1981; Posavac and Carey, 1985). To assist readers in understanding the ombudsman program planning process and to provide some guidelines for program development, each step is reviewed in some detail.

Step 1: Conduct Environmental Analysis: The External View

A planning group for a troubleshooter program may first conduct a "scan of the organizational environment" as the initial formal program planning activity. Two or three members will assess whether the current external environment will support an alternative dispute resolution/ombudsman system. Through a series of meetings, the planning group will scan the environmental areas for support or rejection of the ombudsman concept. These areas would include such topics as law, culture, technology, education, and politics.

Ombudsman program planners must determine whether general external environmental trends support a complaint mechanism as a useful addition to the organization. It is an attractive activity *if* it can help to avoid outcomes such as the cost of the sexual harassment settlement. But beyond cost savings, what does an ombudsman program accomplish, either positively or negatively, that would generate support or resistance from the environment? Members of the planning team might divide their scanning into the areas of the organizational environment that we have surveyed earlier (law, economics, technology, politics, and so on).

After a series of meetings and extensive research, a memorandum will emerge that identifies the degree of fit between the proposed ombudsman program and current trends in the business and public arenas. The following review is illustrative of this scanning activity and its output.

EXHIBIT 1: MEMORANDUM

To: Senior Executive Group
From: Ombudsman Program Planning Group
Re: Environmental Review

Background. We were asked to examine the ombudsman concept because the company is faced with increasing litigation, and it has dual interests in improving the quality of working life and removing barriers to productivity. This part of our report addresses external issues.

Analysis. The first area we reviewed was the *law.* There are some current trends and considerations of great interest to the corporation. Recent settlements of wrongful termination and sexual harassment cases (among many other types) are increasingly recognized for their legal and economic impact. But further probing uncovered other legal issues for the organization.

Many private corporations and public agencies have always used outside counsel. However, the growth in outside counsel's expenses has been phenomenal, especially over the past ten years. Both private and public organizations are seeking ways to diminish the use of outside counsel. Recently, they have begun to build their own complement of internal corporate legal staff. In some organizations, management has announced the need for a program for reducing legal costs. Many organizations have grasped the fact that there must be alternatives to court settlements of issues and problems related to corporate activities. It is clear that legal pressures in the organizational environment are pushing for alternative ways to settle disputes. This one area of the organizational environment shows support for ombudsman development.

Closely allied to this is *economics,* the second subject of our scanning. In many organizations, there already is recognition of the high cost of ignored complaints. There is no "environmental data" indicating that future complaints will be lower in numbers or that the financial impact will be lessened. If anything, prevailing experience suggests that as higher settlements in suits of all types begin to emerge, they become "data" for analysis by certain interested parties (potential plaintiffs and their attorneys). This is illustrated by the medical malpractice cases. Both attorneys and future complainants tend to watch the size of the settlements and, in some cases, the ease with which they are arrived at, using these observations to determine their future interest in pressing a case.

In short, it appears that all organizations' costs of handling complaints — either by ignoring them or by allowing them to go to court — will eventually become unacceptably high.

A part of this concern about complaints stems from the general recognition that *culturally* (the third environmental area) more employees and customers are becoming assertive about their individual rights. The rise in corporate legal expenses and in part the increase in legal involvement in customer and employee concerns is a cultural phenomenon. More consumers are concerned about their rights and about producer obligations. This was initiated with the widely known activities of Ralph Nader. In the 1970s and 1980s, this trend continued in the direction of employees' rights (Ewing, 1977; Westin and Salisbury, 1980; Ewing, 1983). This change in employee/consumer assertiveness became an increasing challenge as more members of the culture *believed* that they had employee/consumer rights that they could assert. This changing culture, especially in North America, contributed to an upward rise in consumer complaints. This trend shows no sign of abating.

This cultural trend toward more complaints is linked to the increasing *educational* level of the population (a fourth environmental area). Although there is relatively little data, the speculation is that those people most likely to complain are those most educated about their rights and the demands that they can make on public and private organizations. The rising educational level of the population is thus seen as a potential contributor to an increase in complaints. This educational level creates a need for a formal mechanism to allow educated persons to voice their concerns and to have a fair hearing. Additionally, educated persons are less likely to be fooled by or satisfied with the public relations-oriented activities of corporations and their image-making representatives. In short, an educated population is more likely to see through a corporation's superficial attempts to smooth over or finesse a problem, resulting in further complaints or a quick trip to the courts.

The high-tech world of the past thirty years or so is a part of the fifth environmental area. The educational level of the population is related to the phenomenal growth in *technologies* in almost all organizations. This phenomenal growth is hardly surprising, nor is it thought to be a situation that will either disappear or level off. Along with technological growth comes an increase in the sophistication of the work force and the complexity of the work systems. Both sophistication and complexity result in more potential areas and points for conflict between the organization and employees and consumers. It is assumed that the rise in technology and the change generated by the inclusion of new technology in existing work systems has and will continue to create much employee anxiety and, inevitably, complaints about the way the organization responds to these problems. It has also created generational conflict in that young adults have never known a world without computers yet many senior managers are still uncomfortable with the wired world. The wired world is also a world that is always "on." People may have the freedom to work from home but they are also expected to respond to calls from electronic devices while on a weekend getaway. Additionally, increases in new technology yield problems in new-product performance and in product understanding and use by consumers. Technology is thus considered a primary contributor to the growth in complaints.

Politics is the next environmental topic. In past years, there has been a belief that government in one form or another would step in to help resolve individual versus organization conflicts, or at least would offer a mechanism for doing so. However, politics in the first decade of the 21st century has been caught up in a conflict between those who oppose government intervention in all forms and others who reluctantly accept government bailouts as necessary evils. Whatever the political future, organizations need to create their own mechanisms for responding to complaints.

Two final environmental trends are significant but less primary contributors to the pressure for ombudsman programs. One environmental pressure is *sociological.* Human resource staff are especially aware of the changing patterns of relationships among employees and the emerging stresses of all sorts, such as two-career families, for example. This has generated difficulties in transfer and hiring/recruitment. It is expected that these changes in the work force will continue to place upward pressure on conflict levels. For example, the pure logistical difficulties of transferring two career-oriented employees means that corporations will experience more complaints about movement of employees around national and worldwide sites.

Related sociological changes include a "back-to-roots" and "family life" orientation that makes corporate employees less open to transfer. At any point of difference between "usual organizational behavior" (for example, openness to transfer) and an employee's new sociological changes/directions, there is increased conflict potential.

The final concern for ombudsman program planning is the issue of *demography.* The workplace has changed in two ways: increasing immigration has led to concerns about diversity and conflicts and questions over which cultural behaviors can be accommodated in the workplace, and which cannot (for example, how will a company deal with a request for prayer rooms in the workplace, extra religious holidays, cultural or religious dress?). The aging of the population means that at some point the corporation will again have to address issues such as mandatory retirement where this is still permitted by law or culture. While organizations are moving to resolve this with competency-based tests and other mechanisms, the problem of how to manage increasing numbers of aging employees is pressing. Many of the baby boomers are about to retire? Who will replace these employees, especially if highly skilled? If they choose to remain at work, will others perceive them to be selfishly hogging all the privileges and benefits of workplace power and seniority, blocking opportunities for a younger generation?

Consider the educational level of the population now and the increased sophistication of the baby-boom generation, the first to claim its own space and voice, and possibly the first group of people in late middle age who still think they are rebels. This is the generation that has shaped the past 40 years and led changes in laws and workplace practices, such as family insurance for same-sex couples. This is a generation that questions authority even now, when it is the generation in power.

Phenomenal growth in the aging group is already upon us. Is it not more likely that this group will be inclined to act in its own interests, presenting complaints to the corporation's management about the way individuals are treated? The emergence of the aging population's power means that this is an environmental pressure that should not be understated. Planning to manage the complaints they will continue to generate, probably to their last breath, is critical because the workplace of the future will be made up of competing interests: highly educated and skilled immigrants who will not accept being sidelined for promotion (and who may decide that lack of promotion is racism); younger people who want, finally, to get the corner office with the perks and good pension that their parents had and, lastly, the 70-something boomer who simply won't stop working, not only because he can, but because the last recession ate away at his capital.

While this list is not an exhaustive scan of our corporate environment, it does show significant pressures for development of a mechanism for resolving complaints. The planning group has sufficient evidence to suggest that systems designs should be explored. In fact, several pressures (for example, legal and economic) are independently significant enough to generate support for an ombudsman program, irrespective of the contributions of the other pressure points.

After this environmental scan, the program planning group needs to determine how well an ombudsman program concept fits their organizational culture. This leads the group to analyze the organizational culture, with attention directed toward the degree of fit between culture, the company's current status, and the ombudsman program concept.

Step 2: Assess Fit with Corporate Culture: The Organization's Internal Status

A *culture review* or *culture audit* is an analysis of the match between the organization's characteristics and the ombudsman concept. The planning group concentrates on defining and describing the five items below:

Participants and their characteristics.
Occupations of the work group.
Power and specific interest groups.
General organizational characteristics.
Corporate trends and current financial status.

The purpose of this internal analysis is to determine whether the organization would accept an ombudsman program and whether the timing is right. With the help of brainstorming sessions, the above topics are expanded, using this list as the starting elements for consideration. All of these are reviewed, with the highlights of the findings presented in a summary memorandum.

Participants and Characteristics. The planning group first considers who in the corporate culture would have a stake in a new problem resolution system (a stakeholder analysis; Mitroff, 1983). The analysis begins at the top, focusing on the chief executive officer and senior vice presidents (or their equivalent in public sector management: secretaries of cabinet-level departments and their deputies). These individuals need to believe in and support the ombudsman concept right from the start in order for it to become viable. The chief executive officer must believe in employee/consumer communication and be willing to back it with resources. The planning group must determine whether the CEO has a management group that will tolerate and, more important, encourage open communication. Communication between management and employees up and down the organization needs to be supported, since without this communication base, the ombudsman concept has no chance.

In order for the planning group to feel that top management is open to the concept, they must find a ombudsman program to be a logical extension of management's philosophy and activity within the organization. How, for example, does management usually address issues like policy conflict, interpersonal conflict, and alcoholism? Are the problems openly confronted and addressed? Or are they submerged and ignored? If a key member of the senior executive team is violently opposed to open confrontation of complaints, start-up will be difficult.

The planning group must also consider the views of middle management, professional staff and employees. Are they accustomed to a culture that encourages open dialogue and communication? When the program concept is announced to the employees and to consumers, will they see this as an attempt to *continue* to solicit employee suggestions and complaints, or will it be new?

In summary, will a ombudsman program be consistent with most of the personal philosophies of management and employees that define the organizational culture as a whole? If not, the ombudsman program will be an intended (or unintended) part of cultural change — from closed to open communication with all of the attendant problems that major change entails.

For example, the secretary in our opening case can take her complaint to an ombudsman (new to the company) as the "first case" to be openly addressed *ever*. The level of shock will be much higher than in a company where problems and issues were confronted and resolved by a peer review program (Olson, 1984) or other complaint system (Rowe and Baker, 1984).

Occupations. A second planning area involves employee occupations. Are there occupations that do not fit with the ombudsman concept? We know that ombudsmen are at work in organizations where there is a mix of highly sophisticated engineers and research and development personnel (Bell Labs), in those with manufacturing personnel (McDonnell Douglas), in those where production-oriented clerks (Blue Shield) or assembly line workers (General Motors) are dominant, and in a wide range of public and semi-public agencies:

educational institutions, health care agencies, hospitals, the police, military, correctional institutions; welfare departments, even churches. The program is most consistent with a work force that has experienced openness, including opportunities to speak out and be heard.

Some organizations would not allow discussion of a sexual harassment case. Others would discuss it as an individual *personal* problem of one employee. Ombudsmen need at least enough freedom from the culture to support confronting the problem as a single case, and as a possible organization-wide issue.

Power and Interest Groups. The planning group must address the question of power. This design issue involves the need to have the ombudsman report to someone high in the organization, someone with enough authority and power to permit the ombudsman to do his or her work. In many organizations, the chief executive officer is the logical choice. Unfortunately, many top executives have a passion for attending meetings in other cities, for making themselves highly visible to their divisions throughout the country and to community and professional groups. Given this situation, practicality often means that the CEO is not the choice for ombudsman supervisor. Instead, a frequent choice is the senior operations manager, senior vice-president or senior vice-president for human resources, since the ombudsmen concept in the context presented in this book is predominantly people oriented. In some cases, the ombudsman reports to the board. The ombudsman is not usually part of the line-management structure.

Lodging the ombudsman office with human resources is sometimes not a good choice, since power in private corporations does not always rest with human resources/personnel people. However, when a chief executive officer with tenure and recognized performance personally supports the senior vice president for human resources, the setup will work. When human resources has the ear of the CEO and this fact is well known, he or she is a good choice for a power base for the ombudsman. Few other formal positions lower in the organization are thought to be viable as ombudsman reporting links.

Regardless of the position, power and reporting relationship are interlocked, and depend on a good relationship between the ombudsman and the executive to whom he or she reports. With a good relationship, an ombudsman can present and discuss sensitive cases such as suicide, sabotage, and sexual harassment. Without that relationship, those cases will not be addressed or even brought to light.

General Organizational Characteristics; Finances. The fourth area for consideration is the fit between the ombudsman concept and certain organizational characteristics; the fifth area involves finances. Here the planning group offers its review in a memorandum.

EXHIBIT 2: MEMORANDUM

To: Senior Executive Group
From: Ombudsman Program Planning Group
Re: Organization's Status

Purpose. We reviewed the organization's current status to assess the degree of fit between where the company is now and the ombudsman concept. This memo covers three areas — history, character, and financial status and trend.

History. The organization has been in business since 1910. It has experienced no labor/management difficulties but has operated for its full history without a union. There are some 35,000 employees in this particular branch of the organization. The corporation holds a 32 percent market share in a market that is fairly competitive — a dominant share. The company was founded by a family who turned over management of the business to professional managers some twenty years ago but still maintains large stock holdings. They tend not to interfere in the business. It is not expected that the board would have any difficulties with the addition of an ombudsman.

Character. The corporation tends to be activist-oriented in terms of public positions in support of environmental protection, community development, outdoor recreation activities, and general community services. The corporation has a long-established and excellent community reputation, both within its geographical locale and in the national business community. The program planning group feels that corporate members and family stockholders would not be concerned about the potential for "bad image" publicity if someone found out they had a "complaint taker." If the media discovered that the corporation allowed employees to file complaints, it would be an indicator that the corporation had the courage to confront the issues, typical of its earned reputation.

In short, this organization's history and character were viable and healthy in early periods and they are today. A financial review of the corporation reinforces this status.

Financial Status and Trend. The corporation seems to be in a significant growth trend. Its financial status was termed "very healthy." There is no question that the corporation could financially afford the addition of a nonrevenue-producing position. The planning team believes that this kind of issue would not even arise for discussion. Profits for the past year were the second best in the organization's history. Financially, the timing is right for making an addition to the problem-solving mechanisms of the corporation. It would be regarded as moving forward in a positive, future-oriented sense and can be billed as a mechanism that would remove potential negative impacts on the future bottom line.

In summary, the planning group's brief review of these internal characteristics of the organization (participants, occupations, power, internal characteristics, and finances) indicated that there were no obstacles to the design and development of this ombudsman program. In fact, the timing appeared to be quite appropriate for the addition of the program to the organization.

The planning group next outlined the goals, technical system, and management design for the ombudsman program. This was a participative process that involved senior management, middle managers, and employees.

Step 3: Design the Ombudsman Program

Planning must encompass the actual design of the troubleshooter program, although not yet the operational issues, the day-to-day activities of the ombudsmen. The purpose of this planning is to develop an overview of the goals, technical work, structural arrangements, and management of the program. This analysis is divided into five areas of planning work, according to one model of organization and management (Kast and Rosenzweig, 1985; Ziegenfuss, 2007). The planning group must define the program's (1) goals, values, and culture; (2) product and technology; (3) structure; (4) psychosocial aspects; and (5) leadership/management. This is an organizational systems analysis of the ombudsman program concept (Ziegenfuss, 1985c, 1985a, 2007). The following overview details typical findings of a ombudsman planning group with respect to design issues.

Goals, Values, and Culture. A first planning consideration involves defining the philosophy and nature of the program, including the culture it will promote. What are the purposes of the program? How would the mission and purposes of a new ombudsman program fit with the culture of the organization?

As a start, the planning group must establish that the mission of the program is a developmental one. There should be complete agreement that the values and philosophy of the program are "helping," not "policing" in orientation. The problem resolution program should be *designed* for the purpose of helping the organization. It helps by assisting employees and management to resolve barriers to productivity and it helps by increasing the quality of working life and the quality of consuming life. Some investigation-type complaint programs are established with policing functions; their primary purpose is accountability, which may conflict with the helping mission of the ombudsman. Other programs (e.g., in hospitals) may encourage individuals to avoid dealing directly with ward or clinic management issues. Problems ensue when, for example, a nurse or physician encourages patients to complain to the ombudsman about issues unresolved by senior management. Sometimes an employee tries to launch a campaign of aggression against another employee by deliberately encouraging complaints to the ombudsman.

We have seen that the objectives of ombudsman programs are to increase employee productivity, communication, and participation, and to improve the quality of working life. These goals in turn imply certain values: (1) the sharing of problem responsibility and open communication, (2) employee and consumer participation, (3) a commitment to a high quality of employee work life, and (4) open confrontation of both individual and organizational problems. These values are represented by the "rituals" of complaint confrontation and resolution that become embedded in the corporate culture (Schein, 1985).

Rites and rituals are the "culture transmission method" that communicate the goals and values of the ombudsman program to managers and employees, a means for establishing the program's presence on a regular basis. For example, once a month the ombudsman is invited to the senior executive meeting (a usual ritual) to present a critique of the kinds of complaints (such as policy problems, personnel and/or consumer complaints, and harassment) and the types of resolutions used (for example, negotiated compromise, reprimand for manager, department-wide or specialist training). A second example of embedding the ombudsman's work in existing rituals is to make the complaint summaries a part of the executives' quarterly and six-month reports that are reviewed in depth by the executive team. Through formal presentations and informal discussions, this establishes the ombudsman's presence in the organization, ensuring his or her place in the cultural network of senior executives.

The presence of the ombudsman in the cultural network involves several concerns. How does he or she fit into the structure (for example, at what level), and how is acceptance established? This individual must have access to senior management meetings on a regular basis, needing only to notify senior management that he or she would be attending. If real top-executive support exists, this should be affirmed most of the time. Ombudsmen invest time in senior management meetings, both as a way of marketing the adviser service and as a way of getting to know key executives. In hospitals and universities, the ombudsman would meet with division heads or physician committees.

There are two useful networks to which the ombudsman must be connected. The first is the senior management group just discussed. The second network for employee ombudsmen is the human resources group. This group includes human resources personnel such as the employee assistance program, personnel counselors, and the EEO representative. Involvement in this network is not so important for power and status in the organization. Instead, this is the group of working relationships that will generate referrals and linkages for the ombudsman program, for example referral of a complaining employee with an addiction problem to the employee assistance representative or referral of a policy problem from EAP to the ombudsman. Without close and ongoing linkage to the executive network, there will be no power and authority. Without linkage to the human resource network, there will be no referral sources or resources for support.

We have reviewed goals, values, and ombudsman linkage to the cultural network that already exists. There is an alternative to harmony with the existing culture. The issue of whether or not the ombudsman program would initiate cultural change within the organization must be addressed.

One basic question with regard to cultural maintenance or change is whether the presence of the ombudsman indicates a move toward much higher levels of employee/management or consumer/corporation communication. Some organizations have very open communication and operations as a starting point. In these there is little fear that a ombudsman would be a contradiction to the corporate culture. In public and private organizations with open communication, the presence of the ombudsman simply formalizes the openness that already exists, creating a good match between the existing organizational culture and the new position. For an organization interested in moving toward a more participative, open culture, the ombudsman becomes a part of the change process. Instead of repressing complaints, they are now brought out and addressed directly, often meaning that initial discomfort with the ombudsman will be high. In a "closed culture," the sexual harassment case is quietly resolved by suggesting that the secretary leave or transfer to another division. With a push for cultural openness, this case is still confidentially solved, but the issue is raised on a corporate level (without disclosure of the parties involved). Problems and issues can acquire a high profile as needed. In organizations with closed cultures, on the other hand, fierce resistance to a new program of this type would be expected. Where cultural change is the agenda, a plan will be needed if the ombudsman program is part of a planned change effort.

This completes the review of ombudsman program goals, values, and culture issues. The ombudsman represents goals and values that may or may not be a part of the existing corporate culture. If not, cultural change is an intended or unintended outcome. Planning must assess this starting point before moving to the technical design questions, the next planning topic.

The Products and Technology of Ombudsman Activities. Planning must address a series of design questions. Ombudsman program design involves eight topics:

Determining the target group of clients.
Specifying the primary duties of the ombudsman.
Defining allowable complaint topics.

Selecting problem resolution techniques.
Setting the degree of formality of the effort.
Establishing confidentiality guidelines.
Providing feedback on individual and complaint groups.
Defining data use.

All program elements are more fully detailed later, but it is important to define some broad guidelines for these technical issues from the start. Each is briefly described in the memo that follows, a sample of how one corporation might present the operational design for an ombudsman program for employees. The topics are identical for a customer-oriented program; they only need to be altered to fit the consumer focus.

EXHIBIT 3: MEMORANDUM

To: Senior Executive Group
From: Ombudsman Program Planning Group
Re: Ombudsman Program Technical Design
  This memorandum addresses eight technical design elements of our proposed ombudsman program.

  1. Target Group of Employees. The ombudsman is to be used by all nonunion employees at all levels except top management. Union employees in the various divisions have their own formal grievance program. Top management executives are excluded. They would not be able to get much satisfaction by complaining to a ombudsman who reports to a colleague. Additionally, the conflict of interest inherent in the ombudsman working for one colleague while taking complaints from another would not be functional.

  2. Primary Duties. The planning group looked up the various ombudsman websites and decided to send one of their group to an ombudsman conference on setting up an ombudsman program. They were particularly impressed to see that a leader in their own field was one of the featured speakers. These are seen as good starting descriptions of the complaint program, which could evolve and be adapted as necessary over time. The functions included the following:

   A. Complaint processing
    1. personal communication
    2. confidential advice and counseling
    3. investigation or inquiry, conciliation, and mediation
    4. complaint resolution, adjudication where required or permitted
    5. upward feedback

B. education and training

C. consultation

These are considered to be the primary activities of the new ombudsman.

3. *Complaint Topics.* The types of complaints to be taken comprise the third technical design topic. It was decided that the scope of complaint topics would *not* be narrow. There should be wide latitude in choice in the interest of stimulating complaints and in avoiding the problem of a single type of complaint being the "identifier" for the system. The design team is interested in promoting the use of the system; attempting to define excluded topics would decrease utilization. Nonetheless, it should be made clear what the ombudsman cannot do for the client, such as investigate concurrently with a lawsuit, for example.

The group brainstormed a sample list of expected employee complaint subjects as follows: promotion, discrimination, sexual harassment, policies, benefits, personality conflicts, unfair treatment generally, dismissal practices, and physical environment.

It was expected that this list would expand, with the topic boundaries being nearly unlimited. However, it was recognized that if the company developed related programs like employee assistance and equal opportunity, some of the complaints taken by the ombudsman would be referred to one of these offices for a response. This would limit the ombudsman's time in these areas to complaint identification and referral.

4. *Techniques.* The planning group addressed the question of whether this program would be primarily an interpersonal type of response in terms of complaint investigation and follow-up. The option at the other end of the method continuum was to create an online or a paper-and pencil-based system of inquiry, complaint and response. Some ombudsmen emphasize face-to-face or telephone meetings; others prefer written systems, either email or letter.

The design group recognized that it was possible to establish a complaint program using either type of technique, that is, heavy personal interaction via meeting or phone or written interactions, via email, comments solicited via the company website, or letter. However, the design group felt that the primary technique should involve individual interpersonal exchange. This was recognized as a much more expensive design but one that would ultimately establish more intensive communication within the organization.

5. *Degree of Formality.* The design group felt that the ombudsman program should maintain a high level of informality. While complaint processes should be documented, it was important to keep it relatively informal in order to stay away from the "legalistic" complaint resolution system designs. It was generally assumed that all ombudsman programs face internal *ongoing pressures*

toward increasing documentation and formalism. To begin with an informal emphasis on resolution of problems, not documentation and legalism, is felt to be the best base for strong complaint processing productivity and acceptance (a humanizing, people-first approach).

This would lead naturally to selection of ombudsmen who resist keeping formal reports and/or extensive transcripts of conversations, notes, persons interviewed, and data sources collected for each of the complaints. Some of the complaint programs examined in the public and private sectors do use extensive documentation as a basis for their work. In this planning group's view, they were considered to be bureaucratic in nature and not much better than the legalistic systems they are designed to be an alternative to.

6. Confidentiality. All complaints and complaint responses are to be absolutely confidential. Only those people essential to the investigation of the complaint need to know the nature of the complaint and names can only be released with permission. The only qualifying clause was the "duty to warn" in the event of threatened harm by a complainant to another person in the corporation. For example, there would be a duty on the ombudsman's part to warn a potential victim if someone threatened to murder a supervisor and named the supervisor, time, and place. In the legal literature there is generally an established precedent that the listener, whether he or she is a counselor or psychiatrist (or probably an ombudsman), has a duty to warn the target about the impending danger.

7. Feedback. The questions related to confidentiality and the extent of documentation and written reports also involve consideration of how much information is fed back, to whom, why, when, and how. What is reported about a sexual harassment case? The primary feedback goes to the complainant, since this person has a need to know about the outcome of the problem. This should occur very soon after the resolution of the problem, within hours or days (constrained somewhat by the work schedule). When the committee reviewed some of the complaint program designs in existence, they found that they were on a continuum with regard to feedback. Some programs provide extensive information on the outcome of the problem; others simply tell the complainant that it was solved. There was a split within the planning committee about how this feedback would be given, whether in person or in writing. In keeping with the push for informality, the general belief was that the feedback should be given orally, with no written feedback. Had the committee decided that the email or letter-based system would be recommended, there would have to be a written response documenting the resolution of the complaint.

8. Data Use. The design group recommends that some statistics regarding the nature and number of the complaints be kept and that these be passed on to top management. The ombudsman would develop simple frequency counts, complaints by month, and complaints according to a categorization (of types of complaints). They would not be detailed in any way that could lead to identification of the specific complainants who filed them. There was some vigorous debate about tracking complaints to individual units (departments, divisions, floors), although this was seen as quite valuable to the organization developmentally. Some felt it allows identification of the complainant in highly unique and sensitive complaints. However, units would be able to use the data to spot organization and management problems if they could receive the data in the aggregate, protecting confidentiality.

This memo outlined the technical work system of the ombudsman program, focusing on eight design elements: target group, primary duties, allowable topics, problem resolution techniques, degree of formality, confidentiality, feedback, and data use. This work system is embedded in a structure that is a combination of the arrangement of the ombudsman program parts and the whole organizational context. Planning group discussions and decisions about structure are summarized next.

Structural Issues. The planning committee addressed eight structural aspects of the ombudsman program design, including standardization, specialization, formalization, complexity, centralization, personnel configuration, professionalism, and authority (Daft, 1983; Ziegenfuss, 1985a, 2007). All of these are briefly discussed as they would be presented in a planning document developed by the ombudsman program group.

1. *Standardization.* It was quickly recognized that the ombudsman's complaint-taking process and certainly the responses could *not* be standardized. Each complaint is viewed as an individual situation that should be dealt with individually, leaving much space for innovation and creativity. There was considerable concern that the ombudsman should not be confronted with bureaucratic attempts to standardize the process at the outset of development. How, for example, would one standardize sabotage, transfer, or sexual harassment cases? Facts and outcomes in all cases will be unique. Process and procedures, however, could be specified in somewhat standardized fashion.

2. *Specialization.* Should the ombudsman become a *specialist* in certain types of complaints, for example, in discrimination, hiring/firing, harassment, policy, or promotion issues? The design intent was that the work structure be broad and encompassing, with specialization left to other units (such as the employee assistance program or EEO office) as required. This program was to be a generalist-type problem-solving effort. Ombudsman work should be diverse and broad, not constrained or directed at only certain types of problems.

3. *Formalization.* How formal should the structure of the program be? It was agreed that there should be formal recognition from the chief executive

officer, appearance on the organizational chart, and inclusion in formal news releases and information memorandums within the organization. These would be evidence of the formal presence of the program. However, as already discussed, the work emphasis is on informal problem solving. The differentiation is between formal recognition of the program in the structure versus formal bureaucratized demands on the problem-solving process. The design group was clearly in favor of a formalized presence in the structure but with wide latitude for informal problem solving, which they believed would be more effective over time.

4. Complexity. A clear concern for controlling the potential complexity emerged. The planning group felt that the structure of the program should be "light," "informal," and low in complexity. There were design committee members familiar with legalistic approaches to problem solving, such as arbitration, hearings, and appeals. Their view was that an ombudsman program is an alternative to complex legalistic systems. Ombudsmen are most effective if the level of complexity is kept to a minimum. This translates often to a design push for informality, as previously discussed. Specifically, forms and reporting and feedback mechanisms are all kept simple and direct.

5. Centralization. Should the program be centralized? The program was to be initiated in one of the five divisions of the corporation. If all divisions eventually have an ombudsman, how will control be maintained? For example, how will a number of hospital ombudsmen in a multi-hospital system be structured? Should all of the ombudsmen be under centralized control or should the function be decentralized with significant autonomy?

The planning committee favored decentralization, with each ombudsman having individual autonomy and freedom. Obviously, there is a need for them to network for support, and to combine data, for example, on the nature and volume of complaints. However, it was felt that strong centralized control would push the program toward formalization, legalization, and bureaucratization, thereby diminishing its effectiveness.

6. Personnel configuration. The sixth structural concern translated into a discussion of the type, background, and selection of the ombudsmen. It was decided that the type of person was more important than his or her particular training, whether in human relations, counseling, social work, law, or some other field. There was general agreement that the person should come with very high references as a problem solver. There would be less reliance on specific background training and experience in the corporation, with greater emphasis on personal characteristics. However, the planning group did note that ombudsmen are not likely to do very well if they are very young or very new in the corporation. It was agreed to locate the ombudsman in the central building but down a discreet corridor, to ensure confidentiality.

7. *Professionalism.* One of the committee members asked whether or not there was a professional society of ombudsmen. He discovered that in 2009, the International Ombudsman Association had developed a Board of Certification, complete with exams and an accountability system for ombudsmen (Ethics Boards). The ombudsman would be encouraged to apply for certification and join other, relevant, associations such as those related to the industry. This would be particularly important if the ombudsman did not come from a field with already established standards, i.e., law, psychology or social work. However, membership in the International Ombudsman Association was considered to be most important in honing ombudsman skills, teaching the neophyte ombudsman how to assume the authority of the role and offering valuable guidance from members in an established field.

8. *Authority.* The structural question of authority was addressed and here again, the interest of the committee was that significant authority be vested in the ombudsman, a level of authority that would make it possible to respond to and resolve the most significant complaints. Without this, the ombudsman will be neutralized, lost in the bureaucracy, identified as a paper shuffler or a public relations flunky for "higher-ups."

These structural suggestions became design guidelines for program development. Some of them raised psychological issues.

Psychosocial Issues. Design attention turned next to the acceptance and feelings of the corporate members. The complaint program itself has a "psychosocial" component. The group felt it was necessary to consider how individuals and groups of employees would react to the ombudsman program; for example, what are their attitudes toward such a program? In their review, the planning group considered six areas: expectations, attitudes, commitment, communication, intergroup conflict, and resistance. This material is presented in summarized form.

1. *Expectations.* With regard to expectations, the planning group felt it was necessary to ensure that employees knew how the program was to work. New programs of any sort can create considerable anxiety. There was concern that employee anxiety be minimized in the start-up process. This meant providing potential complainants with as much information as possible on how the program would work and on its expected benefits for the organization as a whole and for individual employees. The nature of an ombudsman program means that addressing expectations is critical.

2. *Attitudes.* What will be the attitudes of the employees toward the new ombudsman program? Will they be suspicious of the rationale and/or the use of the complaint data? Will they be concerned that it is more a public relations exercise than a real problem-solving mechanism? A particularly important

question is how managers will feel about it. Will they be afraid of what the number of complaints will mean to their department and how they will be treated by the senior executive group? In short, the design group felt it was critical to communicate the philosophy of the program (an organization development/helping intention) to potential users and to lower and middle management so that they would accept it as an effort to improve the quality of work life.

3. *Commitment.* How will employees develop commitment to the program? Fully informing and educating them at the outset would contribute to this commitment. But the design group felt that real commitment would emerge only as a result of the use of the ombudsman program. The "seeing is believing" notion would be the determinant. If initial complaints are handled fairly, professionally, and with behaviors that actually provided help — not with a policing or an adversarial approach — support would be forthcoming. Policing and the resulting adversarial relations would be capable of killing the program in weeks.

4. *Communication.* The communications concern of the planning group focused on how the purpose, process, and outcome of the complaint program was to be communicated to the organization's members at large. It was decided that a series of memorandums and in-person small group meetings would be held with both managers and employees. The memorandum as a process for communicating organizational change was not thought to be terribly effective. The in-person sessions between some leading members of the design group and later the ombudsman would be used to communicate firsthand the purposes and workings of the program. Additionally, this would give the ombudsman the opportunity to meet the people and to begin to develop relationships.

5. *Intergroup Conflict.* There was some concern that the introduction of the ombudsman would produce group conflict among groups already offering complaint resolution services. The design group took special care to involve these people (employee assistance program staff, affirmative action, personnel) in the design work and felt that the potential for intergroup conflict was minimal.

6. *Resistance.* The last area of concern was resistance to the program. The design group felt that if all the above steps were carried out appropriately, resistance would be minimized. However, there was some concern that any resistance that got going would be detrimental to the program. Special care should be taken to monitor the acceptance of the program during the first few months of its existence.

These six areas recognize the importance of the psychological side of program design and development. Management has the entire responsibility for these aspects and more.

Managerial Issues. The final topic of concern to the planning group was the management of the new complaint program. Discussion focused on five topics: planning, organizing, developing, directing/leading, and controlling. All of these issues were felt to be critical to the ultimate success of the program. That is, the ombudsman program must be managed just like any other program in the organization.

1. *Planning.* The planning group was aware that its initial work was essentially strategic in nature. That is, it focused primarily on mission, goals and objectives, and design at a fairly abstract level (Ackoff, 1981; Below, Morrisey, and Acomb, 1987; Ziegenfuss 2006; Ackoff, Magidson, Addison, 2007). It was recognized that detailed operational planning would start when the ombudsman was appointed. He or she would lead the operational planning process. The planning initiated with this design work could continue with the design group as an advisory board. Membership could also involve related persons such as the Equal Employment Opportunity representative and the employee assistance program director.

2. *Organizing.* Creation of the program management structure is done by the ombudsman. The process could begin with an analysis of the ombudsman program structures that exist in other organizations, continuing the work of the design group. This could also include visitations to existing programs. Since the "program" is small — one person — there is not an extensive organizing requirement. However, one area of concern was that the information system be developed fairly quickly. It is critical that the information system design be thought through well enough to ensure that the initial complaints become part of future data analysis.

3. *Developing.* "Developing" activities would involve both the program and the individual. Before seeing the pool of candidates, it was not possible to assume that the ombudsman would have extensive experience. With or without experience, he or she could benefit from exposure to other ombudsmen and to training programs in negotiation and dispute resolution. The ombudsman was expected to design a one-year self development plan that included a mix of visitations to other programs, readings of relevant books and papers, and participation in three relevant workshops which could include those sponsored by ombudsman organizations or more general workshops in communications skills or dealing with the angry public.

On the program level, the ombudsman concept design group agreed to initiate a series of quarterly reviews to identify developmental needs useful to continuing the progress of the program. This developmental review would include a consideration of whether goals and objectives were on target; an analysis of resources required; and a review of the start-up process, specifically targeting those topics that will need attention, such as employee and manager acceptance.

4. *Directing/Leading.* Who will direct the program; that is, who will be responsible for the ombudsman? There was some question here about the reporting relationship, as discussed earlier. It was decided that direction should come from the chief executive officer of the corporation. This would enable the authority/power linkage to be maximized, providing the direction and leadership necessary to ensure that the ombudsman program is an integrated component of an overall organization development strategy.

5. *Controlling.* Control of the program is defined through a series of control guidelines (see Chapter Nine). The design group in an advisory capacity and the CEO would be responsible for initial reviews. As noted in the development section, these reviews would occur quarterly at the outset to ensure that the program was on track.

Management of the ombudsman program is fairly simple and straight-forward, a two-person job involving the ombudsman and his/her superior. Since there is not an extensive staff or program, the control and management are personal and highly visible. Still, an evaluation following start-up step 4 is useful, as noted in step 5.

Step 4: Start Up and Operate

There is not much to discuss about start-up. This is the "do it" stage. One cautionary note seems appropriate. Ombudsmen need some luck and an inclination to delay confronting the "most major" conflict in the first six months. Until presence and credibility are established, attacking a high-visibility, politically involved problem could cause the program to be killed. An example might be the suspected fudging of sales performance figures by the division sales manager who was personally hired by the CEO. It is better to collect additional data and absolutely secure the position before initiating a review requiring a full-scale test of acceptance and power.

Step 5: Periodically Evaluate Progress

This step calls for a periodic review of the progress of the ombudsman program. The design group felt that no design was perfect and that periodic adaptations are necessary. A review would need to include level of effort, documentation of case types, frequencies and outcomes, and some inquiry as to how managers and employees feel about the program. Chapter thirteen, on bottom-line benefits, presents the issues to be addressed in examining ombudsman impact.

The preceding review of formal program start-up should illustrate that a ombudsman program can be systematically planned and developed, like any other program or product. History, environment, internal host organization characteristics, and the program design itself must be considered.

However, the formal path is only one route to program design and start-up. Many programs begin with an informal effort initiated by an employee or a customer representative, a volunteer or someone else with a deep interest in solving problems.

There is no "standard" way to report an informal start-up. An employee with a real commitment to productivity and work life quality, or with dedication to excellence in customer service, might "drift" into an ombudsman role. Hospitals provide one common example. Patient representative programs began in North American hospitals almost 40 years ago but, over time, the function became formalized. While some programs began as tentative, part-time or even volunteer-staffed positions, they have evolved into full-time professional departments staffed by appropriately qualified ombudsmen.

The focus of the role has also changed. Many patient representatives were originally hired to assist with public relations; in fact, some even worked in or for the public relations unit. Their job was to help keep the hospital image clean and tidy. Smooth the problems, pacify angry patients, placate egotistical physicians, they were told. They were not directed to engage in real problem solving, work that would involve clinical and management staff confrontation and change. Some hospitals were afraid to; others did not have the idea of problem solving and organizational development as a program concept. Nevertheless, many patient representatives from the first saw themselves as ombudsmen for both patients and hospital. Informally, they attempted to use their individual cases and their knowledge of the hospital to achieve change. They became highly skilled at conflict resolution involving angry patients, aloof physicians, and management that was caught in the middle. Patient representatives have been hampered by several barriers, however: (1) a lack of recognition of their true role, (2) a low-level reporting relationship without access to power and authority, and (3) poor data system backup that would enable them to fully document the problems and the problem patterns they encounter.

If they are "informal ombudsmen," they follow the general work activity plan outlined in Chapter Four, and they work with a wide range of complaints that take them through all parts of the organization. Over the years, executives have come to recognize their help in solving difficult problems and in avoiding litigation.

Summary

In this chapter, we considered how the ombudsman program emerged as a viable entity in one organization. We followed the planning of a formal program through a historical and environmental analysis that considered the kinds of trends that led the organization to develop such a program.

A review of the internal characteristics of the corporation then analyzed the degree to which the ombudsman concept fit the organization. The topics surveyed included employee characteristics, occupations, power and interest groups, organizational characteristics in general, and the corporation's trends and financial status.

The planning and design group presented their findings regarding the feasibility of introducing the program to the corporation. These considerations involved goals and values, technical aspects of the complaint work, structural design issues, psychological and social issues, and the management of the program. Each of these areas was briefly reviewed with regard to planning considerations.

After a few comments about start-up and evaluation, we turned to the subject of informal programs. An illustrative group of informal ombudsmen—patient representatives—was discussed. The emergence of their ombudsman role has been gradual over the past twenty-five to forty years.

In this chapter, in short, we focused on one design and planning experience, the development of an ombudsman program in a corporation. We now need to hear in some depth about the authority and power of ombudsmen, the kinds of cases they encounter, and how their performance is controlled.

Chapter 6

Using Authority and Power as Tools for Effective Problem-Solving

In this chapter, the sources of the ombudsman's authority and power are examined. The position of the ombudsman in the organization and the amount of his or her power — the ability to get things done, to solve problems — is reviewed. Authority and power are linked and it is their convergence that enables the complaints to be resolved and the organization to be developed. Consider the following example.

Firing with Due Compensation. A real estate salesman working on a commercial property sale for nearly a year was fired just before the sale was completed. He protested to the company that he was still due his commission since he put the package together and worked extensively on the project. In a brief telephone call, the company division manager refused his request and afterward would not return telephone messages. The former salesman sued the company.

How would the ombudsman become engaged in the salesman's commission problem without some level of authority? Where does the power to initiate change come from?

Authority

The management literature includes well-known definitions of types of authority (Max Weber's original view, 1947; Kast and Rosenzweig, 1985; Hellreigel and Slocum, 2010). Although a bit "ancient," these major types are known by many managers, and most important, they are understandable in a commonsense way. Professional authority is added to Weber's original set of charismatic, traditional, and rational/legal forms of authority. They are noted here as authority sources that converge to become the total authority base for ombudsmen. Each of these authority sources is reviewed with an example.

Authority Source 1: Charismatic Authority. The first source of a ombudsman's authority is charismatic authority. The ombudsman's personal traits and attributes determine in part how much authority he or she has as a complaint taker and problem solver. This authority source differs from the others in that it is based on the personal characteristics of the person in the ombudsman job (Weber, 1947; Kast and Rosenzweig, 1985; Hellriegel and Slocum 2010). Each ombudsman has a different level of charismatic authority. Different levels of charisma are functions of traits such as personal and social likes and dislikes, interpersonal relationship skills, and abilities to negotiate, to be diplomatic, and to be assertive and persistent.

Consider the chapter's opening case, for example. When the ombudsman is called into the salesman's commission problem, how is he or she regarded? The participants immediately relate to the ombudsman's traits — will this person listen, be fair, be creative in finding a solution, is he or she a bureaucrat, and so forth? If negative images come to mind based on the ombudsman's personal traits and demeanor, the charismatic authority level of the ombudsman will be low. If personal traits produce an image of charisma in the mind of the real estate salesman and his division manager, charismatic authority will be high.

For the authors, this is the most important source of authority for the ombudsman. This authority is not based on formal organizational position (people in certain positions have authority because of that position), but on character traits, interpersonal abilities, and style. Charismatic authority is derived from the behavioral and interpersonal history of the ombudsman in the organization, particularly if there is a long employment history, for example, as vice president for personnel, or as executive assistant to a senior person. This is because ombudsmen with long tenure in the company have had the opportunity to develop personal sources of support. Ombudsmen who are charismatic establish people linkages that provide support for themselves and their activities (such as problem solving and negotiation of difficult conflicts).

If the ombudsman does not have personality characteristics suitable to the job — for example, fairness, sincerity, trustworthiness, persistence, and determination — the other sources of authority (professional, traditional, and rational/legal) are significantly undermined, if not totally useless. They will not add much authority to a base of "charismatic deficiency." When a patient ombudsman arranges a meeting to solve a doctor/patient conflict, the physician will only make sincere problem-solving efforts if the ombudsman's credibility is well established. Credibility depends first on personal characteristics, then on other sources of authority.

There is no real separation of an ombudsman's charismatic authority source from traditional, rational/legal, or professional authority sources. Many ombudsmen recognize that ability to work effectively with complainants, subjects of complaints, and "innocent bystanders" is determined to a large extent by personal credibility. A patient ombudsman colleague with very strong charismatic authority has been investigating complaints for more than eleven years, the last six years in a hospital. Her charismatic authority is based on her unique set of personal characteristics, which I would list as important to all ombudsmen: warmth, determination, fairness, sincerity, ability to listen, assertiveness, and an outgoing personality. When this patient ombudsman arrives on a unit, she is greeted as a warm, supportive problem solver who will fairly and sincerely attempt to solve a problem. There is little or no doubt that the problem *will* be confronted and resolved, no matter how much time is required. That image communicated fully to employees and consumers provides the basis for her charismatic authority. But she also depends on additional authority sources.

Authority Source 2: Professional Authority. The second authority source for ombudsmen is professional authority, the ombudsman's standing in the organization as a professional problem solver. It is derived from the ombudsman's ability to satisfy the criteria for professionalism, including

- Knowledge about problem-solving techniques and theory.
- Official sanction of the ombudsman's role nationally, regionally, organizationally ethical behavior in terms of confidentiality and fair treatment both training and experience in problem solving and complaint taking.

The professional authority of an ombudsman is based on the extent to which he or she is a professional with regard to complaint-taking/problem-solving, education, and consultation actions. Professional demeanor and behavior must be recognized by members of the organization. In some professional settings, such as universities and hospitals, a professional degree can serve to enhance the ombudsman's authority. However, without charismatic authority, it will be meaningless and will not automatically confer credibility.

Belief in the professionalism of ombudsman activities is based only in part on formal training and public recognition. Ombudsmen themselves do not all, even now, agree that they have a distinct professional identity. In the early days, many joined the fledgling Corporate Ombudsman Association or the Society of Patient Representatives. Since then, the field has become high profile with journals, codes of ethics and standards of practice. The International Association of Ombudsmen offers training programs with accreditation. The Forum of Canadian Ombudsman Institute offers various professional courses. However, even many years after the first ombudsmen entered the corporate world, the professionalism of ombudsman is based more on a connection with allied fields such as dispute resolution, negotiation, industrial relations, arbitration, law, psychology, and organizational behavior and development. Each of these fields has a set of generally accepted principles, behaviors bounded by ethical constraints and expectations for the role of persons who identify themselves with the field (the traditional aspects of professionalism; Vollmer and Mills, 1966). To the extent that ombudsman work is similar and/or identical to work in other fields (for example, psychology, labor law), the professional authority base is established and developed over time by the connections with that field. An ombudsman who is a professionally trained labor negotiator has the benefit of the recognition, guidance, and support of the people and practices in that field.

Some ombudsmen are trained industrial psychologists (at the Ph.D. level). When they come into a unit as official ombudsman, staff recognize their credentials, including the expertise and ethics and the weight of the profession. The total of all of the implied elements of professionalism creates the authority. Others are faculty, nurses, and engineers with similar professional roots.

Ombudsmen without this identifiable connection to a professional field build an image of professionalism based on their behavior and knowledge. Executive assistants or former managers will be recognized in time as having authority that derives from their professional manner of problem solving even though they may not ever be identified with a "professional" problem-solving field.

Authority Source 3: Traditional Authority. The third source of ombudsman authority is tradition. Authority through tradition (Weber, 1947; Kast and Rosenzweig, 1985; Hellriegel and Slocum, 2010) is established only by ombudsman who are in operation over a long period of time. After five to eight years of successful work, the program is accepted by the organizational culture. Acceptance means that complaint taking, problem solving, and the ombudsman's approach to enhancing productivity have become part of the "tradition" of the corporation or public agency. Company tradition says that the ombudsman has recognized authority to mediate conflicts, assist in removing barriers to productivity, and generally promote the quality of working life through open communication.

In one hospital ombudsman program, it took about five years for the patient ombudsman to develop the tradition of problem confrontation and problem solving. Part of the time requirement was due to the years needed to generate complaints hospital-wide. Tradition had to be developed from ombudsman experience in all units of the hospital. Secondhand experience — comment from colleagues who dealt with the ombudsman — is also necessary but is not sufficient for full tradition building.

There is one way to develop this "traditional authority" without waiting for the years of official ombudsman experience. When considering candidates for the position of ombudsman (a newly established formal position), select an employee who has had both wide experience in the organization and who throughout that experience has established his or her own personal tradition of problem solving, fair play, and productive actions. This is an approach to selection that is based on the assumption that all organizations now have ombudsmen but do not officially recognize them!

At least one corporate ombudsman program at a large bank uses this mechanism to assist in establishing the authority base (Tillier, 1987). A career senior executive is chosen to be ombudsman for the final years prior to retirement. Traditional and charismatic authority are linked — the person chosen has strong personal characteristics and a successful corporate history. Authority is established by the tradition of performance and the confidence vested in that executive over decades.

Consider again the case of the salesman's commission. Contrast the reception given to a ombudsman who was a relatively new employee of the company (less than five years) with that of a senior executive with a long and successful corporate history. Common sense indicates that the senior official would begin with higher levels of authority. The organization trades on the personal history of the individual to begin to establish an ombuds tradition.

There is a fourth authority source derived from relations with the law.

Authority Source 4: Rational/Legal Authority. The fourth source of ombudsman authority is rational/legal authority derived from the ombudsman's function as a quasi-legal interpreter (Weber, 1947; Kast and Rosenzweig, 1985; Hellriegel and Slocum, 2010). The ombudsman interprets/explains/teaches the official rules and regulations of the organization — policies and procedures — as well as the practical implications of internal (individual and group behavior) and external (industry-wide) perceptions and pressures. The complaints that arise in the organization are often related to or directly involve quasi-legal issues. For example, many patient complaints could have medical malpractice implications. This authority base is founded on the need to ensure that official policies and procedures are the guidelines for employees' behaviors.

With regard to the salesman's commission case, what is the organization's official position on payment to a former employee? If there are written policies, they may only need to be shared with the complainant. Is there a need for a formal legal opinion about whether the employee is owed the commission? If uncertainty exists, the ombudsman can assist the organization in making the decision, including concern for precedent.

Organizations operate somewhat rationally, guided by a set of policy and procedural guidelines that determine the acceptable behaviors of organizational members, or at least the boundaries of behavior. As interpreters of official rules, ombudsmen have rational/legal authority to resolve conflicts and complaints. A hospital patient has a right to be informed about the purpose, process, benefits and risks of a given medical treatment? The physician may be resisting the requirements of informed consent, but by law and by the hospital's medical policy (which the physician may have forgotten), the patient must be told. The authority is rational/legal, backed by the full weight of the organization.

This authority from the ombudsman's position in the organization and the official rules and regulations are used to help guide consumer and employee behaviors. Prescribing behavior via rules does not fit very well with what we know about how organizations work. Employees do not behave according to a set of rules. Rule and policy interpretation helps to establish a base for problem-solving actions. Many employees and consumers relate only to the "enforced authority" of official policies, changing their behaviors only when regulations and laws are cited. Some physicians may not voluntarily inform a patient about all details of treatment in response to a request, but they would provide information in compliance with the law. The ombudsman uses this authority when applicable to the participants and the case.

The primary authority source used by ombudsmen is likely to be different, based on their individual differences. Some rely more on their charisma, others on their professionalism. It is the total constellation of authority sources that creates the authority base for the ombudsman programs. This authority base remains intact when an ombudsman leaves, but a new ombudsman may switch the primary source of authority from charismatic, for example, to professional. Traditional authority will increase as the "tradition" of ombuds work flourishes in an organization (over time with different people).

All ombudsmen need power to encourage and to ensure the changes that effectively resolve problems.

Power

Power is the ability to get things done. As with authority, there is no single source of power. One commentator offered a set of six sources that ombudsmen rely on to generate "action abilities" within the organization (Filley, House, and Kerr, 1976; also see Ziegenfuss, 2007). As in the case of authority, these six sources converge to create a power base. The convergence of diverse power sources produces the ability of the ombudsman to achieve problem-solving and organizational development objectives. Just as ombudsmen draw on different sources of authority according to who they are as individuals and according to the needs of the situation, power to initiate change comes from a similar set of sources. The whole set of power elements accounts for the level of the ombudsman's power. They draw on one or more power sources according to the situation they are in and the people involved in the case. A brief explanation of each power source identifies the nature of this action ability.

Reward Power. Reward power is often the first noticed by managers and employees. It is one of four sources of ombudsman's power representing the organization's dominant influence on its members. Reward power derives from the ability of the chief executive officer to distribute rewards to those employees who are productive and punishments to those who are not (Filley and Grimes, 1967; Filley, House, and Kerr, 1976; Ziegenfuss, 2007). Ombudsmen know that there is widespread recognition and some fear that the number of complaints in one's department can negatively affect the extent of the rewards one receives (promotions, bonus, additional staff). How many division managers will receive bonuses after firing a series of salespeople who sue?

The reward power of ombudsmen is based on the realization that a list of complaint topics with frequencies may affect the rewards that an executive or department director receives, such as compensation, access to capital, or staff support. In talking to an executive or other employee about the need to solve a problem or to negotiate a conflict, ombudsmen directly or indirectly imply that a refusal to engage in the problem-solving process may affect future rewards, personal and/or departmental.

Use of a direct threat to deny rewards will negate the acceptance of ombudsmen and turn the program into a police action. Few ombudsmen do that. But the possibility is always present.

An example of this is the case of the hospital admissions department director. The admissions department director was interested in promotion to a higher level of management within the hospital. But there were a large number of complaints in the department about the scheduling of work, errors on admissions forms, and conflicts with other units. When a patient complained about unnecessary admission delay, the patient ombudsman was confident about a sincere attempt to respond when she presented the complaints. She knew that the fear of losing the desired promotion would motivate the admissions director to solve the problem. This did not have to be mentioned directly, at least not to this manager. Complaint levels and managerial willingness to respond are indicators of managerial effectiveness. While the ombudsman does not control the reward system, the perception of a close relationship with senior management may motivate good behavior; an actual close relationship with senior management guarantees her input to decision making.

Power Source 2: Coercive Power. Coercive power is the second power source for ombudsmen. It relates directly to the threat inherent in a request to negotiate a solution to a conflict (Filley and Grimes, 1967; Filley, House, and Kerr, 1976; Ziegenfuss, 1985, 2007). Ombudsmen arrive at the conflict situation with an ability to force change if necessary. Under somewhat ideal circumstances, all employees and consumers realize that ombudsmen are mandated by the organization, supported by the chief executive, and have top management's coercive power behind them (although it may not be used often). For example, one corporate ombudsman had difficulty getting two managers to meet in order to solve a personality conflict involving a sales and a production unit. In an attempt to resolve the stalemate, the ombudsman referred to his ability to coerce a solution by drawing on his relationship with the chief executive. The managers agreed to meet.

It is important to recognize that coercive power is not an effective means for solving many problems, or for solving even a few problems over a long period of time. When employees are forced to change, they tend to do so without commitment, lacking the persistence required for follow-through. The coercive power base exists more often as an implied threat that is not put to use by ombudsmen, at least not by the good ones. As with reward power, coercive power is always there but is rarely used.

There are, however, some managers and employees who will not respond to anything but coercive power. Whether by training, experience, or personal preference, they relate only to authority backed commands.

Power Source 3: Legitimate Power. Legitimate power is the third power source in this connected set. It is based on the ombudsman's mandate by the organization, including recognition by the chief executive and senior management that the ombudsman is "a legitimate part of the organization" (Filley and Grimes, 1967; Filley, House, and Kerr, 1976; Ziegenfuss, 1985, 2007). This power tends to come "on line" only after some period of operation, during which the ombudsman concept and the person in the role demonstrate performance sufficient to convince senior management of their value. An important point here is that ombudsmen are not outside resources coming in on an informal or infrequent occasion to lend a hand. They are a recognized and official source of problem solving within the organization. When legitimacy is established, the ombudsman has a standing similar to the corporate legal office, the Equal Employment Opportunity office, and the staff units that work to improve organizational process and functioning (for example, personnel, planning). The legitimizing of the function occurs through placement in the organization with reporting responsibilities to a high executive. Promotion of the function within the organization creates a power source based on legitimate recognition.

This legitimizing can be done with the help of titles, office placement, salary, and meeting access. One corporate ombudsman is special assistant to the president (title). A patient ombudsman's office is located on the first floor of the hospital with high lobby visibility (placement). Some corporate ombudsmen are well paid ($80,000 to $125,000+), while others are allowed to attend any and all meetings they feel are relevant to their problem solving work (access). One international bank's ombudsman is a senior career executive (World Bank) (history). One airline troubleshooter is a senior manager who also represents the company to government agencies (Air Canada) (representation). All these are "legitimizing" factors that produce power.

Power Source 4: Referent Power. The fourth source of power in the ombudsman job is referent power. This is the power of the ombudsman derived from the chief executive officer or senior manager to whom he or she reports (Filley and Grimes, 1967; Filley, House, and Kerr, 1976; Ziegenfuss, 1985, 2007). Quite simply, this means that the ombudsman achieves some significant degree of power through his or her relationship with the senior manager. If the executive is powerful, that power will "spin off" to the ombudsman.

For example, in one company the corporate ombudsman reports to the senior vice president for human relations, who has a well-established track record for successfully promoting both productivity and employee quality of working life. The vice president had a hand in selecting the ombudsman for the position and was very active in informing employees and management of the purposes, work activities, and expected benefits of the ombudsman's work. The senior vice president was instrumental in beginning to establish the power base for the company ombudsman. Those employees and managers who would not initially acknowledge the ombudsman's power *would* recognize that he reports to the senior vice president, who has thirty-five years in the corporation and many connections.

Ombudsman referent power depends on a combination of the position and personal characteristics of the supervisor. Unfortunately, some ombudsmen report to persons who are not powerful in their organizations, as in the case of a patient ombudsman who reports to the social work department director. The patient ombudsman's referent power is significantly diminished because it is dependent on a unit that has limited power, a director lower in status and prestige in the medical pecking order.

These four types of power sources — reward, coercive, legitimate, and referent — relate to the organization and are derived from it. To a great extent, the ombudsman does not have much control over these sources of his or her own power. Rewards are given out by the chief executive officer. The degree to which both the ombudsman and senior management want to be coercive is determined largely by that manager's group. Whether or not the ombudsman is legitimate is determined by the status given the ombudsman function in the organization. Finally, the referent power generated by referral to the reporting senior manager is outside the control of the ombudsman as well.

Two other power sources — expert power and personal power — are related to the ombudsman personally. That is, ombudsmen can develop expertise *and* they have a certain set of personal characteristics that comprise their personal power base.

Power Source 5: Expert Power. Expert power is based on the amount of expertise the ombudsman has developed (Filley and Grimes, 1967; Filley, House, and Kerr, 1976; Ziegenfuss, 1985, 2007). Expertise in this job pertains specifically to the three main ombuds activities, including complaint processing, education and training, and consultation. Expert power is derived from the ombudsman's ability to fulfill these core functions of the job.

This type of power is visible to employees and consumers as they watch the ombudsman in action. Expert power does not derive from personal style but from the level of technical skill. Conflict participants — employees and managers — ask themselves:

• Is the ombudsman a good negotiator?
• Is the ombudsman a conflict resolution expert?
• Is the ombudsman an effective listener and teacher?
• Does the ombudsman generate effective and lasting solutions?

When the answer to these questions is yes, this data is added to knowledge of the ombudsman's character, training, and experience to create a judgment about the level of expert power.

Power Source 6: Personal Power. The final source of power for the ombudsman is personal power (Filley and Grimes, 1967; Filley, House, and Kerr, 1976; Ziegenfuss, 1985, 2007). This is power developed as a result of the individual traits and characteristics of the ombudsman. It is how ombudsman interacts with people on a day-to-day basis; whether they are able to resolve problems in a fair and equitable way; whether they relate to conflicts with objectivity, determination, and openness; and whether they have an ability to appreciate the goals and values of individuals, of individual units, and of the organization as a whole. Here again the personnel characteristics defined in the discussion on charismatic authority are relevant. Does the ombudsman have sincerity, fairness, interpersonal skills, creativity, and determination? This unique mix of the traits of individual ombudsmen and their behavior over time develops a personal power base that determines whether the troubleshooter will be personally effective within the organization.

Summary

In this chapter, the elements of authority and power of ombudsmen were presented. They are a diverse set that in combination become the power and authority for the entire ombudsman role. Authority was defined as a merger of four types: charismatic, professional, traditional, and rational/legal. The four types vary in importance for each ombudsman.

Power was defined as a derivative of six types: reward, coercive, legitimate, referent, expert, and personal power. These sources also vary by level for each individual ombudsman. And, both the authority and the power of ombudsmen are related to their information processing and communication work, i.e., how they function in relation to senior management.

Chapter 7

A Day in the Life of an Organizational Ombudsman

One of the best ways to understand what an ombudsman does is to sample a "typical" day. This chapter outlines an ombudsman's activities from one day's start to close. It is a representative day, although this particular set of activities is a composite of a number of days of activities. Activities are obviously not the same every day and it is unlikely that any one ombudsman would have a day exactly like this. The variation in the tasks and nature of the work activities during the day is much like general ombudsman work, though. It does represent the work of ombudsman colleagues who have read this description of a sample day.

As you will see in the following pages, a day in an ombudsman's life can involve a wide-ranging set of activities, including

- Receiving and interviewing complaint presenters.
- Taking phone calls.
- Investigating old complaints by checking files.
- Meeting with in-house attorneys to resolve complaints that have already gone too far.
- Emailing or meeting managers, professionals and employees to gather facts for complaint investigation.
- Active listening and personal counseling.
- Writing reports.
- Meeting with complainants to counsel them about seeking assistance elsewhere.
- Making referrals to various other offices within the corporation.

At the conclusion of the review, the outstanding characteristics of a typical day in the life of the ombudsman are summarized. The description is presented as if one ombudsman were telling the story of his or her daily activities.

96

This ombudsman is in a formally recognized position in a corporation of 3,200 employees. The report is in the first person, written as if the ombudsman offered this in a conversational account of a day's work. It is a daily diary.

An Ombudsman's Day

8:30 A.M. I frequently begin my day by completing complaint reports from the previous day. I have to admit that as a people-oriented person, the notion that I have to write reports is somewhat objectionable. I am much more interested in the meetings with complainants and in the group sessions with department heads, managers, and employees that I use to resolve the problems.

I can usually get some of the reports written first thing before I lose my ability to control my time. I begin by spending about half an hour writing up complaint reports. The reports include the facts collected as a part of investigation, summary thoughts on ways the complaint could be resolved, people with whom I have already talked and those with whom I have yet to talk, and some target times I expect can be met for successful resolution of the complaint.

I tend to rough these reports out quickly, passing them on to my secretary. I have found that once the reports have been at least partially committed to paper, it is easier for me to edit them, refining as I go along.

9:00 A.M. If I have no early morning complaint appointments or meeting sessions, I am usually doing some background investigative work. This morning I need to check files relating to old policy statements on sex discrimination within the organization. I recently had a complaint from a female employee who was beginning to feel that she was a victim of discrimination. She was not aware of any policies against sex discrimination that the organization had developed during her ten years of employment and thought that it had not done very much to combat the problem. She wanted to know if the apparent absence of a policy was one of the key points to her case, or at least an indicator of the depth of the problem.

Inquiring at the personnel office, I found that there was a history of policy proclamations on this issue dating back to 1978. I quickly noted the number of policy statements and their starting dates so I could pass this information back to the complainant. Then I asked personnel to send me copies of the policy statements so that I could see how their content would affect this case.

9:15 A.M. Before I could follow up a bit more with the woman who filed the sex discrimination question, the phone rang. My caller wanted to file a complaint about management relations and concerns about certain production areas. Like most of my callers, he wasn't sure how to file a complaint. Although the company had announced the opening of my office and clearly displayed my phone number on bulletin boards and in the company directory, nearly every caller was not sure I was the person to contact. And despite my "publicity," nearly everyone who called heard about me from a friend of a friend of a friend that I had helped. I mentioned that I was open to taking a wide range of complaints, but if he was a union member and wanted to file a formal grievance, that was his first option. I asked him to use his union first. He stated that he was not in the union and that his complaint had to do with some questions about quality control in production.

The caller provided some of the details of the question, and it sounded significant enough for us to meet in person. He said he would try to bring along some further information outlining his case. We made an appointment to meet in two days.

9:30 A.M. Interview. I had my first complaint interview of the morning. An engineer came in from one of the divisions with a complaint about the manager of his unit. The manager was an engineer in his late thirties. The complaining engineer was fifty-nine years old, just about to turn sixty. The manager had talked to him about trying to increase the speed of his work. After several discussions in which the pace of the work was a concern, the manager suggested that perhaps he was slowing down and nearing retirement.

The complainant felt that this was "not so subtle" pressure to retire! He wanted to know whether or not this was age discrimination. But more important, the engineer was concerned about retaining his job and rebuilding a working relationship. He frankly noted that he didn't have much of an understanding on how to speed up his work and would like some further information in that area. We talked for about half an hour. I suggested that we meet again in two days after I had an opportunity to talk to the manager and to see what kind of assistance I could get for him.

10:00 A.M. Meeting with in-house lawyers. I next attended a meeting with two of the corporate attorneys. They had been told that one former employee had sued us over concerns with his dismissal. The employee was angry about the dismissal, thinking it was unfair and that he had not had an opportunity to address the concerns for which he had been dismissed. His brief, filed by his lawyers, insisted that the organization had no mechanism for filing complaints in-house and, secondarily, did not encourage employees and managers to resolve their problems.

The attorneys wanted to know how widespread the knowledge of my existence was in the organization and whether or not this particular employee had used the system. This raised two rather delicate questions. First, we needed to consider how widespread the existence of my program was within the organization — a subtle review of both the extent of my recognition and my power. The second issue was potentially much more significant. The question was, had this former employee ever used my services as a complaint resolution expert within the organization? We stress that complaint information is confidential. The concern was that if I informed them that the employee used the ombudsman, it would be a violation of confidentiality. The problem was rather easily resolved in this case, since I was able to answer freely that he had never used the system.

After some further discussion about the nature of the case, the lawyers said that there was a chance it would be negotiated out of court. They asked whether or not I would consider being involved in the mediation of the dispute. I remarked that I would be glad to do anything they thought would be helpful, but only as a neutral party.

10:45 A.M. A No-Follow-Up Problem with an Old Complaint. Since I was in the attorney's office, I realized I was not far from one of the managers' offices who was involved in a prior complaint. I thought I would drop in to see how the proposed actions to resolve the problem were working. I already knew that, to date, no action had been taken. The complainant had called me with regard to the continuing problem of fellow workers taking frequent smoke breaks and leaving him to shoulder what he felt was an unfair load of work. The complainant felt that smoke breaks should be scheduled in an equitable manner and that he, too, be allowed to take a non-smoking break. The manager felt that the complainant was not a team-player and so far had taken no action.

I wanted to encourage the manager to try to take care of the situation before it got worse, but he was not in. Just as I was about to leave, he did come in, but by then I had to rush to an 11:00 A.M. meeting. He quickly told me he had not taken action yet but seemed willing to get cracking on the problem by finding out how much time was actually lost in smoke breaks. I made a mental note to get back to him the very next morning.

11:00 A.M. Counseling. At 11:00 A.M., I had a meeting with a junior manager from one of the marketing divisions. This manager was concerned about her performance to date and particularly how it would affect her promotional possibilities. She had an M.B.A. from a reputable school and was concerned that she was not moving up quickly enough in the corporate hierarchy. She seemed to have some definite notions about how quickly she should be at what level in the organization. She was concerned that her performance was not measuring up. In a previous session, she stated that some of her performance problems were related to unfair treatment by senior managers in her unit. She felt her youth, and her energy and enthusiasm, threatened them.

She had been with the company about one and a half years. It seemed to me that in this second session, I was really engaged in counseling the young woman. The problem was at least in part her own insecurities and anxieties stemming from her youth, the fact that she was new in the corporation, and the fact that this was her first job following graduate school.

This second session was useful, I thought, even though a preliminary probing of that unit did not turn up any harassment by senior managers. This counseling provided needed reassurance for the young woman and would probably help to avoid problems with senior management. If she continued to have this type of problem, I would suggest a referral to a professional career counselor, either inside the corporation or outside it.

11:25 A.M. Report Writing. At this point, with a few spare minutes before lunch, I went back to writing complaint reports from the previous day. This allowed me to get some of this out of the way before lunch, clearing my desk for the afternoon sessions. The afternoon sessions rarely ended early, so this was all the report writing for today.

Noon. Lunch with the EEO Representative. I scheduled a lunch with the Equal Employment Opportunity representative in our corporation, Jane Thomas. We met at a small restaurant across the street, since whenever we meet in the employees' cafeteria there is talk by management that we are conspiring to make their jobs more difficult. This is a regular monthly meeting that we use to ensure that we are working well on cross-referrals. We also use it to clear up any questions that we might have in our own complaint taking that closely involved each other's area. This is the technical side.

Since we are both basically in the same work, the meeting is also a support session. Obviously, the EEO representative understands the stresses and trials and tribulations of the corporate ombudsman's work and vice versa. It's an opportunity for us to commiserate about the difficulties in promoting change with people and in confronting and resolving the problems in the corporation at large. I finish the lunch refreshed.

1:05 P.M. Call from Colleague. After lunch, I return a call from a colleague concerning promotion for this year's corporate ombudsman conference. The ombudsman association of which I am a member is trying to develop a network among ombudsmen in major private corporations across the country. There are several reasons for this linkage. One key reason is the support and assistance each ombudsman will receive in developing his or her own job and role in their corporation. The association also promotes the existence of the ombudsmen around the country, furthering the concept of in-house problem solving. It parallels other ombudsman groups such as Society for Health Care Consumer Advocacy of the American Hospital Association. And last, it gives companies an opportunity to publicly link with other corporations that are already engaged in this activity. We spend about twenty minutes talking about mailing lists and persons to contact.

1:30 P.M. Chief Executive Officer Briefing. I meet with the chief executive officer to brief him on the status of the complaints I was taking in the corporation. The CEO was particularly interested in hearing the employee perspective on how we were doing. This emerges from the nature of the complaints and exactly what the corporation was doing to resolve them. His concerns were (1) that the corporation was seen as responsive, (2) that he was informed about what employees felt about the corporation and how things were going, and (3) how the corporation was doing in resolving complaints (to keep down the cost of litigation and low productivity). The company had just lost a multimillion-dollar suit by a former employee. The CEO knew that the court award was only a part of the cost of resolving the problem. There were a lot of hidden staff expenses in preparing for the litigation, as well as attorneys' fees and finally the settlement. He had *no interest* in his management or his employees generating follow-up cases.

I followed a general pattern for the monthly briefing that we had established at the outset. I gave him a simple one-page summary of the volume of complaints from the different divisions, the nature of the complaints in each of the divisions, and a short list of examples of the problems—a phrase or a sentence, explanations of the nature of the complaint. This type of report gave him a sense of "the numbers" in terms of how they were doing, and also a more extensive understanding of the nature of the problems, without overburdening him with details.

We talked briefly about the strategies that I am using to resolve the complaints. He offered to be of any further assistance I might need in carrying on with the job, specifically suggesting that I could feel free to call on the corporation's attorneys for help.

2:15 P.M. In-Person Complaint. Following the CEO briefing, I returned to my office to take another complaint.

This complaint involved research work in one of the laboratories. The complainant was a young and dedicated scientist in the industrial research and development laboratory. She was working as a part of a new-product team that was developing a new artificial sweetener. One afternoon, she noticed a discrepancy in one senior scientist's reports and checked it. It appeared he was "fudging" the data but she was not sure. He was an irascible guy. Since he would be responsible for her promotions and her continued work on the project, she was afraid to ask him about it. She did not want to embarrass or anger him and had no idea what to do, so she just watched and worried, becoming more and more distracted.

This was the first time I heard this complaint. I listened attentively, asking her for details about what data, when was it altered, how much by whom, did she have proof or was it speculation.

I told her that I would begin to look into the case but would not yet confront the other scientist nor would I reveal that she was the complainant. She left feeling satisfied that a start was made.

I thought that I should begin by addressing general questions about the type of problem to several senior scientists who I knew well. I also needed time to think through a verification strategy (that I thought, would be most challenging). I made a note to move quickly on it.

3:00 P.M. Referral to the Employee Assistance Program. I took a call from an employee who was concerned about his colleague's drinking on the job. He wanted to complain in some ways but also wanted to ensure that his colleague would receive some assistance. He was asking if I could help with this problem and/or what he should do as a start. We talked about the nature of the difficulty and the level of the problem; was it a beginning problem, a fairly well-developed one, or at an absolute crisis stage with danger involved? If it were the latter, I would join him immediately on the unit and see if we couldn't get some action today. He remarked, however, that he felt it was more in the developing stage but that it was clearly a pattern and one that was getting progressively worse.

I suggested that the best referral was to the employee assistance program, which specifically dealt with personal problems of employees on the job. I gave him the name and telephone number of the director of that unit, suggesting that he start there. I told him to get back to me within a day to inform me of progress. If he needed additional assistance, I would make sure that he received it.

3:30 P.M. Referee for Two-Manager Conflict. At 3:30 P.M., I worked on the resolution to a problem that involved two managers with joint control over an employee in both of their units. This company is operated with a matrix organizational design that combines functional areas with specific project teams. The problem involved an organizational development specialist who reported to the human resources vice president and who was working on a project team to develop a new product for the company.

The product team leader requested that the organization development specialist assist him in some team relations work that the organization development specialist felt would not be productive. The team leader wanted to mandate a two-day weekend sensitivity group to "shape up" employee attitudes. When this problem was raised with the two managers, they immediately got into a shouting match because of past conflicts and communication problems. They were not able to resolve it. The organization development specialist suggested that I sit in to try to referee the meeting.

The meeting was heavily emotional and very tense, not what you would call the lighter part of my day. However, we were able to discuss it with a somewhat lowered or at least controlled level of emotional involvement. We were able to arrive at a temporary compromise by which the request would be put on hold until we found a successful way around the methodological barrier and the conflict in objectives.

5:00 P.M. Conclusions. At the end of the day, I had a bit of time before I would leave. I spent this time completing reports, returning phone calls from employees who wanted to file complaints, and setting up a management team briefing, which I also give each month.

7:00 P.M. Follow-Up. I thought I was done for today but I had a telephone call from a senior computer scientist. He was angry about a management decision to cut back financial support for his project. He told me about it the other day, feeling that the decision was a result of internal politics. He was talking now about his severe disappointment and that he may want to get even. I agreed to meet him for coffee. When we met, he was very upset, implying that both suicide and sabotage were options for him. We talked for two hours, after which he agreed to sleep on it until we met again the next day.

I went home to bed emotionally and physically exhausted.

Summary

The diary just presented reflected a day in the life of a formal corporate ombudsman. Consumer ombudsmen such as patient representatives and "unrecognized ombudsmen" such as executive assistants, employee and human relations managers, and others tend to have the same kind of day. They take complaints, make written and oral reports, meet with their referral and support networks, and counsel members of the organization. Except for labels and the types of persons seen, a day in the life of a corporate ombudsman is a somewhat standard one — it can be generalized to many/most troubleshooters.

What does this summary of one day of ombudsman activity tell us about the characteristics of the job? The following general job traits emerge:

Varied. As one can see from the above set of activities, the day is full of very different tasks — it's a nonroutine job.

Interesting. All of the aspects of the job are interesting. The complaints are not boring; they're unique and individual problems.

People-oriented. This is a "people" job from start to finish, involving talking, interacting, resolving, mediating.

Hectic. This is a fairly typical day, in which there are many activities scheduled back to back. The activities are often very different, and so the pace is more hectic and harried than serene.

Unpredictable. While the days themselves are somewhat predictable, the nature of the problems and the tasks on any given day are fairly unpredictable.

Stressful. Any time you are dealing with people and their conflicts, stress is high. Mediating these conflicts is a high-stress job.

Lacking in closure. Most of the tasks initiated on any given day are never actually finished on that day; thus you don't often get the sense of final closure to a problem.

Rewarding. There is keen awareness that you're removing barriers to productivity and increasing the quality of working life of fellow employees in the corporation.

Technically challenging. The work requires a very high level of interpersonal competence and clinical/counseling/negotiation/teaching skills.

In short, this is a day that is interesting, that requires no clockwatching, and that is highly demanding and fulfilling on a level much like a combination of clinical work and highly successful management productivity. The cases presented in Chapter Eight will further demonstrate these characteristics.

Chapter 8

Ombudsman Experiences: Learning That All Problems Are Important

Employee and Client Complaints

One way to further understand the nature of the ombudsman's job is to examine a set of cases. Of course, an individual ombudsman may have more of one type of case than another, and not all of the topics treated here will be addressed by an ombudsman during a given period of time. The first section of this casebook chapter concentrates on cases presented by employees, to be followed by client complaints. Employee complaint topics include: research data fudging, interdepartmental conflict, discrimination, supervisory conflict, sexual harassment, physical conditions, salary, personal problems, and production/sabotage. Some of these cases will appear to be more important than others (for example, sexual harassment and sabotage versus hot work areas); however, it should be remembered that an ombudsman considers *all* problems important, since some less significant ones eventually point to larger conflicts.

In each of the cases, an abstract of the ombudsman's actions is presented that touches on the five common steps of identification, investigation, feedback of facts, development of responses, and monitoring to ensure follow-up action. In all of the cases, the responses are sketched in extremely brief fashion. They are offered to provide a flavor of casework, not exhaustive detail. Also, it is important to keep in mind that many readers will perceive the problems and the responses as having alternative interpretations, with many options for other action. That is true of nearly all cases, and attests to the difficulty of the work.

Case 1: Research Data Fudging

The Complaint. Tony Rodriguez was a five-year employee working as a marketing researcher in a food-products company. He had been involved in studies of various products and their market research potential since his arrival at the company. He was mostly a "numbers cruncher" without very much exposure to the committee meetings and board briefings at which his numbers were presented. His supervisors were increasingly interested in moving him up the market research ladder in the corporation, especially in the last year.

At the conclusion of a recent study, he was asked by the market research director (to whom he reports) to make a presentation to the new-product group of the corporation. The market research director said a quick review of the data from the new study would be useful, suggesting that he and Tom should go over it prior to the briefing.

During the briefing about two days later, the director saw that the market data did not reflect strong support for the new product. Noting this, he suggested that some changes could be made. Tom was not clear about this and asked specifically what he was talking about. The director suggested that new products were tough to get off the ground in this corporation. The way it was usually done, he said, was that the market studies were conducted but the data was "boosted" by a factor of about 20 percent. He suggested applying this factor to the data to show greater market support.

He said that the senior officers in the corporation were generally too conservative to adopt new product ideas very easily, but if they saw strong market data support, they generally went ahead. Almost always, these product ideas were successful. He couched it in an "overcoming the bureaucracy" sort of concept and strongly suggested that Tom do it.

Since this suggestion was followed by a comment on the possibility of Tom's moving up the career ladder, he went to the ombudsman for consultation on what he should do about it.

Ombudsman Actions. The complaint as the ombudsman saw it was a dual one involving both the ethics of the decision to "fudge the data" and the issue of corporate culture. The ombudsman investigated, asking some of his contacts whether this was, in fact, true. The investigation uncovered that it was generally the case. Data fudging was a bit of a time-honored tradition for breaking through the corporate conservatism.

The ombudsman asked the market research director about the situation, which he at first denied. When the ombudsman mentioned that he had confirmation from other independent sources, the director admitted it was true. He had no suggestions on what to do about it. He could choose to play it straight but he did not feel it would be helpful to the company. He also did not want the issue to focus on him personally, saying he was only one of six market research directors.

The ombudsman suggested that it could be taken to the executive group as a problem using a product or products that were established some five years ago. The market research director agreed that that might open the topic, which then could be expanded to address corporate conservatism. The ombudsman agreed to do that as a first response and reported this back to the complainant.

The ombudsman saw this as both an individual-level problem (one employee/one conflict) and a system-level problem (corporate culture and values issue).

Case 2: Interdepartmental Conflict

The Complaint. The ombudsman received a complaint from Harold Thompson in the computer product services department. Harold was concerned that customer demands on product services were becoming too heavy. Customers were becoming dissatisfied about the timeliness with which the corporation could respond and whether or not the company was being forthright in terms of how quickly responses were made. He complained that the salesmen were saying that product services were available practically twenty-four hours a day. When customers called, they *expected* immediate attention. After one or two false starts at problem solving in the end they had to wait several days for a response, it was quite disconcerting, to say the least.

Both the sales department and the product services director were aware of the problem. However, the two directors did not get along and were not able to even hold a discussion regarding the problem. This was attempted some four or five months ago, but the meeting quickly dissolved into a shouting match and was ended before any useful suggestions emerged. Harold only knew that at his level, customers were unhappy. Even when he was able to address the customers' problems, they were dissatisfied because of the time delay (mostly an expectations problem, he felt). Harold could see that increasing dissatisfaction among customers would result in a detrimental effect on the company at some point in the future.

He asked for suggestions on how to handle the inter-departmental conflict.

Ombudsman Actions. The ombudsman agreed to look into the case, suggesting he would be talking with other employees in both units before he talked to the respective department directors. This he did, finding that the complaint was essentially true. The obvious first action seemed to be to initiate a meeting of the two department directors with the ombudsman as third-party mediator.

The meeting was held. Both directors, at first, expressed surprise over the existence of the problem. On assurance that it was fairly evident from the employees, they both admitted its existence. A one-hour session probing possible solutions degenerated into a near shouting match. The ombudsman suggested another meeting to try to resolve it independently, without higher involvement. The directors agreed, but that meeting too was unsuccessful. Some possibilities for department changes emerged, but they could not be agreed on.

The ombudsman requested a third meeting, to which he invited their already informed senior vice president (after telling them he would do this). Both were emotional and somewhat stubborn but were able to resolve it with the senior VP present at the next meeting.

The ombudsman would continue to follow up on the meeting's action plans over the next six months.

Case 3: Discrimination

The Complaint. Mary Matthews filed a complaint about discrimination in her office. She was a junior marketing representative who was interested in promotion to marketing services coordinator. The district supervisor had been very nice to her on hiring and remarked at the time that it was "quite nice to have a woman and an ethnic minority, no less, in the business." Mary had long grown accustomed to snide comments about her gender and her ethnic origin and just sloughed it off.

However, three sales representative coordinator positions had come open in the last two years. She was eligible and applied for each one. However, she did not get any of the jobs. After the third final selection was made, she went to the district manager and asked directly what the problem was.

Although he made no direct references, he did suggest that it was important to have a good match between the personnel coordinating the team and the makeup of the team. He did not offer to explain this and Mary did not follow up with additional questions.

She remarked to the ombudsman that, in part, she was afraid that she already knew the answer. She was unsure about government and company policies with regard to racial, ethnic group and sex discrimination and wanted first to know what official positions were, as well as what informal actions have been taken in the past. She also wanted advice on how to handle the problem.

At the same time, she remarked that her father was an attorney active with the ACLU (American Civil Liberties Union). If she did not get satisfaction within the company, she intended to take it further and expected to receive full support at home.

Ombudsman Actions. The ombudsman investigated the complaint, finding that Mary Matthews' allegations were true. Three positions were open; she had applied for all three. In the last two cases, it appeared that she was more qualified than the persons selected. The ombudsman asked the district supervisor about his selection process. He informed the ombudsman that it was his decision (with clear resentment at the probing).

The ombudsman thought this case had potentially significant impact on the corporation both as a guide/model and in terms of potential litigation cost. The ombudsman went to the senior vice president for personnel, who immediately initiated his own review. He called in the district supervisor who admitted that he felt the employee would not fit in because of her ethnic origin. The supervisor was given a one-week suspension without pay. He was directed to redesign the marketing services system to make room for one more coordinator, based on an expected expansion that was emerging. This was not satisfactory to the district supervisor, but it was accepted.

The complainant was satisfied with the corporation's response and her own new situation as the fourth sales representative coordinator.

The ombudsman suggested that the corporation present a training program on recruitment and promotion policies and practices. This was done, but only on a one-time basis in two of the departments.

Case 4: Supervisory Conflict

The Complaint. Frank Smith filed a complaint regarding what he felt to be unfair treatment from his supervisor, foreman John Thompson. Frank was a single parent whose wife had passed away a year ago. He had two small children, ages six and eight. Frank's job began officially at 8:30. However, he informed the foreman that in order to get the children safely off to school, it was difficult for him to leave the house before 8:30. He asked if he could make up the fifteen minutes either over lunch or at the close of the day, when a neighbor was already watching the children.

He noted that his job on the shop floor was independent. He could start fifteen minutes later than his colleagues without impeding work in any way. Since his colleagues were also aware of the situation with the small children, he did not feel that they would object to this special treatment. He communicated his request to the foreman.

He reported that the foreman expressed shock at the request and insisted that absolutely not, under any circumstances, could this be done. After several days, he went to the foreman and made the request again, suggesting that there was no easy way for him to arrange babysitting for a fifteen-minute period the first thing in the morning. The foreman insisted that there was no way he could start a new company precedent allowing individuals to receive special treatment. Frank did not want to make trouble, but at the same time, he did not know how he could continue his job and care for his children. He asked if there was any way that he could get help with this problem.

Ombudsman Actions. The ombudsman "investigation" was brief. He needed to establish the school and work times and the character of Frank Smith's job. This he could do with some telephone calls. The ombudsman then went to the shop floor manager to see what might be done in the way of a response. He suggested that he would be afraid that many persons would want this kind of exception.

The ombudsman then went to the personnel executive to see if "flextime" was being considered or had ever been discussed. He said it had not but that he had read much about it and would be interested. The ombudsman suggested using this one employee's problem as part of a pilot test. The personnel executive agreed.

The ombudsman organized a meeting with the personnel executive and the shop floor manager to talk it over. The group agreed that it seemed an ideal case. The group then brought in the foreman and discussed the problem and this proposed solution. He was reluctant at first but gradually became convinced of the fairness (or at least recognized the pressure). He was somewhat interested in the possibilities, mostly negative.

This new arrangement was done. The ombudsman monitored it after three months to see if it was working well, which it was.

Case 5: Sexual Harassment

The Complaint. The ombudsman received a telephone call one day from Kathleen Collins, a computer systems marketing representative in the local division of the company. Kathleen had not been with the company more than about nine months but was now having a problem with the district manager for computer systems marketing. He travels with her on her marketing trips about once per month to supervise and to offer suggestions for performance improvement. The first three trips were very professional. But on the last several trips he made suggestions about their need to travel overnight and about the possibility of sharing accommodations.

The suggestions for "accommodations sharing" were at first very subtle and were offered in somewhat of a joking fashion. As the suggestions continued, she said she expressed no interest at all. His suggestions then became more direct and during the last trip, somewhat strident.

Kathleen said that she was concerned that her performance ratings would suffer and that her career with the company could be in jeopardy. She had

had no performance ratings since the start of the suggestions, but was due for one in three months.

She had never encountered this in her quite young career and did not know how to handle it. She was asking for guidance on how to discourage the advances in a way that would protect her job and career. Also, since she liked her supervisor, she did not want to offend him.

Ombudsman Actions. In this case, it was not necessary to further identify the nature of the complaint. Typically, an investigation would involve the confrontation of the supervisor with the question of "did this happen?" The ombudsman asked Kathleen if she would like to try once more to discourage him (with some guidance) or would she like the ombudsman to confront the man with the question directly? Or a simple "general visit" to marketing to raise the question could be made.

She said that there was another trip well before her ratings were due. She would be willing to try once more to stop the advances. After that, she definitely wanted outside help. She also wanted a record that she complained, since she was afraid of the impact on her ratings.

The ombudsman agreed to this as well, informing her that frequently "merely inquiring" into the problem was sufficient intervention. The ombudsman also suggested that he could send a policy memorandum/reminder to the marketing department. Sometimes this was effective.

The ombudsman and Kathleen decided that another try from her, the policy reminder, and the ombudsman's beginning inquiry would be the response. They agreed to meet after her next trip.

Case 6: Physical Conditions

The Complaint. Martha Worthington filed a complaint about conditions in one of the manufacturing sections that developed components for computers. She noted that she was in one of the old buildings in one of the old wings that was scheduled to be renovated in the next few years. She noted that in the summer, temperatures in the building climbed into the mid to high nineties on hot days.

When she and the other workers complained about the conditions, they were informed that the company would not invest in air-conditioning for this old building. They were told that it was about to be renovated. However, they were first told this about a year and a half ago but no work had begun. When she raised the question again, she was told to drop it.

She said she simply wanted to get across the point that their productivity was suffering, since by early afternoon most of the workers were going at about half-speed or less because of the heat. She thought that an investment in some sort of portable air conditioners would probably be recouped by the additional productivity. She wanted to know how to express these concerns without getting herself fired.

Ombudsman Actions. The ombudsman investigated the situation by talking to several other employees of that unit. They confirmed the problem, which the ombudsman further verified by walking into the unit one afternoon. It was unbearable.

The ombudsman then contacted building maintenance to see what could be done. They said they were already backed up with projects and were constrained by a limited budget. The ombudsman suggested the productivity problem might be costing more, but that assessment was clearly beyond their level of concern.

The ombudsman then went to the operations vice president, who did recognize the problem (and did recognize the ombudsman's power to force resolution if necessary). He thought there might be an intervening step that could be taken. Perhaps portable air-conditioners and fans could be leased for the summer. He would request a quick engineering and cost review.

This was investigated and found to be feasible without too high a cost. It was completed ten days later.

Case 7: Salary

The Complaint. Barbara Bosworth filed a complaint regarding her secretarial salary. She had been with the corporation for some five years, beginning as a Secretary I. She had recently advanced to Secretary III and was making $32,000 a year. She was interested in further promotion but knew that the next rung on the career ladder for her was administrative assistant. When she had an opportunity to be transferred to another unit, she jumped at it, thinking that this was the chance to become an administrative assistant. When the job was offered to her, she neglected to ask to be sure that the official title said administrative assistant. The administrator interviewing her referred to the jobholder as his assistant, who would be pretty much in control of the office. When the decision was made, he informed her that she would get a 5 percent jump immediately and another 5 percent in three months after satisfactory performance.

After three months, she realized that she was working as an administrative assistant pretty much in control of the office as he had suggested. However, she did not hear mention of any forthcoming 5 percent salary increase. When she raised the issue, he said he felt her salary was appropriate for her duties. She remarked that her responsibilities were considerably beyond what she was doing as Secretary III and that the new higher salary after three months' satisfactory performance was one of the conditions of the job. He did not respond but looked fairly agitated about her suggesting the point.

She did not know how to pursue this issue further, but felt that she was unfairly treated with regard to salary and the movement to the new position. She was afraid that pushing it further with her boss would cause her problems on the job and wanted to know how to handle the situation. She remarked that she would not stay in the job without additional salary.

Ombudsman Actions. The ombudsman investigated the situation by examining her workload and duties and comparative salaries. She was correct in her assessment. The ombudsman passed this information on to the personnel director, who reviewed the case and agreed. The personnel director called in her supervisor (a private meeting) and suggested that he revise her salary to fit her new duties and responsibilities. The man was immediately compliant with the request, seeming to be afraid of consequences if he did not. He offered only a halfhearted presentation of his position.

Case 8: Personal Problems — Addictions and Marriage

The Complaint. David Stern was a relatively young sales representative in a district manager's office. He was one of a crack team put together by an equally young district manager who was beating the competition easily. David was a friend of the district manager, since they had gone to school together. He was aware that the pace of sales was quick and that it was important for the district manager to take clients out to lunch quite frequently. However, David noted that his young boss seemed to be indulging in more lunchtime martinis than he had seen him drink in the early part of their careers. He also knew, since their wives were friends, that his district manager and his wife were having marital problems.

He felt that these two difficulties — the heavier drinking, which he was not sure was really an addiction, and the marriage problems — were linked. He wanted to suggest to his friend that he seek treatment or seek some sort of support but did not know how to go about it or even whether the suggestion was appropriate in the work context. He also knew that the district manager was becoming increasingly short-tempered with the staff. They had had very good working relationships over the past five years.

He wanted to know two things: whether it was appropriate to raise the addiction and marital issue in the work context at all (or whether he should just raise it as a friend out of work at some point), and whether or not the organization had assistance available for this kind of problem.

Ombudsman Actions. The ombudsman spent some time telling David about the policies of the corporation and the programs the corporation has for addressing the personal problems of employees. The company had long supported assistance as a means of retaining good people.

The ombudsman referred him to the employee assistance program director, who would offer a series of strategies for getting help to his friend. This was to be done quickly. The ombudsman called while David was there to set up the appointment. The ombudsman talked a bit more about the usual forms of help — the educational role — and suggested that he call back in a month to report on progress.

Case 9: Production/Sabotage

The Complaint. Ronald Smith filed a complaint relating to difficulties on the computer assembly line. Someone in the line appeared to be sabotaging some of the equipment during the production process. He was aware that some of his supervisors understood that there was a problem, but no one seemed to know quite how to deal with it. He had been approached on one or two occasions to ask if it was his doing. He did not admit to it being his problem, nor did he know who was responsible on the line. Although the supervisors leaned on him heavily, they did not discover the cause of the problem.

All he knew was that the defects showing up in the assembly line seemed to be a regular and purposeful process. It was not the kind of mistake that would be made easily without some conscious attempt to do so.

Ombudsman Actions. The ombudsman's brief investigation suggested that this seemed to be a real sabotage problem. The products were at the technological cutting edge and were of special concern to the company. The ombudsman immediately referred the problem to plant security after telling the complainant what he would do. The complainant agreed to help security with the problem, which was regarded as significant, possibly criminal, and well beyond the people-conflict situation.

Customer Complaints

To represent ombudsmen that handle customer problems, the casebook must also include illustrative customer complaints. These complaints are similar to ones mentioned throughout the book, and are handled in essentially the same manner as those of employees. The following cases indicate examples of customer problems handled by ombudsmen. The complaints involve or come from a patient, a prisoner, a citizen, a welfare recipient, and a customer of a gas company.

Case 10: *The Patient's Treatment*

The Complaint. Two parents were at a dinner party one evening when the host received a telephone call. The caller asked to speak to one of them. The caller informed Mr. Jones that his three-year-old son was in the hospital and that he needed permission to treat him. The father, obviously upset, said, "What hospital? What's going on?" His grandparents were babysitting with him. The caller identified himself as a physician and asked for permission to treat. Mr. Jones said, "Well, I need more information," whereupon the physician said, "I need permission to treat your son. Will you give it?" Mr. Jones replied that he would not give permission until he knew about the nature of the problem and what was going on, whereupon the physician hung up.

The next person to call was the nurse, who called back within a couple of minutes and said, "Your son has fallen and cut his head. We need permission to treat." This time Mrs. Jones answered, and asked for further information. The nurse said, "It's a fairly deep gash in his forehead requiring probably seven to fifteen stitches. Do we have permission?" Mrs. Jones said, "Is he basically okay?" The nurse said, "Yes, but we need permission to clean and close the wound." Mrs. Jones said, "That's fine with me; my parents will monitor. Go ahead." She hung up. The next call was from her mother, the boy's grandmother. She said, "They need permission to do this, but will not accept our permission." Mrs. Jones said, "Okay. Tell them to go ahead."

At that point the nurse called back and said, "Aren't you going to come? It seems like you really should be here." At this point, becoming outraged, Mrs. Jones said, "We've just been trying to find out what's going on. Of course we're going to come. We'll be there in fifteen minutes."

When the parents arrived at the hospital, the nurse immediately began to lecture them on how they did not know the appropriate procedure and shouldn't parents be a little bit more caring about what goes on? Mr. Jones, who happened to be a professor of health and medical care systems, was outraged at the notion and wanted to file a complaint. He asked if the hospital had a patient ombudsman at the hospital, but was told (mistakenly) that there was none.

Ombudsman Actions. There was no one on duty at 9:00 P.M. Saturday night to take the complaint because the ombudsman office was a one-person, part-time and poorly publicized position. Fearing retribution or poor service or both, the parents did not complain to anyone. Instead, they waited until their son was clearly all right, and then wrote to the chief executive of the hospital who sent their letter on, unacknowledged, to the part-time ombudsman. Meanwhile, the Jones family told many people of their bad experience at the hospital and about their inability to complain.

Ombudsman action would have helped, but there was none in this case.

Case 11: A Prisoner's Complaint

The Complaint. Henry was a twenty-one-year-old inmate in a county prison with not much experience in correctional institutions. When he first arrived in the prison, the guard ordered him to clean his cell three times as part of the "welcoming initiation." The young inmate gave him some wise backtalk and refused to do it. Following that opening incident, the guard began a series of subtle and not-so-subtle harassments of veiled threats, denials of opportunity for recreation time in a couple of instances, and references to what could happen to him in the prison environment. After several weeks, the young inmate realized he had made a major error in the prison culture. He wanted to complain about the way he was treated. He went to the prison ombudsman to file a complaint, fearing harassment or even threats to his safety if he talked to the warden.

Ombudsman Actions. The prison ombudsman listened to the problem with sympathy and understanding. He suggested the inmate try to handle it himself by toleration and no response (hoping the harassment would just extinguish itself since it produced no return from the inmate). The ombudsman also suggested that he (the ombudsman) take the complaint to the warden to initiate a general "meet and discuss" with guards (of that unit first, then other units) over inmate harassment. At this point, there would be no direct action with the guard in question. The inmate was to report progress every other day and to alert the ombudsman immediately if the harassment became stronger. This was considered a first action, to be followed quickly with stronger action if needed.

Case 12: A Citizen's Complaint

The Complaint. Sam Johnson lived on a well-traveled, somewhat rural, road, which was rapidly developing as a main route to a number of new housing developments. Following one particularly hard winter, a rather substantial pothole opened up on the road. Sam decided that he would call the department of transportation. He informed the department that the pothole was both substantial in size and potentially dangerous, because there were several trees quite close to it on one side of the road. Somebody veering to avoid the pothole or going through it and losing control would go immediately into a tree. Sam filed several complaints with the department of transportation, but it appeared there was some dispute over whether it was a county road or a state road. No one would clarify who had the responsibility.

After some weeks of trying to sort it out, Sam decided to see if there was someone who could help him get the problem resolved, an effort that he thought was in the interest of public safety and good citizenship.

He called on the department of transportation's ombudsman for assistance.

Ombudsman Actions. The ombudsman took the details of the location and who had been contacted and told Sam she would get back to him in the next several days. The ombudsman called the streets unit to find out if they knew of the problem and whether corrective action was to be taken. Although it was near a juncture with a county road, it was clearly state responsibility. The unit cited general workload problems and denied knowing of the complaint. The ombudsman cited the need for quick action and asked if senior management should be involved. The unit director replied that it could be repaired in the next several days but would not specify when. The ombudsman suggested that would be okay but made a note to follow up, assuming she would have to do so. Case open.

Case 13: A Welfare Recipient's Problems

The Complaint. In one state, welfare recipients received their check by mail. One mother with two small children and a missing husband was having difficulty ensuring that the welfare department send her checks to the correct address. It was true that she had to move several times in order to arrange suitable living arrangements because of the breakup of her family. However, the checks were repeatedly sent to the wrong address.

After all the necessary change-of-address forms were filed, the checks first went to the wrong address, an old address, and were returned to the department. The next set of checks went to another previous address, but did not arrive until a significant time later, since they were forwarded by a friend who helped informally. The third time she attempted to correct the problem, they got her address right but spelled her name wrong and she was unable to cash the check. After repeated calls to the welfare department (the bureau of names and addresses or some such department), she called on the troubleshooter for assistance.

Ombudsman Actions. The ombudsman was able to get the facts by telephone — correct name, address, and to whom she talked. The woman had to receive a corrected check immediately. After identifying the correct department, she requested a quick correction from a staff member. The response was a series of reasons why it would take days, if not a week. The ombudsman said that would not do. She told the staff member she would need a meeting and would call back in several hours. The ombudsman next called the unit director and explained the situation, including the need for immediate action. The director offered one view of "immediate" that was not acceptable. The ombudsman and the director agreed to meet with the complainant at 4:00

P.M. that afternoon to resolve the problem — to secure a new check. The ombudsman called the welfare recipient to tell her to come in.

Case 14: Complaint from a Gas Company Customer

The Complaint. Mr. Davidson had just purchased a property from the estate of an elderly woman. The woman heated the three-story house, now converted to apartments, with gas heat. Mr. Davidson wanted to rent out the apartments and began to do so, incorporating payment for the heat in the rental amount. He retained responsibility for paying the heating bills.

As the winter began, the gas company sent a bill based on the estimated previous year's cost, which appeared to Mr. Davidson to be astronomical. On calling about the cost, he found that the elderly woman was apparently a very heavy user of gas and kept the building very warm. Mr. Davidson explained to the utility company that he would make radical changes in gas use, and through insulation and construction, would be reducing the gas bill substantially. The gas company said that it would read the meter on a regular basis.

After two months, the gas company indicated that it had not been able to read the meter but again submitted a very high bill. Mr. Davidson suggested that its representative come out to read the meter and agreed to meet him or her there. The meter reader never showed up at the agreed time. Mr. Davidson complained.

Meanwhile, the gas company sent another bill, this one based on the previous year's heat cost, and demanded payment. Mr. Davidson said that he would not pay until they got a real reading of the correct amount of gas usage under his new ownership. The gas company threatened to cut off heat to the facility.

After attempting to negotiate a solution with the payment collections department, Mr. Davidson called on the ombudsman for assistance.

Ombudsman Actions. The main ombudsman action from the company's customer representative involved scheduling and attending a meeting of the customer with representatives from the meter reading group and billing department. As facilitator in a tense meeting, the customer representative was able to negotiate a time and place to read the meter — that afternoon. He was also able to establish a regular time for meter reading that was to be passed on to the tenants and posted in the apartment. He expected all parties to honor the solution — old bills and collections letters were destroyed — although the billing and collections people were not fully pleased. Neither was the customer, since no apology was directly made. All agreed that further time on the problem was not useful.

The customer representative made a note to follow up.

Summary

Customer-involved cases are much like employee problems. Many times they are people-based conflicts with the core action being confrontation and resolution meetings. Often the ombudsman does not have a sense of whether the solution was immediately and permanently successful. In short, the cases lack closure.

The sample cases cited provide a sense of the nature of ombudsman work — varied and interesting. What is probably not apparent from these brief descriptions is the high level of emotional involvement in each case. The cases are stressful and loaded with conflict. The seeming ease of resolution is only an artifact of the telling. Most dispute resolutions are hard, involving change for both people and organization; neither is willing to change easily.

These case examples reflect the work of formal ombudsmen, those officially recognized by title and position. They are also representative of the informal ombudsman's caseload. This means that these cases are also likely to be the ones addressed by human and employee relations managers, executive assistants, sales representatives, and trusted senior people who have "adopted" the role. The degree of formality with which the problem solver solves the problem is the differentiating element between formal and informal ombudsmen, not the nature of the case.

The cases are representative of the caseload of both consumer and employee troubleshooters. The types of actions taken — formal and informal fact finding, meeting arrangement, personal counseling, communication to senior management — are representative response actions of all ombudsmen. Some ombudsmen are concerned with products and services, others with work and work related performance.

Ombudsmen for both employees and customers must successfully solve problems. How the organization tracks the ombudsman's performance is the subject of Chapter 12.

Chapter 9

Value to Top Management

This chapter reviews the contribution of the ombudsman to the top management of the organization. There are three questions that illustrate the potential benefits to the organization. Why are we using ombudsmen in today's public and private organizations? How does the ombudsman contribute to top management's investment in effectiveness? What are the benefits to the leaders, executive team and ombudsman?

We have discussed some of the benefits to the organization and its leaders in the chapter on the needs for an ombudsman. In this chapter, we will focus on the specific contributions of the ombudsman activity to the leader and the top management team. This takes us to several key questions:

- How does the ombudsman contribute to the competencies of the leader and the top management teams?
- How does the ombudsman contribute to individual, team, and organizational effectiveness?

We will illustrate the answer to these questions through two sets of organizational behaviors, namely the competencies of the leaders and top management team and the execution of key roles of the leader. Leaders must address issues with their customers and their employees. Let's began with the competencies as defined by expert authors in the field of organization behavior.

Competencies

The following competencies are listed as critical to the performance of senior executive/top management duties (adapted from Hellriegel and Slocum, 2009).

- Communication.
- Teams/teamwork.

- Diversity.
- Ethics.
- Across cultures.
- Planning and change.
- Self knowledge.

The authors contend that these seven competencies are the key characteristics of senior executives capabilities. Let's take them one by one.

Communication

Communication is thought to be the building block of the organization. The underlying concept of organization is one of a social system with individual and interpersonal interactions that both formally and informally drive organization behaviors. Thus it is the duty of the senior leader and top management personnel to develop better personal trust and to build a common ground or common culture with a combination of structure and directed behaviors. First and foremost, leaders must be able to communicate out of the organization to the board of trustees and down the organization to the management team and toward employees at all levels. As we will see, ombudsmen support this activity in a number of ways.

First, the presence of the ombudsman demonstrates the structural attribute of openness. Staff, employees and customers are welcomed with their questions and concerns. Not all staff and customers feel comfortable in going to an organization member in the line of hierarchy with sensitive concerns. The ombudsman demonstrates by his or her very presence an openness to questions and concerns.

Second, the ombudsman contributes active listening to staff and customers. Not all managers are comfortable discussing the range of subjects addressed by the ombudsman. Sometimes customers and employees merely need someone to talk to.

Third, the ombudsman is relied on for constructive feedback regarding the various activities and behaviors in the organization. At a well-known international airline, flight attendants were unhappy with a new policy mandating a rotation through long and short flights. Several attendants had nearly back to back flights that did not allow for the proper rest period. Direct appeals to management resulted in nothing. They took their concerns to the ombudsman.

Finally, the ombudsman assists top management in mediating cultural differences that arise in an organizational world that is increasingly diverse. In all of these ways, the ombudsman supports the core competency of communication whether it is oral, written, up to the board, or down to the staff.

The ombudsman is not a replacement for the communication capabilities of top management. Instead, the position is one more supportive link to successful communication capabilities within the organization.

Teams/Teamwork

There are a number of issues involving the development of teamwork that ombudsman once again support. The first of these is underscoring the norms of the culture. Ombudsmen demonstrate that one of the key elements of culture and values is openness, that is, allowing teams to question the direction and behaviors of the organization.

The ombudsman also contributes to cohesiveness of the teams by allowing an escape valve for concerns by team members. In some cases, ombudsmen operate within special functions. For example, in one large health insurance company, the turnover among computer systems analysts and engineers was very high. The company established an ombudsman for the Information Technology section, a service that was not made available to the rest of the company.

In the present day of specialized functions and products, we need some mechanism to cross functions, for example, to build the linkage between marketing and engineering, between finance and manufacturing, between human resources and sales. Conflicts arise that cannot be handled within a given function. In this sense the ombudsman functions as a "silo prevention" mechanism (silos being departments that are isolated with little interaction with others to the detriment of the company as a whole). Modern employees tend to work within functional and product silos across which little communication and conflict resolution occurs.

The ombudsman is also helpful in self-managing teams when the team is unable to address the issues within themselves.

Last, the ombudsman offers mutual and personal accountability by testing the degree of fit between the organization's announced values and its actual behaviors within its teams and in relation to the outside. For example, nuclear power managers insisted that they were in total compliance with all existing safety rules and regulations. Citing security terms they would not detail their compliance. After outside advocates protested the lack of transparency with a series of "front page news articles" the utility created an ombudsman to hear both customer and employee complaints.

Diversity

The concern for diversity in today's work force is now apparent to nearly all employees and customers. The changing work force has increased interest in finding mechanisms to address a variety of values and behaviors. Employees and customers come to the organization with different attitudes about work, about service and about inter-personal relationships based on their cultural differences. Again, the organization needs a mechanism for addressing these changes. The ombudsman is but one part of a package of strategies for managing diversity, meaning gender, age, ethnicity, and ideology.

The ombudsman helps to create an environment of inclusion. The ombudsman's mere structural presence signals to the workforce that there is a top management supported mechanism for addressing concerns by any of its members, whether employees or customers. The ombudsman helps us to learn from those with differences by processing complaints and concerns and passing them on to the executive leader and top management personnel as well as to board members. The presence of an ombudsman is part of the mechanism by which the organization communicates and supports diversity at all levels of the organization. The executive is recognized as a leader interested in confronting bias, one who has established a mechanism — the ombudsman — to handle concerns and complaints.

At a large import export bank with some 30 international locations, women employees went public with their concerns, concerns that ranged from relatively minor dress code issues to allegations of harassment in certain foreign locations. The complaints again went public, as no internal structure existed for listening. An ombudsman for all locations was created.

Ethics

We discuss ethics in a separate chapter altogether (chapter 11). Here we're concerned that top leaders abide by the basic principles of ethics with regard to their internal organization, behaviors that affect their decision making with regard to products, services, customers and employees. The ombudsman contributes to ethical decision making by ensuring that all courses of action are reviewed even when there is potential dissent. In some cases, management is interested in going in a given direction without regard to downside concerns about customer or employee impact, or product safety for example. The ombudsman again allows a voice to be heard, ensuring that a full and open discussion about alternatives is presented. In some cases, natural ethnic groupings can require different styles of management when, for example, dealing with the labor subgroups hired for construction, farm work, and other short-term commitments.

Ethics also means concern for the application of government laws and regulations. In the rush to deliver products and services in an efficient and effective way, both managers and employees are tempted to play the gray areas with respect to law and regulation. In recent years, we have certainly seen this orientation with regard to the financial services industry and large scale corporate endeavors.

Ethics also implies a concern for the dignity and respect of both employees and customers. Part of this respect is demonstrated by the presence of an ombudsman who offers a point of view that may be in opposition to expected directions. The ombudsman suggests that the culture values honesty and openness without hidden agendas designed to take advantage of either customers or employees.

Last, consistency with regard to core principles of ethics requires leadership commitment. That commitment means that the ombudsman is an illustration of the leadership's values and follow-on behavior. For example, failing tires were reported to have caused sport utility roll over crashes and other accidents. Information was available both within the tire and auto companies that would have alerted senior management to the seriousness of the problem. But there was no mechanism for employees with concerns to responsibly raise them within the organization without seeming disloyal. After disastrous litigation and bad press, an ombudsman was created along with a path for the complaint data to reach senior management.

Across Cultures

Following closely with the concern for diversity is the allied issue of cultural differences. Each organization, each complete group and each customer base represents some uniqueness with regard to a given organization's culture, whether in health care, banking, the military or some other field. The presence of the ombudsman helps to surface recognition of this cultural uniqueness by allowing differences and conflicts to be confronted and addressed. The ombudsman is also concerned with work-related values as some employees are part of cultures that value individualism, while others value the community over the individual. Work practices will tend to reflect these opposing orientations.

The successful organization needs to meld this concern with individual needs for productivity with shared concerns for teamwork.

Part of the ombudsman's efforts are directed at continuing to motivate those with different values and attitudes by providing active listening and a mechanism for addressing concerns. In large organizations, ombudsmen confront concerns with language, with behavior patterns, and with working relationships. In multinational organizations with subsidiaries in foreign countries, they are able to set up unique ombudsman offices which reflect customs at the local level. Thus the company is able to think on a global scale but to act in relation to local concerns.

For example, military deployments take officers and enlisted men and women and their families to distant locations in foreign cultures. In some assignments families face safety issues while women in particular are restrained as to their movements and dress. Other deeply sensitive issues, with an ethical dimension, concern the offering of gifts to those with whom one wishes to do business or after an agreement has been reached. What one culture defines as bribery might be interpreted quite differently in some parts of the world. An ombudsman can be used to alert senior staff as to the degree of difficulty encountered in managing these location concerns.

Planning and Change

Ombudsmen have been used as part of a planned change process. Planning requires attention to direction, destination, and decisions (Ziegenfuss, 2006). In the first concern the organization is trying to determine if it is currently going in the right direction. The second question addresses how the organization will know when it gets there. In the third question one asks what decisions have to be made and how past decisions have been received. The ombudsman contributes in several ways to these three planning elements. Ombudsmen offer many employees an ear for their concerns about the plan's direction. They offer an ear to those concerned that the desired direction has not been attained. And the ombudsman's presence allows for questions regarding the planned decisions and their impact on both employees and customers. By using the data generated by the ombudsman, the leader and top management members are able to determine how their actions have affected organizational behaviors and subsequent organization progress toward a desired future. Some companies in the private sector have used the ombudsman as a feedback mechanism to determine the success of planned changes including both the way in which changes have been handled and progress toward the desired direction (in some cases an idealized design, or most desired redesign, Ackoff, Magidson, Addison, 2006).

The ombudsman's role with regard to change is closely linked to the "planning for the future" activities of senior management. The complaint data and accompanying analysis is one of the mechanisms for establishing a diagnosis (i.e., what is the state of the organization today), a database with regard to needs and readiness for change. In today's public and private organizations, technological change is significant across nearly all fields. Feedback from the ombudsman regarding how to account for resistance to change and for technological accommodation is a strategy useful to top management. Leaders expect resistance to change on both the individual and organizational level. Those accustomed to leading change recognize that a feedback channel is needed to test the degree of success. While there may be public forums for presenting concerns organization-wide (e.g., the increasingly prevalent "town hall meetings") less often is there a mechanism for individual expressions of concern. The ombudsman is often the most appropriate person to receive and address individual concerns. As noted, the implementation of change requires individual, team and organizational adaptation. Ombudsman data can be used to help assess the degree of accommodation to planned change, alerting leaders to a troublesome pace or the potential for internal and external backlash. In this sense, ombudsmen are a part of a process of continuous improvement. Although leaders expect that they are pursuing the correct direction and pace of change, feedback from employees and customers can help them improve the change process. In managing change, leaders learn to accept the presence of feedback and manage the use of it.

Self Knowledge

The final competency area for senior executives and top management is self knowledge. The leader must employ knowledge of his/her own personality and attitudes toward employees, toward customers, and toward the responsibility for designing the organization of the future. The ombudsman is able to contribute to this self-knowledge by providing feedback from individuals and groups, including patterns of concerns regarding the executive decisions about direction, destination and behaviors. While an individual and a senior management team can become isolated, organizational aspirations involve employees organization wide. Whether there is agreement with the organizational goals and/or the process of their development is again the mechanism by which the ombudsman contributes to both formation of "executive personality" and the personality of the culture as whole (Schein, 1985, 2004). Thus the ombudsman provides the data that enables the executive and senior management team to manage themselves and their careers. Feedback from a wide range of the employee and customer stakeholders is critical to understanding the impact of decisions both large and small. The data and feedback help to provide a continuing awareness of the individual and team members' perspectives on the organization's current state and its progress toward the future. The presence of the ombudsman requires that the leader and the senior team be able to accept "data" on their leadership and management effectiveness. This data may be used "formatively" to assist the executive and his senior members in culture building and effectiveness. The board of directors, however, may use the ombudsman data in a "summative" way, part of a database for its decision making regarding the performance of the executive and senior management team. The ombudsman contributes simultaneously to the individual self knowledge of the executive and·the "group," self knowledge of the executive team as a whole. Hearing the degree to which one's decisions are accepted and supported is critical to organization progress.

Role Performance

Along with the support for the development of competencies, the ombudsman contributes to the role performance of executives and top management leaders. In two well-known presentations of the role of top executives, the roles were described as informational, interpersonal, positional (Mintzberg 1975) and designer, teacher, and steward (Senge, 1990). Let us take them one by one establishing the points of the ombudsman's contribution.

Informational

As noted above, the role of the ombudsman is designed to provide information to the executive and other top management leaders. The complaint data information is collected and analyzed, helping to describe the structure and process of the organization's "current state." This information can be communicated up to the board, down to the staff, out to employees and to customers and shareholders. The ombudsman has a minor role in this informational distribution, but the complete data is a part of the database for senior management communication. When the CEO asks, "What is the work climate like — hostile or friendly?" managers have actual data with which to respond — data developed by the ombudsman's complaints. While not definitive — other streams of data are needed concurrently — this is another source for informing senior management.

Interpersonal

The senior executives and top managers must know the condition of the psychological climate within the organization. It is hard for them to personally assess the level of collaboration, conflict, and competitiveness within the organization's various teams at various levels and through various functions. Senior executives want to know whether the psychological climate — the inner personal relationships in daily work tasks — are supporting productivity and quality innovation or, if the climate is undercutting these key outcomes. Senior managers depend on their interpersonal capabilities to make these assessments and to build stronger social and psychological relationships within the climate of the organization. Ombudsmen signal, with their structural presence, a willingness to be concerned with these issues on the part of leaders. The ombudsman's work also demonstrates "confidence" in the management and leadership. Leaders are not afraid to be open, to be attentive to concerns.

Positional

We have already talked about the planning required for moving the organization to its desired future. Ombudsman data provides decision support information that helps executives to determine both the direction and the degree of progress that has been made toward the desired future. Senior executives need to know "what is happening on the ground" at subsidiaries. For example, do employees feel the need for more resources, faster decisions, help with conflict resolution or other actions?

Designer

Senior executives and top managers are responsible for the architecture of the organization of the future. Some years ago a manufacturer of American automobiles decided to introduce total quality management philosophy and practices at several plants around the country. The approach calls for wide participation of employees in all areas of operations. Senior managers were convinced that a component of the company's future should be a strong quality improvement effort. Implementation of new manufacturing processes is always uncertain. This company used the ombudsman's feedback system to help to assess progress and implementation barriers.

In thinking through the design for the organization's future, leaders must understand the current state of operations, meaning strengths and weaknesses. One data stream for this analysis is the ombudsman's complaint data. For example, at the auto manufacturer, employees' complaints about managers' interference in the quality teams would signal a need for additional education and training for both managers and employees.

Teacher

Senior executives and managers must understand how to diagnose, plan for, and act on any barriers blocking progress toward the desired future. Leaders are the founders and reinforcers of the corporate culture. As such we look to leaders to guide us in our approach to management problems, our views of the external business environment and what is known as the company's core values, e.g., "customers are our focus," "we are patient centered," "kids come first." Leaders teach us how to behave to achieve success in the organization. But they also use managers and staff to conduct training sessions, to address sensitive issues from fraud and abuse to harassment. In some companies, ombudsmen provide training/teaching help on ethical issues, and on employee and customer relations.

For example, in a large multi national company with far flung subsidiaries, sexual harassment complaints were coming to the ombudsman's attention. While they were addressed on a case by case basis, the volume and regularity indicated a need for training regarding harassment — subsequently provided by the ombudsman.

Stewardship

Managers are required to carefully conserve human resources for use by the organization. As part of their stewardship they are responsible for the removal of obstacles to productivity and innovation and for collaborative team work. In many industries such as defense, concerns about compliance with rules and with fraud, waste, and abuse are common. Whistleblowers have a contribution of sorts when they take these concerns public. But the ombudsman's purpose is to enable an airing of concerns within the organization, hopefully changing behaviors before public damage is done and litigation results.

For example, in a large insurance company the information technology department seemed to have an extraordinary level of turnover. Analyst and programmers were leaving shortly after signing on. Two actions were taken in an effort to intervene as turnover costs for the few available recruits were quite light. Leaders first conducted a survey of employees to assess the quality of their working life (feedback on climate, structure, level of management support, policy barriers and so on). As a second initiative, leaders created an ombudsman position to address the continuing stream of concerns arising between analysts/programmers and managers of the IT department. After two years they were able to cut turnover from 47 percent to 22 percent, a significant savings in recruiting and training costs.

Summary

Thus we can see that the ombudsman contributes to top management by assisting in the building of managerial competencies and in some cases providing activities that reinforce and teach in the competency areas. Additionally, the ombudsman supports the informational, interpersonal and positional roles of top leaders by providing data and feedback on organizational climate and progress toward the future. Concurrently, the ombudsman assists in the design, teaching and stewardship roles at the center of the leader's responsibility.

Chapter 10

The Ombudsman in the
Structure of the Organization

A medical resident observes the increasingly erratic behavior of a senior surgeon. The surgeon is getting older and is not as steady as before. She is increasingly impatient, speaking irritably to those around her in the operating room. On one occasion, the resident thought he detected the odor of whisky when he stood near her. This young doctor is torn between speaking up so as to protect patients or keeping quiet so as to protect his future career. A nurse suggests he call the ombudsman.

The ombudsman does not receive complaints from employees or doctors but she is empowered to ensure that patients are protected. She listens carefully to the story, aware that certain elements may be missing. The resident told the ombudsman he couldn't sleep at night, not so much because it was difficult to be assigned to an erratic and sometimes bullying surgeon, but because he feared that one day, the surgeon would make a serious error. She helped the resident identify the issues and offered contact information on those to whom he could report.

Information can come from surprising sources when the ombudsman is trusted. A hospital ombudsman may learn of unethical practices from the ward clerk. A junior secretary may impart confidential information about a professor to the university ombudsman. A financial services worker may quietly tell the ombudsman that she suspects dishonest practices.

In the absence of an ombudsman, such potentially inflammatory information may be sent to television news bureaus, posted on blogs or circulated, scurrilously, round staff rooms. The media delights in stories of malfeasance at the top and health care, policing and finance are favorite targets. After exposure, much hand wringing ensues and whistleblowers come forward to say that no one listened to them or, worse, fired them. Even in cases later proven to be false, the corporate image may still suffer. Ombudsmen can provide a safe space for individuals to air their concerns. Ombudsmen are also empowered to discover whether or not these concerns have merit or are motivated by malice.

Ombudsmen do not have to solve every problem and frequently are not authorized to do so, but effective ombudsmen understand the structure of their organizations because they interact with people at every level and are part of the structure themselves. We can enhance our understanding of the ombudsman concept by considering the fit with elements of organization structure. In this chapter we address the following:

- Physical Location and Organization Size.
- Hierarchy, Authority and Independence.
- Centralization.
- Formality, Informality and Confidentiality.
- Employment and Compensation.
- Complexity and Connected Units.

Let us begin with a somewhat straightforward consideration of location and size of the organization — the physical structures.

Physical Location and Organization Size

The physical location of the ombudsman's office is an element crucial to the independence of the position. If the ombudsman's office is located in the executive wing of the institution, then the ombudsman is perceived to have power and authority (by virtue of physical proximity and referent power). The downside of such a prestigious position is the implicit and perceived threat to confidentiality. The ombudsman's office needs to be easily accessible, convey an impression of authority but, at the same time, positioned to be as private as a psychiatrist's office. No one is going to visit the employee ombudsman if the human resource director's secretary is next door. Gossip, along the lines of "Guess who I saw visiting the ombudsman?" should be guarded against at the outset. Some ombudsmen solve this problem by maintaining an office but meeting clients in separate meeting rooms.

The office may vary by size of the organization — some large organizations have a team of ombudsmen located in "headquarters." Others would have a decentralized group with an ombudsman staff member located in different subsidiary and geographic structures (e.g., European office, Western Region, each separate hospital). No matter the structural location, each ombudsman's success depends on the degree of autonomy and the relation to the power structure (or hierarchy).

Hierarchy, Authority and Independence

Effective ombudsman programs have the following features: the ombudsman reports to the highest authority in the organization; the ombudsman's office avoids organizational roles that present a conflict of interest; the ombudsman maintains strict confidentiality and does not report details of cases to managers beyond what is necessary; the ombudsman has no role in hiring or firing employees, or in enforcing policies. Ombudsmen work with related offices but need the stand alone recognition.

According to the International Ombudsman Association, the characteristics that set ombudsman offices apart from other departments, such as risk management, health and safety or employee assistance are:

1. Independence "in structure, function, and appearance to the highest degree possible within the organization."
2. Neutrality and Impartiality. The ombudsman is called a "designated neutral" and thus "remains unaligned and impartial."
3. Confidentiality. Everything told to the ombudsman by anyone seeking help is strictly confidential. This means that nothing is disclosed without permission unless "there appears to be imminent risk of serious harm."
4. Informality. The office is an "informal" resource. It cannot "participate in any formal or adjudicative administrative procedure related to concerns brought to his/her attention" [International Ombudsman Association, Code of Ethics, posted January 2007, retrieved April 25, 2010].

We should consider each of these practice principles. What do we mean when we say the ombudsman is independent? Surely if he or she is paid by the organization, she owes it loyalty?

Independence is a vexed topic in the literature on ombudsmen. Some view corporate or executive ombudsmen as window-dressing and unlikely to be independent in any real sense (Hyson, Stewart, May 27, 2009a, 6, citing Rowat 2007, p. 46). Rowat, in particular, is quite scathing about what he called the distortion of the classical concept with the introduction of university and then corporate ombudsmen (Rowat, 2007, pp. 43–44). Others, such as Linda Rief, speak more favorably of this type of ombudsman presence in the organization's hierarchy (Rief, 2004, p. 24; pp. 38–39). This issue of whether or not an ombudsman can be truly independent continues to be debated in academic circles and in ombudsman organizations, with scholars such as Rowat particularly dismissive of the concept of neutrality to describe a type of quasi-independence (Rowat, p. 46). In everyday practice, however, neutrality, and an independent placement within the structure of the organization, protects as far as possible the effectiveness of the ombudsman.

Ombudsmen navigate a narrow tightrope. Because they are neutral, or impartial, they cannot be perceived by clients to be defending or protecting the institution or having a vested interest in one outcome over another. On the other hand, ombudsmen may find it difficult not to feel part of their organizations, and, thus, to feel some loyalty. But they must avoid at all costs becoming what André Marin, Ombudsman for Ontario, calls a lapdog. Lapdogs "sit quietly and their role is basically to be decorative and comforting to the institutions they oversee" (Marin, 2008).

In the section on independence, the International Ombudsman Association, in its standards of practice, states five requirements: the ombudsman cannot be connected to other "entities" within the organization; he or she cannot hold any other position that "might compromise independence"; the ombudsman has "sole discretion" when deciding how to handle issues of concern that have been brought to her office; she "has access to all information and all individuals in the organization, as permitted by law"; she "has authority to select" her own staff and manage all aspects of her office (International Ombudsman Association, Standards of Practice, posted October 2009, retrieved May 13, 2010).

Can one be independent and yet part of an organizational structure? The way in which the role is structured, what activities are engaged in and even where the ombudsman is physically located, will enhance, or detract from, the power and effectiveness of the role.

In practice, this means that the ombudsman should report to the highest level possible and should not occupy any other post in the organization (for example, the Human Resources manager cannot be the ombudsman and the job should not be linked with Risk Management or Employee Assistance). The ombudsman ought also to be free from influence, internally or externally. In some organizations, the ombudsman reports to or is even practicing as a public relations officer, a human resources consultant, a social worker or a quality and risk management professional. All are potential conflicts of interest. Even if the ombudsman can avoid actual conflicts of interest in her personal dealings with clients, the perception will be that she puts the interests of the corporate institution first.

In the early days of organizational ombudsmen, the role was promoted to senior managers as a way of preventing lawsuits and undue media attention. This remains an important reason to place ombudsmen within the organizational structure. But it cannot be the sole motivation. If it is, then the ombudsman is drained of power and becomes a customer service representative, in the case of clients, or another type of human resources consultant. It may be tempting to install an ombudsman office so as to seem transparent and open. But if the person in the job is not given the tools to do the job, clients will quickly see this as manipulative window dressing and the ombudsman will be neither impartial nor neutral (a "captured" element within the overall structure). This is why the ombudsman, while, perhaps a senior manager in the organizational structure, needs to be as independent as possible.

The requirement that the ombudsman be a "designated neutral" depends first of all upon an effective reporting structure. It insists that the ombudsman not be part of a compliance function such as Occupational Health and Safety and it demands that the ombudsman be unaligned and unlinked with any role that could compromise the perception of neutrality.

Impartiality extends to such organizational roles as committee membership, policy creation and hiring boards. Committee chairs frequently invite the organizational ombudsman to join, hoping, perhaps, to add weight to proceedings or desirous of learning more about client and employee complaints. But membership can be construed as co-option as various stakeholders attempt to influence the ombudsman. Ombudsmen can best serve the institution by issuing special reports to committees and, from time to time, presenting issues of concern (anonymously) at meetings.

In practice, most ombudsmen use their discretion in deciding when to accept or refuse committee membership. One of the authors served for many years on a variety of research ethics committees connected with the teaching hospital's university. These enabled her to know and win the trust of physicians who then actively cooperated in investigations knowing that she respected their professional position. Committees that invite conflict of interest are those that require the ombudsman to draft new policies to respond to problems that the ombudsman identified. If one drafts a policy, presumably, one also endorses it. This is a threat to impartiality as the policies she wrote or promoted may later be challenged by clients or employees (Thacker, 2009, p. 73). Other conflicts of interest include hiring committees, as the ombudsman cannot have a voice in deciding who the organization employs. Attention ought also to be paid to external organizations to which the ombudsman may belong. Every ombudsman, and her organization, needs to reflect upon whether membership in political parties, or protest groups such as those against globalization, or government-run healthcare, are compatible with the position.

Reporting relationships within the hierarchy are critical here. Ideally, the ombudsman is placed just below the board of the institution or, at the very least, reports to the director (president or chief operating officer). Some consider that reporting to any subordinate manager seriously compromises the ombudsman's ability to act independently as he or she may be blocked by a line manager with his or her own reasons to impede action. Some organizations have successfully placed the ombudsman under the chief operating officer and, in other cases, ombudsmen report to the manager of Human Resources. Though not ideal, this can work if both parties pay strict attention to how this may affect the work and how the ombudsman is perceived.

Independence from the line management structure is essential to ensure independence, neutrality and impartiality, and confidentiality. An ombudsman who is also a departmental manager, or who reports to a departmental manager, cannot help but view complaints from the viewpoint of the departmental mandate. The manager of communications service will see complaints as potential media embarrassments; clients will expect someone reporting to social services to fix social or financial problems; the human resources consultant might want to lean on the ombudsman to deal with a difficult employee; risk managers, so often legally inclined, will want information so as to prevent lawsuits. All these are organizationally important, but their mandates cannot be the primary purpose of the ombudsman office.

Total independence is probably difficult to achieve and, perhaps, not even desirable. While some believe that the ombudsman should never be paid by the organization he serves, being part of an organization has its advantages. When the ombudsman is part of the organization, he or she can be relied upon to understand the needs and preoccupations of employees, clients and customers. Outside investigators may have difficulty gaining the trust of those they interview and may have difficulty understanding the specialized mission of the institution. This is particularly so in hospitals, universities and the military, for example. Professionals will not respect an investigator who does not appear to understand their profession. Even if the ombudsman is placed outside the structure, his or her frequent presence may lead her, and those who know her, to believe she is an employee.

Independence is important so that ombudsmen are free from feeling obliged to protect the interests of people in the organization, whether because of subtle pressure, or outright demand. They, like the clients they serve, must be free of the fear of reprisals. However, while an important ideal, one must recognize that absolute independence is probably impossible for most organizational ombudsmen. Lawyer Sarah Thacker concedes that "Organizational ombuds [her term] can never attain the same structural independence as legislative ombuds, whose independence is guaranteed by law and protected by the legislative branch ... [they] are only independent to the extent the entity allows" and, in a footnote, points out that while reprisals may never be obvious, budgetary constraints may be suggested as reason for reducing or eliminating a position (Thacker, 2009, p. 71; p.85 footnote 87).

Centralization

In very large organizations the question of how to address distributed services is key. Ombudsmen can be located in various subsidiaries of the organization with some varying degree of autonomy. Or, the ombudsman service can be centralized with location of the ombudsmen (one or more) in the headquarters operation. In a hospital system of twelve institutions for example, each ombudsman is located at the institutional site but each reports to a chief ombudsman as director of the function for the hospital chain as a whole.

The question of the extent of centralization as a structural element also brings up the degree to which the ombuds processes and procedures are standardized. In more formal programs, rules and procedures for investigations, reporting and follow up are defined. In others the notion of "informal problem solver" allows considerable discretion as to actions and behaviors at each individual site (see formality section below).

For example, one Canadian province's formal, health care center-based program, functions according to rules laid down in law (Government of Quebec, An Act Respecting Health Services and Social Services, R.S.Q. Chapter S42, Province of Quebec, updated 1 March 2010, articles 29–59) that give specific instructions on how to handle disciplinary issues, when to refer and how quickly to respond. Nonetheless, the law leaves ample room for personal decision-making within the parameters.

Formality, Informality and Confidentiality

A design question for ombudsmen is how formal or informal is the effort to be? Tending toward the formal side leads ombudsmen and their sponsoring organization toward a legalistic approach to the work. An informal orientation suggests "problem solving with limited records" (we often use the degree of record keeping as an indicator of the formality of the ombudsman office). The ombudsman supplements the formal channels that exist within the organization because the ombudsman can identify issues and has the power to do something about them. The office itself is not formal, like the legal department. It is neutral, confidential, safe (see Redmond and Williams, 2004, pp. 49–50).

The ombudsman can serve as an early warning system, putting out fires before they explode into conflagrations that destroy reputations and shareholder value. He or she may be able constructively to channel whistleblower information so that it is heard, received and acted upon.

Good ombudsmen respect their institution's goals and mission and exist to ensure that it stays true to its ideals. If one is an organizational ombudsman, it is natural to value the hospital, bank, utility or public agency for which one works. Ombudsmen know their loyalty is to the ideals, in spite of a daily reality that may fall short. Their job is to keep the organization aware of shortcomings, to help correct them and to help to foster systems to prevent future problems.

The demands of confidentiality bear on this question of degree of formality. For example, the issue of privacy makes it clear why the ombudsman may have to withhold information from committees. Consider the advice of the International Ombudsman Association. The International Ombudsman Association, among many provisions, says that communications "between ombudsman and others (while the ombudsman is serving in that capacity) are considered privileged." It states that "the ombudsman does not testify in any formal process inside the organization" and "resists testifying in any formal process outside." even with permission. Records identifying individuals cannot be kept and files must be kept from management with a plan of destruction. Finally, "communications made to the ombudsman are not notice to the organization" (IOA, Standards of Practice, 2009a, points 3.2; 3.3; 3.5; 3.6; 3.8).

What is without question is that all communication between ombudsman and client is confidential and that nothing is disclosed without the client's permission, with the exceptions provided by law, such as threats against self or others. More complicated is the issue of how records are written and maintained. Although the International Ombudsman Association's provisions refer to communications between the ombudsman's office and others as privileged, this may not be so in the private, corporate setting. The issue of testifying in formal processes outside the organization is a matter for state and provincial legislation and cannot be elaborated upon here as a general principle.

Much of the literature refers to ombudsmen taking few notes and shredding all records as soon as feasible (the "informal structure"). However, this has not been the practice of some hospital-based ombudsmen who keep records securely under lock and key, but only destroy them after a period of time mandated by law. In Quebec, local quality and complaints commissioners in health-care settings (see Government of Quebec, An Act Respecting Health Services and Social Services, 2010) are required to keep a complaints file, which is open to the complainant within the designated number of years that is it stored. The Provincial Ombudsman's office has access to this file, with the patient's permission. Laws in the rest of Canada and the U.S. govern how an ombudsman keeps files. In the absence of government protection, perhaps note shredding is necessary.

The underlying principle is that a complainant's contact with the office, and the ensuing conversation, is confidential unless the person complaining permits the ombudsman to communicate the information to those in a position to assist in the investigation. From a practical point of view, shredding records might make it difficult for the ombudsman to follow up if the complainant returns, as many do, sometimes a year or more after the initial visit and may also seriously conflict with access to information legislation according to Ontario Ombudsman André Marin (see Marin, Canadian Department of National Defence, 2007, 17 of 29).

Consider again the advice of the International Ombudsman Association as to the informality of the structure: The Standards of Practice clearly indicate that the ombudsman is expected to listen, give information, help clients to understand the issues and how they might be handled. The ombudsman, in this view, is someone skilled at helping people to help themselves. He or she works informally, "off-the-record." She may inquire into the misapplication of policies or other system wide problems but she cannot "make binding decisions, mandate policies or formally adjudicate issues for the organization." She "does not participate in any formal investigative or adjudicative procedures." If the client wants a formal investigation, the ombudsman will direct him elsewhere. No one is required to use the ombuds office. In this document, the ombudsman is seen as an asset to the organization in that she can identify "trends, issues and concerns about policies and procedures, including potential future issues and concerns." All this is done anonymously, of course, but the ombudsman can certainly make recommendations (IOA Standards of Practice, 2009a, 4.1 to 4.6).

One of the pitfalls of establishing an ombudsman's office is that the office can become, particularly in very large organizations, part of the problem. A danger always exists that the ombudsman herself will structure the office so bureaucratically and formally that clients face one more obstacle to the resolution of their problems.

Frequently the person seeking an ombudsman is simply worn down, exasperated and tired of fighting her own battles. The person visiting the ombudsman is someone who has frequently been given the run-around by a series of low-level clerks and managers. They may have been responded to with a "Thank you for your concern, we will certainly look into this" when what the client wants is lost airline baggage restored, a mistake in a bank statement corrected or the public utility to quickly correct an invoice.

Michelle LeBaron, in her 2008 address to the Forum of Canadian Ombudsmen (LeBaron, 2008), gives a moving example of what an ombudsman can do to sooth the exhausted client who seems to have fallen into a Kafkaesque black hole:

> Weather-worn, an elderly woman struggles in from the cold to warm tea and friendly voices. She has been buffeted from desk to desk within offices; from office to office within branches; from branch to branch within departments. She hopes she has found a place where her voice can be heard [LeBaron, 2008, p. 2].

And that is the key: "where her voice can be heard." The ombudsman may or may not be empowered to investigate. All are empowered and, indeed, mandated to listen and help the client to achieve a solution.

Many corporate ombudsmen, in fact, stop short of conducting investigations. The power to conduct formal investigations is a controversial issue between classical and organizational ombudsmen as we discussed in Chapter 3.

The issue may also depend upon how one defines "formal." The meaning of the standards appears to view a formal investigation as one with legislative power. Larry Hill, examining the Hawaiian experience, describes some "quasi ombudsman" offices as without the power to investigate which he associates with a "posture of advocacy rather than impartiality" (Hill, 2002, p. 37). André Marin's opinion is that "there is no such thing as an 'informal investigation' " (Marin, 2007, 17 of 29).

According to Sarah Thacker, "organizational ombuds do not conduct investigations or issue reports, findings or recommendations stemming from these investigations" because this would "jeopardize their reputations as impartial conflict resolution resources" (Thacker, 2009, p. 72). This seems to be the hallmark of many organizational ombudsmen.

Nonetheless, some organizational ombudsmen have the power to conduct investigations, issue recommendations and even take on an investigation without the specific request of a client (see LeBaron, 2008, p. 8).

Ombudsmen who make recommendations for change do so as their work may show clusters of system dysfunction that needs to be addressed. As Marin says, one can be impartial while gathering the information, yet still advocate for solutions (Marin, 2008, 7 of 8). Nonetheless, even academic ombudsman, many of whom, especially in Canada, enjoy a "quasi-classical" ombuds role (Farrell, 2004, 1, in LeBaron, 2008, p. 8) tend to perform their work informally and also use many forms of dispute resolution.

Employment and Compensation

A solution found by some organizations is to hire an independent ombudsman on contract. Often, this person has a background in the industry in question and is given a private office within or outside the organization. Some industries hire an ombudsman to serve clients of their membership, a system particularly recommended by Donald Rowat (2007, p. 51, and see Rowat, 2003). For example, Great Britain has an ombudsman who serves all the customers of the moving industry. The Canadian banking industry employs a banking ombudsman with overall jurisdiction over complaints from business owners and bank clients.

Complexity and Connected Units

Large organizations usually have risk management and quality departments, public relations offices and a myriad of committees concerned with safety, with ethics, with professional standards. Some of the ombudsman functions may appear to overlap with the concerns of these departments and committees. The ombudsman is well placed to report, anonymously, her concerns and findings, helping the department or committee see the "big picture" and how problems in one area may intersect with concerns in another. For example, an increase in employee sick days may coincide with safety issues; inquiries from various media may indicate a simmering problem with no outlet. As we have pointed out in other chapters, the ombudsman, because he or she is in contact with all departments and with people at all levels of the organization, may serve as an early warning system so that managers can act quickly to reduce or prevent problems.

Summary

Ombudsmen are most effective when they are placed at arms' length from the organization or are given a position reporting to the highest level of the organization. They cannot be line managers, nor occupy any function other than that of ombudsmen. They need to understand their organizations very well, so as to effectively serve their clients; strive to be as neutral as possible so as not to be seen to speak either for management or the client and must protect the confidentiality of what they learn, either about clients or management. They are also most effective when given the freedom to work with people at all levels of the organization, often serving as early warning systems to problems ahead.

Chapter 11

Ethical and Legal Issues

The role of ombudsman is often perceived to be inherently ethical. After all, ombudsmen defend human rights, speak up for the downtrodden, and seek to uncover wrong-doing. However, most know that a belief in one's own essential goodness can be misleading and that guidelines and codes are necessary. Over the years, ombudsmen in various settings have developed codes of ethics and codes of practice.

This chapter will look at ethics and the ombudsman from two perspectives: the ethical codes governing ombudsman practice and the ethical dilemmas presented by clients. The two are intertwined. A key question is "What is the most ethical way for an ombudsman to deal with an ethical dilemma presented by a client?" The answer will be found in the ombudsman's own code of ethics but, where relevant, the ombudsman should also to be thoroughly familiar with the code of ethics governing the profession or group complained about.

This distinction is important because, in some environments, the role of ombudsman can be confused with the role of ethicist. One must distinguish between the ethical principles that guide the practice of ombudsmanship from the role of the ombudsman in protecting the ethical and legal rights of clients and employees. Some tend to conflate the two positions, assuming that the role of protecting rights automatically grants the incumbent the power to rule on ethical behavior.

A human resources paper dealing with corporate governance emphasizes this difference, i.e., that one role remains neutral while the other definitely does not. The office of the ombudsman, because it emphasizes its neutrality, offers a non-judgmental space for people to discuss their suspicions of unethical or corrupt behavior. The ethics officer, on the other hand, must investigate, take action, keep material on file and cannot always promise anonymity (Williams and Redmond in Stopper, ed., 2003, and see Redmond, Daigneault and

141

Williams and Associates, 2006 pp. 6–7). Thus, the ombudsman and the ethicist have complementary functions but their roles remain distinct.

Nonetheless, some organizations hire ethicists to act as ombudsmen and ombudsmen to exercise oversight over ethical behavior. For example, a Midwestern Christian university employs an ethics ombudsman, not as a "morality policeman" or an "ethics compliance officer" but someone responsible for looking into perceived or actual breaches of ethical standards (Oklahoma Christian University, 2008, retrieved November 16, 2009). Others hire an ombudsman to ensure that employees adhere to the in-house or the professional codes of ethics. For example, Energias de Portugal's (EDP) Ethics ombudsman's job is to oversee violation of the EDP's code of ethics (EDP website, 2009, retrieved 16 November 2009). In 2002, the Canadian Medical Association appointed an ethicist as ombudsman for CMAJ with responsibility for publication ethics, varying from truncated letters to the editor to research papers that do not disclose links to the pharmaceutical industry (Hoey and Todkill, 2002 p. 1281). While ethicist-ombudsmen may be appropriate in the culture of some organizations, the general principle and practice is to keep the functions separate.

A Brief History of Codes of Ethics

Many professions and organizations have developed their own codes of ethics. In the case of professions, these are binding upon the practitioner.

While professional ethical norms have a long history (dating all the way back to the sacred scriptures of various religions and to Plato, Aristotle and Aquinas, to name a few), codes of ethics for organizations as diverse as banks, municipalities, universities and the military are of more recent provenance. In a comprehensive article on business ethics, Richard T. De George, refers to business ethics emerging as an academic field in the 1970s. The field, he says, developed in a manner similar to that of the evolution of medical ethics in the 1960s. By the 1990s, De George says, business ethics "was well-established as an academic field." This led to the development of corporate structures designed to "help it and its employees act ethically." These structures, De George continues, may include a code of ethics, an ombudsman or a corporate ethics officer (De George, 2008).

Codes of ethics are usually grounded in philosophical principles such as utilitarian and deontological ethics, which, according to De George, are the forms of argument first introduced to business students (De George, 2008). Others take the opposite approach and append a list of actions to avoid. The Code of Ethics of the Ombudsman for Long Term Care Insurance in Cape

Town, SA, for example, provides many details on prohibited bribes, conflicts of interest, gifts and invitations to social events (Council of LTCIO).

Not all codes of ethics, however, are identified as such. Some organizations create documents with titles like Rights and Responsibilities, Code of Conduct, Principles and Practice. Public radio journalism's original code of ethics (1999) was called Independence and Integrity (Dvorkin, 2004). Additionally, some organizations issue a "bill of rights" for their clientele. Among the best known is the American Hospital Association's Patient's Bill of Rights, first issued in 1973 and revised since. These documents usually parallel a code of ethics governing the professionals·and employees because they clearly point out how the clients might expect the professionals to behave. For example, the requirement that patients be given all the information they need to make a truly informed consent matches the medical and legal codes mandating what the physician ought to disclose.

Codes of Ethics Governing Ombudsman Practice

Codes of ethics for ombudsmen, especially in the private sector, are relatively recent as noted above. The Ombudsman Association developed a code of ethics for organizational ombudsmen in 1985. This association — TOA — and the University and College Ombuds Association (UCOA) were merged and incorporated into the International Ombudsman Association (IOA) in 2005. The IOA Code of Ethics updated from the TOA code in 2007 and is elaborated by two other documents, Standards of Practice and Best Practices (2009). Other types of codes include the Six Principles of Good Governance, issued by the British and Irish Ombudsman Association (founded 1993 in the U.K. and in 1994 extended to the Republic of Ireland).

Most ombudsmen are thoroughly knowledgeable about the codes of ethics that apply to the profession or trade for which they work. In a hospital this would include medical, nursing and other applicable codes. They may give them to clients who seek a benchmark against which to measure their own experience. However, the advent of an official code of ethics for ombudsmen themselves is welcome and important, particularly for those working in organizations managed by people who may not always fully grasp the implications and the importance of ombudsman independence, neutrality and confidentiality.

Below is a brief description with commentary of the code of ethics written to guide ombudsmen practicing in a wide variety of fields in North America. Though developed recently, the IOA code is often cited in ombudsman websites representing an exceedingly diverse group of organizations. The Societé des alcools du Québec (The Quebec Liquor Board) cites in its website the IOA code of ethics, for example as does the University of Hartford and the World Bank. Signaling to potential clients that the ombudsman adheres to an official code of ethics is an effective marketing device in that it promotes the independence and confidentiality of the office and reveals the organization to be honest and transparent.

The International Ombudsman Association enunciates the following four principles: independence, neutrality and impartiality, confidentiality and informality (IOA, 2007). Standards of Practice and Best Practices (IOA, 2009a) flesh out these requirements.

We referred to these ethical standards in other chapters. In this chapter we focus on the ethical implications.

Independence

Independence ensures freedom of action. We have discussed in other chapters what is required if one follows this code. Here we speak of what it means in organizational practice. Crucially, it means that the ombudsman must be independent and appear to be independent in the organizational reporting structure so that she is free from pressure to defend the organization and will not be perceived as a representative of the organization's interests. This is why the position often reports to the board, which is charged with oversight. The senior ombudsman, in large ombudsman offices, is not part of line management, usually reports to the board or the CEO, and has the freedom to contact any individuals or access any documents (within the limits of the law) that will help her fulfill her obligations.

Neutrality and Impartiality

Sometimes clients and staff assume that the ombudsman is a client advocate and cannot truly be neutral. In practice, many ombudsman are not neutral about the issues, but they are impartial. For example, an ombudsman protecting the rights of children could hardly be neutral about the evils of child abuse. But he or she must act impartially when conducting an inquiry.

Neutrality, in fact, requires that the ombudsman be fair and objective and not advocate for any side in a dispute nor show preference for one profession over another (for example, a former nurse biased towards nursing or a former police officer-ombudsman defending police). The ombudsman should have no stake in the outcome of an inquiry. Furthermore, related to the requirement of independence, the ombudsman should not be connected to any compliance function within the organization. The ombudsman must avoid positions that are conflicts of interest or that invite suspicion of conflict of interest, such as serving as a voting member on a policy or hiring committee. If the ombudsman holds another role in the organization, it should be as distinct as possible from the ombudsman role both in reporting structure and office location.

Confidentiality

People trust the ombudsman because he or she is outside the usual organizational hierarchy. The person complaining, and the person complained about, both have the right to confidentiality.

The obligation of confidentiality is much debated in ombudsman circles. In some institutions, in spite of assurances to the contrary, complainants fear that, if they are identified, they will receive poor treatment, which is why some hospital patients may wait up to a year after discharge before complaining. On the other hand, it is very difficult, if not impossible, to resolve anonymous complaints. What the ombudsman can do is assure the client that he or she will control who will get information about the complaint. Practicality dictates that complainants cannot be anonymous if, for example, they want their complaint about a physician to be investigated, as the investigator would have the right (with permission) to consult the patient's chart and the physician would normally have the right to know what was written or said against her.

Another, related, issue concerns how files are kept. Does confidentiality require the destruction of case notes, for example? In many cases it does and is a common practice. Confidentiality extends to written and computerized records and telephone conversations, phone messages, even appointment calendars. They must be secured in such a way that no one, including managers, can see them (IOA, 2009b, 3.6, p. 7). This supplement to the standards of practice advises the ombudsman to keep a database independent of the organization's system. Needless to say, the office files, to which management has no access, should be firmly secured. Many ombudsman offices destroy all written notes and files but some, such as statutory ombudsmen, are usually legally required to maintain files.

Whether or not the office keeps files and notes under lock and key for five years, or quickly destroys them, what is not debatable under the requirement of confidentiality is the right of the complainant to determine who receives information.

The ombudsman must also be discreet about the person against whom the complaint is lodged. A complaint about a manager, a professor or a physician must be conveyed only to those in a position to assist in the investigation. The only exception would be in cases of risk of imminent harm which the IOA Best Practices document suggests should be defined as narrowly as possible (2009b, p. 6).

If an individual alleges wrongdoing, this should be done directly to the organization and not through the ombudsman. If the individual asks the ombudsman to discuss allegations of wrongdoing with a manager, the information should be communicated very generally with the clear emphasis that the allegations have not been confirmed. This is part of the informal aspect of the office. The ombudsman can suggest to the manager how he can obtain information (IOA, 2009b, p. 8).

When issuing reports, the ombudsman provides feedback minus any identifying information. Ombudsmen are frequently asked for statistics about complaints. While the ombudsman may give the aggregate numbers for specific departments within an organization, the information should not be used to set one department against another. The department with the most complaints is not necessarily the one that is badly managed. In a hospital, emergency departments tend to garner more complaints than the palliative care unit because of higher turnover and higher trauma.

Informality and Other Standards

The ombudsman is first and foremost a listener and problem-solver. Informality requires the ombudsman to give and receive information and help individuals identify and reframe issues for themselves. She may talk the client through various options and, with the client's permission, bring in an informal third party.

The requirement to work informally means that the ombudsman may look at wider, systemic organizational problems but she cannot "make binding decisions, mandate policies, or formally adjudicate issues for the organization" (IOA, 2009a, 4.3). She can make recommendations only, presented as neutrally as possible (2009a, 4.6). The organization cannot demand that an individual resort to her in a grievance process (2009a, 4.4).

In chapter three we discuss the meaning of the requirement not to conduct formal investigations. Statutory ombudsmen usually do conduct formal investigations while corporate ombudsman often use the term "intervention" and focus more on understanding the issues and the various stakeholders so as to assist the client in resolving their problem (see Gadlin, 2000, p. 44). Nonetheless, clients frequently present the ombudsman with a clear complaint and the ombudsman needs to discover whether or not the complaint has merit. This will certainly require conversations with those involved. While not a formal investigation in the legal sense, these inquiries are usually conducted in a formal manner, as befits the seriousness of the complaint. However, the inquiry cannot lead to disciplinary action such as dismissal. If the ombudsman learns of wrongdoing in the course of her inquiries, she would discuss with the client whether he or she wishes independently to report the complaint to the appropriate office.

Finally, each ombudsman office needs to develop its own policies and procedures according to the laws governing their state, province or country.

Case Histories

The following case histories will illustrate how these codes are applied.

Case 1. University Ombudsman

An Asian student was accused of plagiarism, given an F and told he would be dismissed from the graduate program. Though the professor had encouraged cooperative research and was also aware that cooperative work was common in what he called "Asian educational contexts," he believed that the student's work had gone beyond what was acceptable.

The ombudsman was Robert L. Shelton. He explains in a paper on institutional ombudsmen in the university (Shelton, 2000) that he learned that another student had been accused of plagiarism but was not punished so severely. All he had to do was make corrections. The professor argued that the Asian student's case was different as the alleged plagiarism was discovered when the project was submitted in its final, not draft form. Conciliation was ineffective so the student asked to withdraw rather than have a failing grade on the transcript and a letter in his file dismissing him from the university.

The ombudsman presented the student's alternative to the professor and administrator but this was refused, because they said they knew the student would probably take the case to the highest level of appeal within the university. The appeal was scheduled and both parties asked the ombudsman to appear and comment, if appropriate.

The appeal board acknowledged "that the instructor had grounds for suspicion," but concluded that the professor's decision to fail and dismiss the student was, in their words, excessive. They recommended that the student stay in the program and be allowed to correct his work. Meanwhile, the student decided that he would not succeed in the program and wanted to withdraw.

The ombudsman spoke to the unit administrator, asking that he be allowed to go, free of "negative claims." This request was accepted over the appeal group's recommendation, the student entered another program and ultimately received a doctorate (Shelton, 2000, pp. 95–96). This was a satisfactory conclusion to an effective ombudsman intervention.

Shelton illustrates how he applied the elements of independence, confidentiality, neutrality and impartiality to his work. First, the university community recognized his independence and experience, which led the faculty members to feel able to speak to him freely and confidentially. He was neutral and impartial and presented the case as such. Furthermore, knowing that the conversation was confidential, the instructor felt free to confide some initial misgivings concerning "contradictions and inconsistencies in the handling of different students" (Shelton, 2000, p. 96). Both parties were conscious of the ombudsman's impartiality, which is why they wanted him to be present "as an observer and as a limited participant" at the appeal hearing. This last request seems to contradict the requirement of informality (not to participate in formal adjudicative procedures). However, his participation seemed appropriately neutral. His role, as someone who recommends rather than adjudicates, was valued and his recommendation appeared to be "much more attractive after the hearing" (Shelton, p. 96).

As we can see in this case, confidentiality did not mean that the ombudsman could not discuss this case with those involved and the name of the student had to be given to the professor about whom he complained. The ombudsman was able to maintain contact with the people with whom he originally negotiated. This is also a fine example of shuttle diplomacy. Experience and sensitivity led to a happy outcome.

Case 2. Employee Ombudsman

An employee with a history of quarrelsome behavior with co-workers and bosses storms into the ombudsman's office, declaring that he "knows" that the boss is helping himself to company funds. He just doesn't know how.

The ombudsman is aware of this employee's work history because his constant grumbling is notorious and many avoid him. He is greatly surprised to hear the complaint about the manager, who is well liked and known to be a deeply ethical person. His first inclination is to immediately defend the manager, but, maintaining appropriate neutrality, he neither agrees nor condemns but asks the employee if he has any evidence. The only "evidence," it seems, is the fact that the boss has taken a vacation in a luxury resort and also has a new and expensive car. The employee demands that the ombudsman "do something about this crook" immediately.

The ombudsman listens, learns that the employee has large debts and that his wife is planning to leave him. He grows concerned. This is a man with huge burdens who seems unable to get beyond his anger. Because the employee has opened up about his personal problems, the ombudsman tells him that: 1. He, the ombudsman, can seek advice, anonymously (i.e., neither the boss nor the employee will be named) from in-house legal counsel but cannot report anything back to the employee. 2. He asks the employee what he would really like from his life and if he has thought of any solutions to his problems. He asks him if he would be willing to speak in confidence to the Employee Assistance Specialist, who is well trained to help people going through a temporary rough patch in their lives. Seeing the grimace on the employee's face, he assures him that this is not a "touchy-feely" exercise but just a practical action to help him manage big problems that are making him miserable and angry. He agrees to this, ending the session with "you can take care of the boss yourself." The employee now seems almost uninterested in the presenting issue and a little more hopeful about his own future.

This type of case is probably familiar to many, if not most ombudsmen. Some people, because of serious personal problems, take out their frustration and misery on those around them, growing angry when they see others enjoying happier lives. This can lead to accusations of malfeasance believed by the complainant but with very little persuasive evidence. Nonetheless, the neutral ombudsman is obliged to look at all sides of an issue. Even a highly agitated person may read a situation accurately. It is therefore very unwise to dismiss such confidences as the ranting of people too emotional to be objective. However, the ombudsman, who is part of the informal system, cannot conduct any type of formal investigation into a complaint about managerial malfeasance. That is why he will seek advice, anonymously, from the lawyer retained by the institution to handle such matters. As the IOA Best Practices document recommends, an organization cannot "take any adverse action" on the basis of flimsy and unproven allegations. Allegations of wrongdoing should be made directly to the appropriate person in the organization. The ombudsman, who is part of the informal system, can help the client to formulate his concern and, if necessary, the ombudsman can then tell him how to make a complaint through the organization's formal channels (see IOA, 2009b, p.8).

The Ombudsman and the Client's Ethical Dilemmas

Identifying ethical components of complaints is an important ombudsman function. For example, a nurse may call the ombudsman, stating that she has a major ethical dilemma on her ward, a patient who refused to eat.

Or a worried daughter might ask the long-term care ombudsman why her mother has not immediately been transported from the nursing home to hospital because she has a cough. The university ombudsman might hear from a student that Professor X's research is being funded by an ethically dubious outside organization. An ombudsman in a financial institution might learn that a senior person appears to be guilty of insider trading.

Many organizations explicitly recommend that faculty, employees or staff consult the ombudsman to determine whether or not ethical issues are involved.

The ability to listen dispassionately and to discriminate among types of problems is an important ombudsman skill as not all, or even many, dilemmas pose an ethical conundrum. In the examples mentioned above, a patient refusing to eat might want to die, may not be hungry, might need her medications adjusted, has medical complications or, quite simply, hates the food. The ombudsman will clarify this before even thinking about calling in the ethicist. The nursing home patient might have an ordinary cold, which can be dealt with on-site; she might have a major underlying medical condition for which nothing can be done; the nursing home's physician might have decided that this patient does not require hospital care. This last might be an ethical issue that the doctor should discuss with the daughter if the patient is not legally competent and the daughter is responsible. When ethical issues arise in a university, the ombudsman might refer the student to the university research compliance officer. For suspicions of financial malfeasance, the ombudsman could refer the client to the ethics officer.

The ombudsman can often be most helpful by first discreetly gathering some basic facts. Individuals often leap to conclusions and may accuse someone who is entirely innocent. The ombudsman herself might consult the institutional officials in her organization such as the ethicist or research compliance officer. If, in a particular institution, this function is exercised by a committee, the ombudsman would approach the chair. In all cases, the complainant will be anonymous. A composite case history will clarify the procedure in action.

Case. Health Care Ombudsman

A young mother is on life-support following a road accident. Her supportive but anxious family, consisting of husband, parents, in-laws and 10 siblings and cousins all beg that "everything be done." The patient arrived with a Living Will (advance directives) buried at the back of her daytimer. This clearly states that in the event that she becomes comatose and unlikely to live, she does not want to be resuscitated nor receive any other form of "heroic" treatment. She has designated a friend as her spokesperson (legal in many jurisdictions) rather than a member of her argumentative family.

The doctors and nurses call the ombudsman, asking what the patient's rights are (this is within the ombudsman's purview) and whether the family can override the patient's written wishes. The family itself is divided and the friend, who has been entrusted with carrying out the woman's wishes, says she feels pressure on all sides. The members of the family compete with one another, exhibiting fear, anxiety and rage.

The first thing the ombudsman would do is verify with the family which person has the legal right to speak for the patient. In this case, it is the friend. She should be the one appointed to liaise with staff so that many different people do not call at different times and seek information from different people. The ombudsman's skills in diplomacy will almost certainly be put to the test as she will probably need to help the friend relate to a family representative.

In this case, the treating team knows about the issues so this part of the inquiry is not confidential. While it may be unusual for a friend and not a family member to be the decision-maker on behalf of the patient, the fundamental ethical principle is that the patient makes her own decisions and, if she is unable, only the person she has previously authorized may do so (how this is applied will vary depending on local laws). In similar situations, but where the now unconscious patient has made no earlier arrangements for proxy consent, the spouse or parent might be consulted. The dilemma itself is clearly ethical, and legal.

The second action the ombudsman might take would be to ask the doctor responsible to seek a consultation with the hospital ethicist and lawyer. The ombudsman might also ask the nurse manager if she has made the family aware that they can consult a social worker and/or a chaplain.

The ombudsman would then explain to the family that she could remain in charge of actual complaints about care rendered, but not about decisions regarding treatment. All issues regarding the right to request or refuse treatment are to be referred to the doctor in charge of the case who may also have consulted the ethicist. In some institutions, the ethicist will meet directly with the family; in others, an ethics committee will hear the issue and make a decision. The ombudsman will usually ask the ethicist or chair of the committee to keep the family spokesperson up to date either directly or through the physician. She may organize a meeting with the family and the treating team. This is usually effective, especially if the doctor in charge of the case or of the particular service is present. As pointed out in chapter nine, the ombudsman supports the core competencies of communication, assisting all stakeholders in the case to communicate with one another.

Thus the ombudsman has referred all ethical and legal issues to the appropriate professionals, she has kept lines of communication open between herself and the family (asking that one be the spokesperson) and has facilitated communication between family and treating team. In this way, a major complaint, a possible lawsuit or unwelcome media attention are unlikely and the family itself is given the tools to manage their grief and feel that they were a part of the decision-making process.

It would, in fact, be unethical for the ombudsman to attempt to investigate treatment decisions, act as counselor or spiritual advisor, or give legal advice beyond the ensuring that the only person granting and refusing consent is the one with the right to do so.

This last point is important. In many cultures, the family, not close friends, is considered to have the right to make treatment decisions for a very sick person. Many doctors, often coming from similar cultures, do not question this. The ombudsman must rigorously protect the autonomous choice of clients in these situations but also be sensitive to cultural values.

An excellent resource to help ombudsmen in health care negotiate ethical dilemmas is the manual *Working Through Ethical Dilemmas in Daily Ombudsman Practice* by Sara S. Hunt, National Coalition for Nursing Home Reform (1989).

Do the Codes Have Teeth?

The Ombudsman of Papua New Guinea, in a 2006 address, said that many people doubt that ethics can solve "the kind of acute governance problems that give rise to scandals in government and business" (Masi, 2006, p. 4 of 9). He quoted Preston, Samford and Connors: "Ethics is seen as too weak and too nice to be of real effect in what is seen as a tough, dirty and unprincipled world. Business and government give ethicists a very polite and respectful hearing. However, one suspects that ethicists are viewed like the Sunday school teachers in a brothel — naïve, totally ineffective and an embarrassment to those who want to get on with their business" (Preston, Samford and Connors, 2002, in Masi, 2006, p. 4 of 9).

Many believe that codes only have teeth when accompanied by laws to enforce them. While the law is persuasive, the authors believe that personal integrity guides many and others recognize that good ethics is good business practice.

The Future

The ethical obligations of organizations and ombudsmen have come to embrace the increasing diversity of many of the societies in which they operate.

Codes of ethics and ethical standards should be based on a deep and sensitive appreciation of the many cultural understandings of clients. This is important not only in multinational organizations but in many large cities in the Americas and Europe. Those who approach the ombudsman may come from cultures in which human rights are not firmly established or honored. They may not understand that they have rights or they may misunderstand the intricate balance of rights and responsibilities which are so well entrenched in western European and Anglo-Saxon cultures. Thus they may bring to the hospital, university or business their own cultural values, some of which may conflict with the values of the dominant society. This is where the ombudsman has an educative function.

Summary

This chapter has distinguished between the ethical codes that govern ombudsman practice from the ethical dilemmas presented by clients; looked at the evolution and content of codes of ethics; commented upon the widely used and promoted ethical requirements promulgated by the IOA (independence, neutrality and impartiality, confidentiality and informality), with case histories to demonstrate their application; discussed ethical dilemmas presented by clients and staff and concluded with a brief comment on the importance of understanding ethics in a multicultural world.

Chapter 12

Evaluation and Control

It is often assumed that once managers are exposed to the ombudsman concept, they immediately recognize its value. However, in discussions of program start-up, managers quickly indicate how afraid of the concept they really are. Executives and managers express concern that the ombudsmen will "get out of control." They fear that ombudsmen will use the power of their position to stir up problems and create conflicts, manufacturing a steady stream of headaches for vice presidents, senior management, and supervisors as well as for professional and technical people such as physicians and engineers. For this reason, this chapter discusses control of the ombudsman, and how the characteristics of controls relate to the nature of the problem-solving job itself.

To systematically explore control issues, we will rely on the work of a well-known management commentator, Peter Drucker. Many readers are already familiar with Drucker's approach to management control. His writings on the nature and characteristics of control can be related quite nicely to the ombudsman function. Before we introduce his views, consider the patient's husband, Donald Johnson, in this chapter's opening case.

The Patient Sues?

Donald Johnson's wife was ill for several months before she was diagnosed as having cancer. Since she was sixty-seven, he realized it would be an uphill battle from the start, but when she died in six weeks he was both shocked and angry. He wondered about the delay in the diagnosis and about the treatment uncertainty. When he tried to telephone his wife's physician three or four times, the doctor was too busy to return his calls. His son told him, "If he won't talk to you on the phone, he'll talk in court. Sue him, Dad." Should he?

154

Donald Johnson's son wants him to sue the doctor, but Mr. Johnson heard that there was a patient ombudsman at the hospital. He contacted her to present his case just to see if she could do anything before he went to his lawyer. She listened carefully to the case asking for details — as much as Mr. Johnson could remember. She thanked him for coming, saying she would inquire into the issues raised, speak to the independently-appointed physician who worked with her on medical issues, and get back to him within a day or two.

Some hospital CEOs and some physician medical staff chiefs would be very nervous about this exchange and the "investigative action" and "interaction" it would generate. Just how is the ombudsman's performance controlled? Controls are derived from control thinking in general.

Drucker begins a presentation in his seminal book *Management* (1973, pp. 496–497) by identifying three characteristics of management controls:

- Controls can be neither objective nor neutral.
- Controls need to focus on results.
- Controls are needed for measurable and non-measurable events.

A discussion of each of these characteristics will reinforce the preceding commentary on the nature and function of ombudsmen and will introduce the various ways of controlling the function.

First, controls are not objective or neutral. The work of an ombudsman cannot be objectively assessed in a pure scientific sense. To begin with, certain constraints are built into the ombudsman function itself. For example, most ombudsmen are not allowed to encourage the employee or customer to hire an attorney and sue the company. While this might be an eventual result of a failure to resolve the problem, management is not interested in increasing the amount of litigation it faces. Management relies on the ombudsman to solve the problem, especially including a solution without litigation. Limits on the encouragement to use the courts demonstrate that the troubleshooter is not there strictly for the benefit of the employee or customer (for example, as an advocate pursuing an adversarial relationship with the organization). Instead, both organization and employee or consumer are jointly represented by the ombudsman, who attempts to maximize the gain while minimizing the loss for each party. Taking the physician to court cannot retract a death, but compassionate explanation by a physician who works independently with the ombudsman, and listening, will ease the pain.

What does this mean from the perspective of the goals and values of the organization and the approach of management? It essentially says that the ombudsman is free to explore solutions within the limits allowed by that managerial style. In other words, the scope and depth of control are determined by the nature of the organizational culture. For example, a corporate ombudsman operating in an autocratic managerial culture would be unlikely to have very much freedom to work in. But when a corporate ombudsman is free to openly pursue various resolutions to a problem (regardless of the issues raised for the executive team), this indicates that the managerial approach is both participative and open, not autocratic and closed in nature. Or in some hospitals, any patient/physician conflicts are open to investigation and resolution, while in others, complaints are quickly smoothed over or repressed if a key physician could be "bothered" by the problem.

Second, in Drucker's view, controls must focus on results. This means that an ombudsman's job is to solve problems, not to create data systems or to establish committees, groups, and interdepartmental conversations. Organizations are not interested in how much paper is generated in terms of complaint reports, progress reports, follow-ups, and recommendations. Instead they value individual and organization-wide problem solving (in such a way that it does not recur either easily or often). This results orientation tends to hold down the amount of bureaucratic control type of paperwork in most troubleshooter programs. Many ombudsmen do not prepare monthly performance reports, for example. Government agencies with statutory authority are often the exception.

Third, the control system must address both measurable and non-measurable events. This is perhaps the most difficult control area. For instance, in the literature on ombudsman work, there is some attention given to the nature and distribution of complaints and the analysis of data on those complaints. However, there is almost no discussion relative to the subtle and indirect effects that the ombudsman has on the organization. Evaluations, research, and management assessments do not often address these questions. What are the attitude, motivation, and expectation changes generated as a result of the ombudsman's presence? What does it mean for an individual employee when he or she knows that the organization cares enough to create a problem-solving position filled by a person sincerely committed to listening to employee or client concerns and to fair treatment? These are challenging evaluation subjects and a part of the problem of management control of this work.

There is a widespread belief by people in the ombudsman field that the greatest impact of their efforts is generated by the indirect and subtle influences of their existence in the organization, regardless of whether they troubleshoot for employees in industries or consumers in hospitals. This means, however, that the most difficult aspect of the field — observing and controlling the ombudsman's unseen effects — is the most important!

A fearful executive might ask, "How do I know that the ombudsman is not using fear, intimidation, and insecurity to solve problems?" While to some extent this concern about an "out of control" ombudsman is legitimate, most ombudsmen will tell you that if they used any of these techniques, the whole organization would quickly know. Power plays may very occasionally be necessary (and even legitimate) for solving a few problems in a few situations. But continued and ongoing use of strong-arm tactics will quickly result in the ombudsman's rejection by the organization. This is because the helping orientation of the troubleshooting mission has been converted into a policing one. These tactics might appear to be successful in a few division or department conflicts, but ongoing use would quickly diminish and eventually eliminate an ability to function effectively as a problem solver.

In summary, it seems that the control of subtle and indirect impacts that the ombudsman has should not be of any greater concern (with regard to documentation) than control of the measurable aspects of the job. The level of subtle and indirect effects is easily known by the informal system and will be quickly communicated to the ombudsman and to management. Ombudsmen will get fewer cases to handle and management will get an "earful of anger" if strong-arm tactics are used.

Ombudsman Control System Specifications

Drucker has identified specifications for managerial controls. These specifications translate into a guideline for designing controls, enabling us to identify the characteristics of management's troubleshooter control system. Managerial control systems must meet the following specifications. The system must be

- Economical.
- Meaningful.
- Appropriate.
- Congruent.
- Timely.
- Simple.
- Operational.

How do designers of an ombudsman program address these control characteristic questions? In one sense, they represent elements of a model control system. How do they relate to a case? Consider an incident with one employee.

The Boss's Home Repairs

Joe Roberts had been a maintenance worker at a school for just two years. At age fifty-four, he had tired of general construction and found he could not handle the workload as easily as before. He had been delighted to get the maintenance job. When his boss asked him to spend several days doing work at the boss's house, he was shocked. He was afraid to say no for fear of being fired. He was also afraid to do the work for fear of being fired. What could he do?

Keep this case in mind as we examine the elements of the control system, asking the question, how do we effectively control ombudsman work?

Economical. Controls must be economical. In management circles, there is a significant debate about how elaborate and formal a control system needs to be. This is true for ombudsmen as well. Do we want ombudsmen filling out contact reports, progress reports, complaint reports, follow-up reports, monthly reports, quarterly summary reports, six-month reports, and year-end reports? Or do we want them solving problems, spending very little time on documentation? Obviously some balance is in order; the question is whether it should be in the direction of higher cost and formality or informality and economical operation.

Ombudsmen such as employee assistance counselors debate how much written documentation should be retained. Currently there is no consensus on this subject. There are clusters of people both for and against documentation that would be part of a monitoring and control system. There are a large number of ombudsmen who feel that the chief executive officer knows firsthand about the quality and success of the work. Conversely, CEOs also learn almost immediately about failure — the employee or customer conflict continues and escalates. The complaints from customers and employees are often significant and sensitive. When they blow up, they do so with loud bangs, not little ones. Impending litigation from a deceased patient's husband is not a trivial situation, nor is the potential suicide or sabotage of an employee.

Because of intimate CEO knowledge, formal ombudsman controls tend to be relatively light. There are some industry differences, however. In the public sector, for example, ombudsman controls tend to be fairly extensive. Accountability is a notable and often-used buzzword in public systems — appropriately so. Public sector ombudsmen such as statutory-based ombudsmen and public advocates need to keep extensive case and report materials to identify the nature, volume, characteristics, and outcomes of the complaints they handle. The control system for public sector ombudsmen is therefore quite extensive, elaborate, and time-consuming, contrary to Drucker's principles of control. Private sector corporate ombudsmen do keep some records and files, but pressures to develop elaborate reports to meet monitoring requirements are not prevalent.

Joe Roberts' problem of working on the boss's house is illustrative. In a public agency, the "official ombudsman" would need to complete a form outlining the complaint, the facts of the case, who was talked to, what records if any were reviewed, and the outcome of problem intervention. This might be written up in a one-to three-page report linked by case number to a formal filing system. A private sector corporate ombudsman might investigate the problem, press the supervisor to drop his request, and record nothing, feeling that the problem was solved or eliminated. The extent of formal control, in terms of documentation, is very different in the private sector. Private systems depend less on formal controls open to future review. Some would say control without documentation is nonexistent — but economical. No system equals no burden.

Meaningful. Controls must be meaningful. The troubleshooter and the chief executive officer must identify the significant results of job performance. What would the ombudsman use to enable the executive to know that he or she is doing the job (the management-by-objectives model)? Many aspects of the ombudsman's work process are potentially measurable. There are a few key elements that help the executive determine whether the function is vigorous and effective. The following are sample measures:

- Complaint contact volume: how many.
- Actual complaint volume: contacts that are fully processed complaints.
- Nature of the complainants: age, sex, race, organizational distribution, job position.
- Nature of the complaints: type and subject.
- Primary list of outcomes: organizational responses categorized (for example, actions taken; policy/procedure changes, decision reversals).

This relatively short list can be used on a frequent basis (such as monthly), to help an executive determine whether or not the ombudsman function is well received in the organization. For example, are many complaints filed — ten complaints a day or only five a month?

The chief executive officer is able to determine from the location data whether complaints are being filed by members throughout the organization, or whether only certain types of employees in selected divisions or departments are filing. Customer groups can be tracked by product and geographical location. Additionally, a "general sense" of the achievements by the ombudsman is revealed by the outcomes data. This is really the bottom line, the benefits of ombudsman work. Are the complaints successfully resolved (yes or no in direct terms), and what were the outcomes (restitution, changed policy, personality conflict resolution)?

By concentrating on volume, nature of the complaints, nature of the complainants, and outcomes (four fairly simple measures), the chief executive officer should have enough meaningful data for control of the ombudsman function. In management-by-objectives terms, these can be considered four key results areas. The chief executive officer can dispense with the lengthy progress reports, data about investigations held, who was contacted, hours of the day contacted, and so on that are used in some public programs. A "lean" control-reporting system avoids this seemingly endless supply of very detailed facts about the process of ombudsman work, ensuring time to support the people orientation of the job and the problem solving.

Appropriate. With the third characteristic, Drucker asks how we know whether the controls concern the significant aspects of ombudsman work. Do the data collected and the controls in total address the critical aspects of the job? Can a judgment be made about the match between the performance of the ombudsman and the objectives? One example here is that instead of simply counting the number of complaints per month or per year, one might begin to distinguish between the number of *significant* complaints. This acknowledges that complaints have "differential potential damage" to the organization — sabotage at a defense plant manufacturing army tanks versus Joe Roberts' dilemma over his supervisor's home repairs. If significant potential damage is threatened, that becomes a priority. A threat to kill a supervisor is more critical than an inappropriate transfer. Common sense says that threats may take on more importance than policy and procedure questions that may come in greater volume but that, even if not addressed, have lower potential for damage. A complaint about a smoking violation in the hospital is important, but far less so than the death of Donald Johnson's wife.

This requires a deeper understanding of the nature of the complaints. In some ombudsman programs, a category entitled *litigation potential* is used. This measure "flags" the potential for litigation as a critical system control element. This can be a simple judgment measure — high, neutral, or low potential. Scanning this data enables the supervising manager to determine whether or not the ombudsman is working with significant complaints and may assist with time management.

An alternative to "formal data review" is a simple "meet and review" meeting with the CEO. A quick presentation of the case topics usually is sufficient to determine significance informally and without extensive paper requirements.

Congruent. Congruency concerns whether the control measures used to gauge troubleshooter performance really do relate to the nature of the work. For example, in order to consider a successful resolution of 85 percent of the complaints over the course of a year (a high level) to reflect excellent ombudsman performance, the nature of the cases must be taken into account. Were they cases that were very difficult with high litigation potential? Or were they cases that were relatively easy to resolve, primarily involving information and education for the work force or for consumers?

This congruency question relates to the key results. Do the control measures reflect the goals of the program? One customer relations ombudsman may spend a long time "listening" to dissatisfied customers. At the end of the sessions, customers are no longer as angry, just because someone would listen. Their problems are not solved with just listening, however. Nor is the organization's development fostered. Action must be taken by employees and managers. Knowledge of the extent and nature of these follow-up actions is critical to determining whether ombudsmen are correctly addressing both organizational and individual problems.

Donald Johnson's dispute with the physician who treated his wife is an example. The physician would not listen — a problem the patient ombudsman can easily solve by listening. But that does not address the more fundamental problem of doctor/patient relations that may be present, if this one case is a reliable indicator of a widespread orientation. If no follow-up action is taken, the data relating to number of patients or relatives listened to can be very misleading. Listening is necessary but not sufficient for the full ombudsman job, in other words.

Timely. How frequently are the controls reviewed? How often does the chief executive officer meet with the ombudsman? This is also the question of how frequently the CEO *should* be meeting with the ombudsman to check performance. Drucker notes that quick and constant control can be destructive to the work process. But in the case of the ombudsman's ability to resolve problems, performance review should be ongoing. Ombudsmen must be in touch with the executive to whom they report, whether it is the CEO or a senior vice president. Reports are not needed. Regular face-to-face discussions about progress on significant cases are sufficient to determine performance. With the significance of the cases, the risk of delayed review and/or inattention is too great.

The timeliness issue is an absolute mandate with regard to some cases. All ombudsmen, like other employees, sometimes fail. Lack of timely control combined with a low level of executive involvement in selected cases could be disastrous for the organization. In our case examples, Joe Roberts could sue for wrongful termination or Donald Johnson could press for a malpractice award. The supervising executive must be involved on an ongoing basis; that is, a shorter control time span rather than a longer one is desirable not only for performance but because a terrific need for information exists with regard to volatile cases.

There is another point about timeliness of controls: the necessity of keeping executives in touch with the problems in the organization. Timeliness is tied to the fundamental organization development purpose of problem solving.

To the extent that executives are distanced from the nature and volume of complaints in their units, departments, and divisions, they have reduced their ability to create timely responses to organizational problems. A time lag between complaints filed and response must be avoided.

This rule also applies to the timeliness of the controls. Limited communication between supervising executive and ombudsman is a sign that controls are weak. There may be an "implied subcontracting" of the organization's problem to the ombudsman. This is especially discomforting because sensitivity to the organization's status — including individual and unit problems- is a starting assumption for the success of an ombudsman program. And subcontracting responsibility for unit problems to ombudsman is one of the great fears cited by executives in resisting program development.

Consider the cases involving Joe Roberts' awkward situation and Donald Johnson's concerns about his wife's medical treatment. Who would want to work in or purchase goods or services from an organization with a CEO who does not care about these kinds of problems? Timeliness of control is inseparably linked to ongoing concerns about people (employees and consumers), the most valuable organizational resources.

Simple. Simplifying the control indicators and the procedure is central to the success of the control process. With problem solving, there is the potential to create many complex documents to support the control system, as evidenced in some public agencies. For example, in reviewing public sector ombudsman programs, high levels of documentation and legalistic complexity seem to be descriptive of the control system. However, the adequacy of the controls is not guaranteed by the paperwork. The bureaucratic approach to the control problem is a "tree killing operation" (using the paper), which often does not result in very effective control at all. Simple control mechanisms should become elaborate over time only if there is a need for complexity. The temptation, especially with the capability of current management information systems, is to begin with the complex and move toward the simple only after disaster strikes in the form of an inability to manage the volume of information.

Operational. Controls must be operational. Successful ombudsmen seem only infrequently to have gotten into trouble with their interpersonal interaction or their problem resolution behaviors. But cases exist in which the ombudsman should have referred the cases to in-house attorneys or to outside sources and avoided the problem altogether. For example, medical cases that are likely to lead to malpractice suits require legal consultation at the outset. In these cases, operational controls need to be in place to help both the ombudsman, and the executives they are responsible to, monitor the work process.

This suggests a need to actually use the control system that is designed. Debates over the level of complexity and the need for simplicity are truly irrelevant if executives do not use the few indicators that do exist. It is much less important whether the design is comprehensive to a compulsive degree than whether the items defined for monitoring are regularly reviewed.

Summary

This chapter surveyed characteristics of the control system used to monitor the performance of ombudsmen by focusing on seven design characteristics. Is the control system economical, meaningful, appropriate, congruent, timely, simple, and operational? The best problem solving system is simple and direct, involving a close working relationship to a reporting superior — CEO or senior vice president. The nature and activities of the ombudsman's job are personal and people-based, not bureaucratic and paper-oriented. The control system should reflect the basic nature of the work.

Chapter 13

Bottom-Line Benefits of Problem-Solving Programs

This chapter discusses the benefits of an ombudsman program that were identified in a general sense in earlier chapters. What happens in the organization as a result of an ombudsman's presence? For readers interested in productivity gains and the subsequent benefit to the bottom line, there are both direct and indirect contributions. Some effects of the work are directly visible (for example, obvious conflicts resolved, litigation avoided), while other effects are hidden (such as those pertaining to human relations). The latter, the indirect benefits, are especially critical but often are not felt or recognized.

Travel Denial

Ms. Jensen had worked for the department for some sixteen years. A program she developed had recently received much national attention. She was invited to participate in a major national conference to present the program for the first time to a large audience of professional colleagues. She was delighted and felt honored at the invitation. The department would receive both public and professional recognition for its innovation. However, her request for travel time and expenses was denied without explanation.

In the case of Ms. Jensen's travel time and expense denial, ombudsman action may quickly secure the required time and support — a visible and direct result. However, a means to complain and receive redress helps to build a corporate culture that pays off over the years. Ms. Jensen's past work and devotion were apparently disregarded by management when they made their decision, the equivalent of shooting oneself in the foot, that is, undercutting commitment and morale.

The description of ombudsman benefits conforms to the view of the host organization as a system, or more specifically, as an interconnected complexity net of five subsystems (Kast and Rosenzweig, 1985; Ziegenfuss, 1985a; Ziegenfuss, 1993; 2007). Public and private organizations are defined as having five subsystems: a goals and values subsystem (culture), a technical subsystem, a structural subsystem, a psychosocial subsystem, and a managerial subsystem. According to this view of the nature of an organization, troubleshooters affect at least one and possibly all of the systems; that is, there are widespread benefits for the organization.

Goals, Values, and Cultural Effects

What are the ombudsman's effects on the goals, values, and cultural subsystem of the host organization? In most organizations, from hospitals to manufacturers, the presence of the ombudsman is symbolic of the corporate culture that the chief executive officer is trying to develop and maintain. An underlying assumption of a culture that includes an ombudsman function is that complaints are to be brought to light, investigated, and responded to in an open, fair, and responsible fashion. In other words, the ombudsman is one means for reinforcing the desired cultural characteristics of openness and fairness.

For example, one can often hear a hospital CEO remark: "In today's competition-oriented business atmosphere, we are true believers in patient [customer] satisfaction." But when you ask whether the hospital has a patient relations manager or a patient representative, he or she responds, "No we don't — they create problems." The presence of an ombudsman/problem solver would signify a commitment to the "desired" cultural elements. The belief is backed up by a position. Resources are committed — money follows the rhetoric about increasing the quality of employee life and quality of consumer life.

What does problem solving contribute to other aspects of the organization's culture, including specific goals and values? One of the critical values reinforced by the ombudsman is the belief that customer and employee viewpoints are needed and are listened to by management and employees. Management values individual participation, including the presenting of complaints. Management backs up this position with a means to help make it happen — the ombudsman.

For example, many public agencies and private corporations promote the notion that employees are free to question any policies or procedures (a core value). This is thought of as great "internal public relations." But any benefits to be gained are lost if the questioning is in fact known (via the grapevine) to produce retribution or other difficulties for the questioners.

This is illustrated by the following typical case. Professor Watson objected to the bureaucratic handling of contracts, to the insensitive dismissal of student registration problems, and to poor facilities support. In return, he found resistance to his deserved promotion and proposed sabbatical.

Suddenly the complainers' rewards are reduced, their policy positions attacked. Few questioners keep going with that kind of "reinforcement." The cultural value of openness is demolished.

A related goal is the promotion of open communication among corporate participants-employees and consumers. The ombudsman's abilities and responsibility for encouraging communication about complaints fosters dialogue in troubled areas, using communication as a first step to resolution. Moving between upper and lower levels of the organization and across management areas, ombudsmen clear channels demonstrating communication openness. This open discussion eventually becomes a ritual, "a part of the way we do things around here."

Rituals may play a negative role, however. What employee is not familiar with the ritual of simulated problem solving? This is not actual problem solving, but a charade in which employee complaints are supposedly encouraged, confronted, and responded to. This ritual is a hypocritical process in which the real activity is often a transparent attempt at internal smoothing over. The organization considers the problem-solving process to be a ritual that it must adhere to for employee public relations reasons but that is not designed to have actual effects. In short, it is not used to address problems within the organization. A response to Ms. Jensen's travel denial would be, "Sure, you can file a complaint talk to your manager, then personnel." The expectation is that the complaint — will be "buried" by personnel or by the process, or by the inherent intimidation of lawyers. A process exists, say the defenders, empty as it may be.

Along with rituals as an indicator of culture, there are rites of passage up the organizational ladder. In many organizational cultures, one rite of passage involves acquiring an ability to tolerate unpleasant experiences. Management actions — transfers, policy conflicts, cutbacks, product eliminations — cause significant discomfort to employees at all levels. This rite of passage to the top requires an ability to take one's lumps and watch fellow employees take their lumps without grumbling about unfairness and damage to both person and organization. While this may be useful for developing management ability to overcome setbacks, it does not help to resolve pressing problems.

The presence of the "grin and bear it" philosophy is part of a developmental process that creates the "heroes" of the organization, leaders who have a negative attitude toward complaining. But this raises the question of who the heroes of the organization really are. Are they the senior executives, department heads, and supervisors who look the other way when problems develop, ignore them as long as possible, or smooth them over without significant confrontation? Or are the "heroic" managers problem-confronting and problem-solving in outlook and action? The presence of a troubleshooter is evidence that the organization wants management, employees, and consumers to identify and confront problems. From this perspective, the heroes of the organization are not the managers and employees who grin and bear it, ignoring problems as long as possible, but are activists who move quickly to understand and address all types of employee and customer complaints in the organization. Therefore, one underlying ombudsman contribution is to help create new management heroes.

How do rites, rituals, and heroes combine to support a cultural network? All organizations from hospitals to manufacturers to banks have a set of goals, values, rituals, and heroes that define and maintain the cultural network. This "in group" (heroes) in good organizations understands that *all* companies have problems and that they must be addressed directly and fairly. The presence of a formal trouble-shooter, a corporate or public ombudsman, means that this cultural network includes someone who continually reminds the members of the group of the necessity to confront and resolve organizational problems.

For example, how is Ms. Jensen's travel denial to be handled? Is it treated as an isolated incident unrelated to morale and long-term human resource development? Or is it treated as a single problem with potentially complex positive benefits to be derived from successful resolution? Using this single incident as a lead to understanding organization behavior sets the problem up as an organizational learning opportunity.

What effects does an ombudsman have on culture change? Many experts have begun to stress the usefulness of changing the organizational culture to continue the organization's development. What impact does the ombudsman have on this process?

In one organization, the ombudsman is assisting in moving the company *away* from an autocratic "I don't give a damn about the people or their problems," "Productivity is all important" approach. The new culture is one that believes that "People are our most important resource" and "One way to protect this resource is to identify, understand, and address their complaints." In this company, the ombudsman is part of a management effort to change the culture. In cases such as this, ombudsmen help change a culture that is closed and autocratic to one that relies on and maintains open communication. They are communication agents that subvert autocracy and closed-system thinking.

In summary, ombudsmen make a significant contribution to the development and maintenance of the organizational culture, helping to change the culture when that is the agenda. They help to develop new "heroes"— managers and employees who fairly and justly deal with complaints in the work force. Ombudsmen foster a cultural network whose membership criteria include: (1) a belief in open communication, (2) the assumption that all organizations have problems, and (3) the realization that the most useful approach to complaints is to identify and deal with them promptly and directly.

Technical Effects

What is the ombudsman's effect on the technical subsystem of the organization? The technical subsystem comprises all of the inputs, activities, and outputs that are regarded as the primary work of the organization in a given industry, for example, health care, transportation, banking. In hospitals, this is the medical and health care services; in the automobile industry, it is the engineering processes used to create automobiles.

How do complaints affect the resources used in the technical process? For example, complaints from one sales unit indicate that information from the marketing group regarding preferences for automobile model and style may not be sufficient to generate corrective action. But in combination with a complaint from the manufacturing division, poor customer preference data can be identified as a significant problem for operations. As a second example, an increasing number of complaints about alcohol abuse on the assembly line should alert managers that the manufacturing process may be exerting too much pressure on employees, or it may simply be too boring.

In other ombudsman cases, employees and customers complain about the quality of products or services produced. These are complaints about the outputs of the technical work process. Some employees are fired as a result of technical system complaints (for example, the whistleblower" cases). In aerospace projects, their complaining was viewed as disloyal and threatening to the defense department, to NASA, and to private corporations. An alternative view is that these employees are performing a service by sounding an alarm about technical process deficiencies. Rather than firing these employees, a good corporation — one concerned with maintaining an open culture as a means to quality and productivity — will use complaint data to identify trouble spots in the technical production of goods and services. The ombudsman's complaint process helps the group to confront and address problems not with an adversarial intent, but with a technical and organizational development orientation. Complaints filed by employees are viewed as one data source by which the programs, methods, and total technical processes of the corporation are monitored; that is, they represent a contribution to quality control (Ziegenfuss, 1985; Ziegenfuss and O'Rourke, 1995; Ziegenfuss, 1998, 1999).

One example was the complaint by an employee about a new computer system the chief executive officer had developed in the first year after his arrival at the company. The computerized management information system was a complete fiasco. Initial heavy-handed use of inaccurate data was fostering fear and anxiety, including cheating about sales targets met and antagonistic infighting among various departments. The employee was afraid to complain to his department supervisor who, he felt, would be afraid to complain to the vice president. Instead, the complaint was passed anonymously to the ombudsman. The ombudsman was able to follow up on this single complaint by conducting a brief investigation, pulling together supporting evidence that the system was flawed. Using diplomacy and trading on his relationship, he gave this information to the chief executive in a way that made the bad news seem at least partially palatable. Since the ombudsman had a close and positive working relationship with the CEO, he was able to pass on the bad news without "getting the messenger killed" (as might have been the case with the employee or vice president). Here the ombudsman was able to contribute to improving the work process in the corporation by breaking the communication blockage and by identifying a technical problem.

Ombudsmen contribute to maintenance and development of the technical work by

• Acting as a transmitter and interpreter of the historical technical practices of the organization.
• Acting as a communication vehicle for informing management when technical errors appear.
• Helping to guard the confidentiality, ethics, and fairness of technical and scientific processes.
• Acting as a feedback mechanism for the technical personnel to inform them that applications are not complete or well prepared.
• Providing data for redesign and new design of technical outputs and the processes that create them.

These are both regular and irregular, continuous and sporadic ombudsman contributions.

Structural Effects

How does the ombudsman affect the structure of the host organization? Organization structure characteristics can be used to track this type of ombudsman effect, examining formalization, specialization, standardization, hierarchy of authority, centralization, complexity, professionalism, personnel configuration. The examples cited are illustrative structural effects of an ombudsman's problem solving. They may not be representative of a specific ombudsman's duties, nor are they exhaustive.

Formalization. Few persons in large organizations would dispute that most large organizations are formalized. Almost everything must be written and discussed, reviewed in meetings, and recorded in a file note. Formalization of private and public organizations has gone to such lengths that when conflict occurs, employees and customers are tempted to hire attorneys to help them through the complex bureaucratic systems. One benefit of ombudsman presence is an alternative to this formality. Ombudsmen solve problems informally without using the often legalistic and bureaucratic procedures of large and small complaint systems. If an organization is less formal, the ombudsman helps to keep informal problem solving alive. If in management's view the organization is regarded as too formal, ombudsmen can be a part of a cultural change process — a means by which informality and problem solving can be injected into the system.

Specialization. Many commentators in technical and scientific fields have noted the phenomenal increase in specialization and the difficulties it causes in terms of cross-specialty communications. Ombudsmen are problem-focused linking pins between and within specialty groups, such as engineers, computer scientists, and physicians. The ombudsman listens to and responds to concerns about specialists' work, or about the discontinuities in production processes that are causing problems for segregated specialists or employees. Specialists build walls around their areas, locking out either competing specialties or overlapping ones, creating barriers to communication. Ombudsmen help keep specialty communications open, becoming one means by which specialties can jointly address problems of mutual concern for which neither has independent responsibility.

Standardization. In the drive toward greater efficiency, major corporations and public agencies use standardization as the mechanism of choice. While standardization does promote efficiency, it often does so at the expense of individuality and innovation. Ombudsmen preserve some of this autonomy and freedom as defenders of individuality and innovation, particularly when employees or consumers are pressed by hostile political forces who insist there is one "best" way. This kind of standardization is a contributor to innovation blockages that are slowing down leadership in creating new products and services.

At the same time, ombudsmen help to ensure that there is increased standardization in certain areas, for example, the fair treatment of customers and employees with regard to a wide range of policies and procedures from recruitment, to transfer, to termination. In several of the cases cited, it was noted that some firings resulted from deviation from what was perceived to be "the way things are done around here," not poor performance. Standardization to increase fairness and justice for all employees in the organization is a most desirable goal, one supported by the ombudsman.

Hierarchy of Authority. Many organizations operate with a hierarchy of authority that is rigid and controlling. The ombudsman represents authority (see Chapter Six) but is sanctioned to bypass the hierarchy where needed. The hierarchy interferes with the communication of problems to executives because no one wants to tell the next level up about a problem. Executives with the power and influence to create change often do not know about the problems. Ombudsmen enable this authority hierarchy to function more effectively by establishing a bridge between levels.

Authority is intact but is no longer a barrier to a quick response to problems.

When sales quotas seemed too high for a sales group — they knew they were working hard in a competitive environment — they did not want to tell the regional supervisor or the vice president of sales. Certainly the desired behavior is open communication. But in a macho-type environment, fear of failure and not wanting to break the "can do" image causes resistance to providing feedback. The intent is not to have salespeople regularly use the ombudsman for this purpose, unless there is no other option. It is better to use the ombudsman than to let the problem exist without addressing it, however.

Centralization. There is a centralizing effect to ombudsman problem solving. Senior management may be centralizing problem identification — but not the problem solving itself. Problem-solving process responsibility and the responsibility for tracking patterns of problems (both within and between units) is now centralized in a person who reports directly to senior management. This enables a picture of the total organization's problem set to emerge as a first step toward taking appropriate corrective action.

Complexity. Ombudsmen work in complex organizations, such as hospitals, major research universities, high-technology firms, major manufacturers. High complexity requires high levels of communication to overcome the difficulties in coordinating various units within the organization. Ombudsmen minimize the negative effects of complexity by targeting specific problems and solutions in this web of technical and social systems.

Complexity confronts employees and consumers right at the start of the problem action. "How do I find out where to go to file a complaint about this problem?" The ombudsman is a "complexity reducer" acting to communicate concern (caring) and acting as a guide to assistance. Ombudsmen can cut through the complex policies, procedures, authority, and resistance to get rapid resolution. From an employee or customer perspective, that IS a significant and valuable contribution to problem solving.

Professionalism. Ombudsmen increase professionalism. Professionals, both scientists with extensive credentials and employees who have had long years of experience and commitment on the job, increase their professionalism by honestly confronting and attempting to resolve problems. Do employees tell customers to "take a walk"? Are employees told to keep quiet? Professional values and beliefs require that employees and consumers must be able to voice their concerns. Professionals also know that the corporation benefits from free and open discussion of customer and employee complaints about the failures of various parts of the organization. In many ways this is part of the concept of professionalism — the willingness to listen, understand, and respond to complaints about goods and services sold.

Personnel Configuration. The presence of ombudsmen means that the personnel structure supports certain values, such as listening to employees' and consumers' complaints. Program startup means that management believes that the structure must include a way of fostering problem-oriented communication and problem solving.

An ombudsman is an indicator of structural flexibility. Ombudsmen are not classified as management or as production employees. They exist within the personnel structure to foster linkages between the two, without actually being a part of either.

Psychosocial Effects

This section reviews ombudsman effects on the psychological and human relations system of the organization. The topics to be discussed are behavior patterns, motivation, expectations, needs, status and role systems, group dynamics, leadership, and power. In both direct and indirect ways, ombudsmen positively affect individual and group dynamics — people relations in the organization.

Behavior Patterns. Ombudsmen demonstrate problem solving behaviors, provide evidence of how the culture values listening (sometimes a new behavior pattern), attempt to understand employee and customer concerns (perhaps a new behavior pattern), and address and resolve employee and consumer complaints (all too often a new behavior pattern). This is *desirable* organizational behavior, since it contributes to the quality of employees' working life and the quality of consuming life.

Motivation. Ombudsmen increase motivation. They do so by supporting employees' beliefs that the organization cares about the problems employees feel need to be resolved in order to get on with the job. Demonstrating concern increases motivation. Anyone who has encountered unresolved problems —

technical and personal — knows how they can undercut motivation. Good problem resolution for customers maintains customer loyalty and buyer motivation.

Expectations. Ombudsmen create expectations. What do employees expect to happen as a result of the complaining? What happened before the ombudsman program existed? If the expectation is that complaints are not likely to be addressed, understood, or listened to, employees begin to look the other way when they encounter barriers to quality and productivity. The presence of an ombudsman suggests that the employee can expect the organization to listen, to investigate, and to act on their complaints. The expectation is that this corporation will remove barriers to quality and productivity. In fact, the corporation has established a means for doing so — the ombudsman program.

For customers, the response is two-directional. If complaints are not addressed, they (1) take their business elsewhere, and (2) tell their friends about their "bad experience."

Needs. Ombudsmen meet employee needs. One employee need is to be able to comment on and affect the workplace from policies to procedures and physical conditions. The ombudsman is one means by which employees can meet their needs for control and power over their work environment.

Status and Role Systems. Ombudsmen have high status because of their reporting relationship to top management. What status issue does this raise for employees and management? Because of the ombudsman's high status, employees and managers who confront and address complaints increase their status. High-status ombudsmen have a status-enhancing effect by passing on to top management information about the good performance of problem solving managers. At the same time, the official presence of an ombudsman legitimizes a role that otherwise exists informally, since as we have seen, there are experienced employees acting as problem solvers in most, if not all, organizations. When the ombudsman role becomes a recognized part of the organization, this is evidence of the importance of this work and testimony to senior management's willingness to invest resources.

Group Dynamics. Ombudsmen affect group relations when they act as mediators. There is a within-group effect when the ombudsman acts as a third-party consultant to groups "at war." For example, in one corporation the manufacturing and sales departments cannot seem to effectively coordinate their schedules. The problem cannot even be discussed because of a personality conflict between the vice presidents in charge of both functions. In this case, the ombudsman is a catalyst for change in the group dynamics and a mediator of an interpersonal dynamic that is a barrier to problem solving and productivity.

Leadership. An executive decision to establish an ombudsman position demonstrates leadership by admitting that organizations of all kinds in all industries have problems and that these problems should be recognized and confronted. Leadership is not just rhetoric about problem solving but a willingness to expend resources.

Power. Ombudsmen decentralize problem-solving power. Ombudsmen have freedom to engage all appropriate parties in conflict resolution. It is a "floating" power base with a capability to move to the problem site. Problem-solving power is not located only in the chief executive officer or the top of the management hierarchy.

This completes our review of the psychosocial impact of ombudsman programs. What are the ombudsman's effects on management?

Managerial Effects

In this section, the effect of ombudsmen on the managerial system is surveyed. We focus on five management activities: planning, organizing, developing, directing/leading, and controlling. How does the ombudsman help to initiate, develop, and maintain these managerial activities? What contributions are made to the managerial work of the organization?

Planning. Ombudsmen contribute to organizational planning by providing data for goal setting. They are part of an organization-wide data collection effort that helps to identify problem areas and needs within the organization that nlust be addressed by management. For example, they may hear increasing numbers of complaints about certain employee personal problems in one unit or location, such as alcoholism at a high-stress military base, for example. This data calls for further investigation to define the problem and to determine what kind of action should be taken. Complaint reports are part of the database for management planning.

This complaint database leads to a managerial "do list." Diagnosis, planning, action, and future evaluation of the status of a wide range of problem topics is required. Ombudsmen are agents and promoters of organizational learning. The organization is able to learn about its strengths and weaknesses by reviewing the complaint data. Weaknesses are to be addressed by individual vice presidents, department heads, and the chief executive officer in the following planning time period.

Organizing. Ombudsmen also make a contribution to the organizational activity of management. This activity includes, for example, the design of an organizational structure, the selection of personnel and facilities, the acquisition of capital, and the creation of information systems. Ombudsmen help the management staff identify "organizing" weaknesses, such as personnel shortages, facilities with poor physical environments, and malfunctioning data systems. We saw earlier that complaints from employees indicated that one unit became so hot with deficient air-conditioning that productivity had dropped significantly. Employees were grumbling on a constant basis about the work environment. As a second example, consider a computer system problem. Management information systems have received increasing attention in the last ten to thirty years. They are now a mainstay for the modern corporation and are becoming increasingly used in public agencies. However, one continuing design challenge is on the people side: attitudes, motivation, group dynamics, and resistance. Ombudsman operated complaint systems can provide insight into the work force. *Complaints are a management information system element targeted at people problems.* Since it is very hard to obtain this type of data, it is an extremely worthwhile component of the overall management information system.

Developing. There are two ways ombudsmen contribute to the "developing" activity of management, one micro and one macro. At the micro level, the benefit is to the person holding the ombudsman's job (see also Chapter Nine). At the macro level, the benefit is in terms of the overall development of the organization. Each area requires brief discussion.

On the micro level, some private corporations are using the corporate ombudsman function as a training position for future management and human resources executives. Performing the troubleshooter-ombudsman job for a period of time

- Teaches the jobholder about the strengths and weaknesses of the organization.
- Develops problem-solving skills.
- Teaches the jobholder about the trade-offs necessary to achieve a negotiated consensus and a solution to difficult problems.
- Exposes him or her to various aspects of operations throughout the organization through the process of complaint solving.

To the extent that ombudsmen need to be fairly experienced before they take the position, individual development does not necessarily occur early in the career. It is perhaps best used as a developmental tool for someone in their early to late thirties. It could be used as direct preparation for more senior positions in personnel or human resources or in general management.

There is at least one model in which micro development does not really occur. In some organizations, the troubleshooting ombudsman is selected because of his or her successful career in the organization, a career that is nearly complete (for example, by age fifty-five to sixty-five). The job may still contribute to individual development but not toward a future career.

On the macro level, development can occur in all of the systems mentioned in this chapter. The effect of the ombudsman is an organizational development one, with implications for the goals and values, technical, structural, psychosocial, and managerial systems of the company. A successful ombudsman program enables the organization to:

- Test goal and value consistency.
- Reinforce certain values.
- Create heroes who address complaints.
- Identify technical and structural weaknesses.
- Test for strong people-problem areas, whether in production or management.
- Develop management in all of the areas mentioned in this chapter (planning, organizing, developing, directing/leading, and controlling).

Ombudsman programs, by bringing out, testing, and proposing solutions to organizational problems, are by their very nature an organizational development tool.

Directing/Leading. Ombudsmen also support the management activity of directing and leading the organization. How? First, they support management activity through problem resolution. Few managers would disagree that a significant amount of time is used up by problem resolution. In effect, some of this time consumption is delegated to the ombudsman.

Bottom-Line Benefits of Problem-Solving Programs. At the same time, the delegation allows the ombudsman to assist in the interpretation of directions and leadership goals that management presents but which may not be communicated clearly. This goes back to the question of the core nature of the ombudsman's function and its involvement with communication. When management provides both direction and leadership, many employees (through no fault of their own and perhaps through limited fault of management) have further questions about the organizational future, about specific policies and procedures, and generally about the way in which the organization works. When these are significant, ombudsmen hear them, passing on to management the need to clarify them.

Additionally, the ombudsman facilitates interaction that is necessary to get the direction and leadership points across. Often the conflicts that result between departments, subgroups, or individuals concern the new directions that management is promoting. The communication required for complaint finding and resolving supports management leadership.

Controlling. Last, ombudsmen are a type of control mechanism, in that the program is used to monitor problem identification and resolution. It is a performance review tool for management. Clearly a unit with many complaints must be examined, or questions relating to productivity and quality of working life will go unanswered.

It is worth noting that there is considerable debate among formal ombudsmen about the purpose and use of written complaint information. The field is divided with regard to the appropriateness of collecting and disseminating information. Many ombudsmen fear that this information will be used inappropriately and that damage to individual employees and managers, possibly including firings, career harm, and harassment — will result. Others feel that if the organization does not collect this information (in aggregate) to help itself identify problems, a valuable organizational intelligence resource is lost. As noted earlier, the authors are in favor of data carefully collected and used with discretion.

Summary

This chapter has reviewed the impact of ombudsmen on various aspects of the organization, including the goals and values subsystem, the technical subsystem, the structural subsystem, the psychosocial subsystem, and the managerial subsystem. The review indicates that effects of ombudsman programs are multidimensional and wide in scope. The final chapter will discuss the future of this approach to increasing productivity and the quality of working life.

Chapter 14

The Future

The last chapter concluded the presentation of the purposes, work activities, and benefits of ombudsmen. Beginning with the pressures for program development, we reviewed considerations about work system design, the actual ombudsman job activities, and such issues as authority and power. Additional topics included the ombudsman as communicator of data from the "complaint information system," the performance controls on ombudsmen, and a review of the benefits of this work to the organization. This final chapter addresses five subjects: the two primary purposes of ombudsman programs, the nature of the intervention that an ombudsman initiates, the "representativeness" of this view of the concept, the benefits to the individuals holding ombudsman jobs, and the reasons for expected future recognition and growth of ombudsman programs.

Purposes

By way of reviewing concepts and activities, what are the two main purposes of ombudsman programs? Quite simply, they are designed to

• Increase productivity.
• Increase the quality of working life and the quality of consuming life.

One assumption of the model is that all organizations, both consciously and unconsciously, create barriers to productivity (and to the quality of working and consuming life). These barriers involve both technical elements (such as production processes) and human elements (including attitudes and behavior). The ombudsman works to reduce and eliminate them on a single-case level and on a system-wide "repeating-problem" level.

In one sales division, several young managers were uncertain about how

178

and when they might begin to look for promotion to other management jobs. The ombudsman arranged for one complaining sales manager to obtain career path guidance from human resources, which he received. The ombudsman also passed on to the human resources director a suggestion about sales division career path orientation for young managers. Uncertainty about career future is one barrier to productivity — a barrier that translates into interference with sales.

The ombudsman program is also designed to increase the quality of working life and the quality of consuming life. For employees, it provides an opportunity to communicate concerns, to question the organization's policies, and to feel that what they complain about will generate action. This increases the feelings and reality of employee control and commitment. If employees can make a difference, they feel good about the level of ownership of their place of work. It is literally in part theirs because they help to "redesign" it on a regular basis through communication of problems and dialogue about possible solutions.

The problems are both large and small — sabotage in a defense supplies plant, poor ventilation when office repainting is underway. Ombudsman strength is based on recognition that both large and small problems have significant impact. Everyone recognizes the fears, anxiety, and negative impact associated with publicized sabotage. Too few managers recognize that the daily indignities of the workplace — inadequate heating and lighted space, no opportunity for relaxation and socializing, poor team spirit — are also contributors to low quality of working life. Ombudsmen must respond to the significant and the seemingly less significant.

The softball competition case cited earlier in the book is a good example. Cheating in an off-hours softball game is in one sense not exactly life threatening to the corporation. However, the level of cheating and the need to do so even in a social game that does not really count may suggest something very profound about the corporate culture. Is there a need for companywide ethics and values discussions?

While quality of working life is a concept that is quite well known by now in management circles , quality of consuming life is not. Who are the consumers/customers seeking a higher quality of consuming life? Based on published reports of ombudsmen at work, they would include patients in hospitals and nursing homes, college and university students, prison inmates, and buyers of all kinds of consumer products. The list is easily extended to nearly all businesses and industries. Few are without some form of ombudsman identified as a customer relations specialist or representative. After all, customers want to believe they are buying quality products and services, and they want action when they have complaints. A company that listens, learns, and responds to customer problems is one that over time creates a high quality of consuming life for its customers. The̦se are companies that have been labeled "customer friendly" (Ziegenfuss, 2007).

Intervention

The purpose of ombudsman work is now clear — increased productivity and improved work life and/or consumer life quality. How are these goals achieved? Do the required changes involve adaptations to the technical and managerial work or to the people side of the organization? The term *intervention* links the ombudsman program to organizational development strategies and methods (called *interventions*). As a form of management action, the ombudsman contributes socio-technical intervention. The key word is *socio-technical,* meaning that actions of the ombudsman are directed at both the social and the technical aspects of the organization (Trist, 1981; Davis and Cherns, 1975). This socio-technical approach is by now a known way of addressing the joint social and technical design elements of any kind of organization, from manufacturing to education to health care. Many business management texts use its concepts as a basis for management problem diagnosis and follow-up action (see, e.g., Hellriegel, et. al., 2010).

Many executives and managers forget that they cannot design and develop new divisions or plants or make major changes in structures and functions without technical and psychological disturbance. When one company cut back from 60,000 to 35,000 employees over a several-year period, there was a flood of questions and complaints from employees. The topics included technical questions of work type and operating procedures and psychosocial questions of layoff fairness, open communication, and stress. Ombudsmen must respond to both types of questions.

Ombudsmen for customers have the same socio-technical responsibility. For example, one woman was shocked to find that her husband died during a relatively routine hospital operation. She wanted desperately to find out what went wrong. The physician told her very little in a somewhat abrupt and arrogant manner. The woman sought the patient representative's help (the hospital ombudsman) to obtain both technical information (about the failed treatment) and psychosocial support (sensitive caring during her grief).

The ombudsman's work is aimed at correcting both social and technical design and operating difficulties that were either built in or are problems that have emerged. One employee ombudsman may offer suggestions to employees in dealing with the stress of layoffs. The hospital ombudsman may secure information on the technical treatment a patient received, having it presented again by the physician or a colleague. Ombudsmen, as good socio-technical consultants, develop jointly optimized solutions to the problems — solutions that include factors of the social system (attitudes, morale, support) and the factors of the technical system (methods, procedures, rationale for results). This is consistent with and of great interest to engineers, for example, in high-tech industries where socio-technical concepts are widely recognized. The point is that ombudsmen should be flexible problem solvers who take both technical and social-psychological approaches.

Representativeness

How representative is the picture of ombudsmen that has been sketched in this book? Does it represent corporate and public ombudsmen, executive assistants, equal opportunity specialists, employee and customer relations representatives, dispute resolvers, and patient representatives? The answer is that it is very representative as a model and guide. It may not be precisely representative of a particular ombudsman position, of course. First, this perspective presents the primary design elements of the ombudsman concept, with the emphasis on commonality across programs. The description reflected an effort to present the similarities based on the increasingly accepted systems view that jobs and programs have many design and activity elements in common across industries and organizational types. In addition, the description may not be very representative of a particular ombudsman because all programs and people are somewhat unique. This qualification recognizes the individuality of human and organizational systems. A patient ombudsman in a hospital works with patients, reports to a professional affairs executive, and may receive anywhere from $55,000 to $95,000 or more in salary. On the other hand, an ombudsman at a major bank works with employees' problems, reports to the CEO of the bank, and may earn a salary of $75,000 to $150,000+.

The design elements and activities of each ombudsman program are numerous and can be varied within the conceptual framework, with the resulting combinations practically infinite. For example, ombudsmen can begin work early or late in their careers, can develop power because of established performance (or not), be friends with the CEO (or not), use a formal data system (or not). Each alternative means a slightly unique way of operating in that organization. This uniqueness, however, is not so great as to constitute a complete departure from the basic purposes and concepts. In short, there is a main concept and a set of procedures that are common to all. This description is thus in general representative of the ombudsman concept.

The ombudsman concept also benefits the individual in the job. We can ask what the career development potential is? The ombudsman's function simultaneously contributes to the development of the organization and it trains future managers. The personal impact of the job on ombudsmen is our current topic.

In a lecture to a group of hospital CEOs about the purpose and use of employee and customer (patient) ombudsmen one listener had a question. The CEO said, "Hey, that's the job I held before I became CEO. My boss said it was good training." His former boss used the post for his successor's development.

What we need to consider are two questions: How promotable are ombudsmen to general management positions; and what points or job characteristics establish the "promotion potential" of the ombudsman? To answer these questions, a set of the characteristics of "good" managers used long ago by one graduate management assessment center is a helpful guide (Cutchin and Williams, 1984). According to this view, there are ten characteristics of a good manager: job knowledge, interpersonal skills, oral communication, written communication, supervisory skills, analytical skills, decision-making skills, planning, stress management, and creativity and innovativeness. It is important to note that these are not necessarily "the" perfect set of managerial qualifications for job success. Instead, they are used to identify and illustrate the promotion potential of the ombudsman.

The topic of promotion potential is important for several reasons. First, there is a renewed interest in management's need to relate to customers and to employees, a central human resources development purpose. Second, there is a related need for a management team that knows the intricacies of relations between employees and customers on the one hand and management on the other. And third, management is now attempting to increase productivity and to improve the quality of working life, key outcomes of the ombudsman work.

This analysis identifies areas of promotion potential to enable ombudsmen and their executives to engage in a dialogue about career options. Some points are obvious, others less so. Each characteristic is introduced with a definition.

Job Knowledge. This is the work-related information developed through a combination of formal training and on-the-job experience that is used for job performance. Do ombudsmen know the business? The answer is clearly yes. Many ombudsmen are technical people with years of experience, including engineers in some companies, nurses in hospitals. They know their business intimately. Their promotion potential is very good, because in management jobs, you must know the business. Ombudsmen who do not know all about the business they are in when they start do know it a few years later. It is impossible to do ombudsman work without that knowledge. And over time, the complaints and problems enrich the ombudsman's knowledge of the business and their organizations' roles and functioning. Problems are excellent teachers.

Interpersonal Skills. These skills form the basis for work with people — not technology — and involve sensitivity to others, interest in and willingness to promote cooperation, verbal assertiveness, and the capability to give and take criticism. This one is obvious for ombudsmen, since effective interpersonal skills are absolutely necessary for mediating conflict. It goes without saying that ombudsmen should *not* be hired without interpersonal skills (neither should managers, for that matter). If they have been hired, they will not be successful in either an ombudsman or a management job.

Some would argue that the essence of the ombudsman's job is interpersonal. Some management analysts would also argue that the essence of management is interpersonal, particularly with the increasing use of task forces and the team approach. The promotion potential of the ombudsman is therefore very strong in this area, especially if one realizes that after a few successful years, ombudsmen are interpersonal experts!

Oral Communication. This of course involves the ability to talk with and understand others, including the ability to present instructions, information, and ideas clearly and concisely and also to listen. This is another primary aspect of the ombudsman's job. Ombudsmen spend all day talking to customers or employees. They provide training, take part in orientations, and conduct meetings loaded with interpersonal conflict. The ombudsman's job is *not* a nonverbal job. Promotion potential is addressed with the question — are there *any* nonverbal jobs in management? The strong verbal skills increase the ombudsman's future value.

Written Communication. This is the ability to communicate the ideas and information of the organization in writing, for example through reports, letters, memorandums, and studies. Here the ombudsman's work can involve reports that include outlining the complaint, the investigation processes and procedures, and the outcomes (although some ombudsmen do not write reports). The factual summaries of complaints are very similar to management memorandums presenting problem analyses. Written presentation skills are developed through repeated practice under strong staff scrutiny. The contribution to promotion potential derives from the ombudsman's ability to write reports and memos.

Supervisory Skills. These could be described as the ability to lead by assuming responsibility and by asserting control. At first glance, the potential here seems to be lower than in the other areas, primarily because few ombudsmen have a staff of even six to ten people. In fact, some only have one assistant.

However, if supervision is considered in the sense of an ability to influence others, ombudsmen are in fact "supervising" many and diverse individuals in the complaint resolution process. This amounts to informal supervision, that is, responsibility for the persons involved without authority. It is management the "hard but effective way," requiring charisma and influence instead of an ordering or directing approach. This influencing ability makes the ombudsman's promotion potential strong, but less obvious than with the other points.

Analytical Skills. These emphasize the ability to identify and assess information used in management planning and decision-making. Here we have another core activity of the ombudsman's job-analysis of problems. How transferable this is depends on the nature of the complaints received. How analytical the ombudsman needs to be depends on how complex the complaints are *and* on how supportive the organizational environment is (that is, its political complexity). A hospital ombudsman may have a caseload filled with patient problems regarding bills and support services such as television and food. Or the ombudsman could spend much time working with physicians on issues concerning diagnosis and treatment decisions that might lead to medical malpractice action. The latter are complex and difficult to analyze and resolve. In general, it must be said that the promotion potential is strong. Ombudsman work is analytical, as are many aspects of management, such as planning and problem analysis.

Decision-Making Skills. These include the ability to decide an issue in situations where an optimal solution is not possible, using information and judgment and a willingness to take risks with minimal guidance from senior management. The key term here is *optimal solution.* There are few, if any, solutions in either ombudsman or management work that are perfect for all involved. Ombudsmen spend a considerable amount of time helping to create problem-solving solutions that benefit several conflicted parties. There is constant optimizing of the individual actor's positions in order to optimize the whole solution. The promotion potential here is very good, since there is much practice in helping others make decisions — a key management task. Ombudsmen encourage but do not force decisions, then must live with many persons' reactions to the decisions they help to forge.

Planning. We could describe this as the ability to create goals and to make decisions consistent with a task to be completed or a vision of the future. There are two aspects of planning that engage ombudsmen. First, there is an ongoing need to consider the alternative impacts of the complaint solutions in the future, the "planned change" that the solutions will create/initiate. Second, planning is a needed part of the management of the ombudsman program, including the core activities of complaint taking, education, and consultation. There is promotion potential here, but somewhat less than in other areas. This is due mainly to the size of the operation and the need for limited planning work. Where there are several ombudsmen and a large program, promotion potential is higher, such as in planning for hospital ombudsmen programs in a multi-hospital system.

Stress Management. This involves the ability to maintain emotional, mental, and physical health in crisis situations, implementing personal change when necessary. How many ombudsmen are not experts in stress management? Those without this expertise are likely to be unemployed. This is clearly because the job is very high stress. Those in it for any period of time must learn stress-coping skills. There is clear promotion potential here. Ask any chief executive officer how many management jobs have not been high stress in the past and how many will not be high stress in the next ten years. Simply put, stress management abilities are preparatory for higher management positions.

Creativity and Innovativeness. These traits are reflected in the ability to identify, develop, and carry out new ideas, programs, or projects. The ombudsman's job depends on creativity and innovation. While some problems may seem routine and somewhat repetitive, solving them is a unique experience in every case. The people and situational contexts of employee/management and customer/provider problem solving demand individualized creative solutions. The strong promotion potential is based on the fact that creative problem solvers are always needed in management.

Promotion Conclusions. Characteristics of the management job were examined to determine the ombudsman's promotion potential. Troubleshooters are customer-and employee-oriented. From this review, it seems that the role is also management-oriented in that it involves internal consulting and a contribution toward productivity improvement. Ombudsmen must have many of the skills and talents of managers. If they do not have them when they start, they soon develop them. Some organizations are already using ombudsmen positions for management training purposes.

Ombudsmen have high promotion potential for many management jobs, and in an age of increasing competition for customers and employees, CEOs should look to ombudsmen for new management talent. It will be worth the search, because ombudsmen know the personal and organizational benefits of putting customer and employee relations first, and they know how to do it.

Expansion of Ombudsman Programs

Both public and private organizations will support the expansion of ombudsman programs in the future. These programs are now beyond the start-up and critical mass stage; that is, they are established in very diverse industries, such as manufacturing, health, education, and corrections. Expansion is likely to occur for the following reasons.

First, for several decades now our society has been moving from a sole interest in high-tech to a joint interest in high-tech/high-touch, a concern for both the technical and the psycho-social aspects of the organization. We are now engaged in a search for the means of maintaining and increasing the "touch," the human aspect. The ombudsman is a personal problem solver working with people in high-technology business and industry. Beyond ombudsmen the future may also see increased emphasis on training front-line staff.

Second, the ombudsman concept transfers across fields and organizations. It has already been tested in a wide range of businesses and industries and in many countries. Public agency ombudsmen have been at work for decades. Ombudsmen serve both employees (for example, in defense industries) and customers (such as patients in hospitals). In short, the concept can be applied to employees and customers in public and private organizations — in business, industry, government, and health care. The widespread testing and use is evidence of both the need for and the contributions of these programs.

Third, to follow up on this point about adoption by many companies and agencies, we can state that the concept is no longer experimental but is well entrenched in many types of institutions and industries. Future expansion can be based on a wealth of experience that is public, private, and cross-cultural in nature.

Fourth, continuing growth in social system and organizational complexity will require some means for humanizing both society and individual organizations. Complexity and depersonalization stemming from technology are increasing. Neither is predicted to decrease dramatically in the future. Ombudsmen will be seen as one of the most important tools for attacking these problems.

Fifth, since litigation is costing both public and private organizations heavily in terms of money, energy, and time, organizations are actively searching for alternative means of dispute resolution. In other words, there is a great need for ways of solving problems outside of the courts and the legal system. Pressures from employee and customer litigation costs alone will be extremely conducive to ombudsman program expansion.

Sixth, ombudsman programs address the organizational problem of "upward feedback." Just how do executives find out what their organizational problems are? Few employees and fewer senior managers tell them, and those who do so comment only at the possible peril of their careers. Ombudsman create data flow leading to executive education.

Last, as we have seen, the ombudsman concept now has widespread support. Nations, governments, hospitals, and corporations feel it is an idea that is aligned with the times and the culture. With participative management and industrial democracy gaining in importance even in cultures to whom these concepts are foreign, ombudsman programs are viewed as extremely appropriate parts of the organizational architecture. And that architecture will surely be affected by disruptive technology as noted above and continuing.

Technology sometimes takes a while to catch up with day-to-day practice and is pushed by clients. One of the authors who works by phone, face-to-face interview, and letter, has noticed an increase in people wanting to email their complaints, which in the hospital setting raises issues of security of confidential information. However, technology can help in the quick resolution of simple complaints. One transport company has an email complaint system and sufficient staff to respond within 24 hours on simple matters like ignored bus schedules, price increases and so on.

The future will probably see an end to the formal, written letter and will be replaced by a complaint system that enables people to complain instantly, via their BlackBerries, iPhones, or whatever technology becomes widely available. Though older people are now considered to favor telephone and snail mail, this is rapidly changing. What technology offers the client is what they enjoy in other aspects of their life: an instant channel of communication and an instant answer. This will necessitate a change to ombudsman practice and staffing. While it is fairly easy to encrypt electronic communications to ensure confidentiality (and electronic signatures are now considered to be legally valid), it is not so easy to find the funds to increase ombudsman office staffing to respond to the increased volume of inquiries and complaints.

Technology has also changed the threat to companies and the individuals working for them if anyone behaves badly. Recently a transport company fired a worker photographed fast asleep on the job at the ticket counter. Police departments know that among bystanders to police action are several people with phone cameras who will instantly send footage to the media. Electronic surveillance of this sort gives the public enormous power and makes it harder for individuals to deny wrong doing. Even though photos and videos can be manipulated and may not always be effective witnesses, they greatly empower the ordinary citizen and add weight to a complaint.

In this book, we have described and defined an innovative concept and process emerging rapidly in organizations in diverse fields. Ombudsman work recognizes that no organizations are perfect. In order to build productivity and to create a high quality of working life and a high quality of consuming life, we must identify, confront, and resolve organizational problems. The use of an ombudsman program indicates that senior management is aware of the problems in organizations, is willing to take action to correct them, and is attentive to employees' and customers' concerns. Executives and managers with those attitudes we all want to work for.

For all of these reasons, ombudsman programs will experience strong support in the present and expansion in the future. The one in your organization will almost certainly be acknowledged or hired in the next few years.

Bibliography

ABA sections seek to clarify ombuds confidentiality considerations. *Dispute Resolution Journal, 58* (3), 6.

Abraham, A. (2008). The future in international perspective: The ombudsman as agent of rights, justice and democracy. *Parliamentary Affairs, 61* (4), 681.

Abraham, A. (2008). The ombudsman and individual rights. *Parliamentary Affairs, 61* (2), 370–379.

Abraham, A. (2008). The ombudsman and the executive: The road to accountability. *Parliamentary Affairs, 61* (3), 535.

Ackoff, R (1981). *Creating the corporate future.* New York: Wiley.

Ackoff, R.L., Magidson, J., & Addison, H.J. (2006). *Idealized design: creating an organization's future.* Upper Saddle River, NJ: Wharton School.

Alderson, M. (2009). Spotlight on ... the removals industry ombudsman. *The Ombudsman: The Newsletter of the British and Irish Ombudsman Association,* December *39.* Electronic version.

Allen, P., Klein, W., & Gruman, C. (2003). Correlates of complaints made to the Connecticut long-term care ombudsman program: The role of organizational and structural factors. *Research on Aging, 25* (6), 631.

Allmendinger, P., Tewdwr-Jones, M., & Morphet, J. (2003). Public scrutiny, standards and the planning system: Assessing professional values within a modernized local government. *Public Administration 81* (4), 761–780.

Alpert, J., & Meyers, J.(1983). *Training in consultation.* Springfield, IL: Thomas.

Altany, D. (1987). Where customers rule. *Industry Week,* June 29, 31.

Ambroz, M. (2005). The mediating role of the ombudsman in the protection of human rights. *International Journal of Social Welfare, 14* (2), 145–153.

American Express Company. (2007–2008). *Office of the ombudspersons: Off the record.* Edition XIV. [Brochure].

American Express Company. (2008–2009). *Office of the ombudspersons: Off the record: Providing guidance on work related issues since 1994.* [Brochure].

Anderson, S. V. (1983). The corrections ombudsman in the United States. In G. E. Caiden (Ed.), *International handbook of the ombudsman: Evolution and present function.* Westport, CT: Greenwood.

Annas, G. J., & Healey, J. M. (1974). The patient advocate: Redefining the doctor-patient relationship in the hospital context. *Vanderbilt Law Review, 27,* 243–269.

Arcimowicz, J. (2002). The ombudsman — one of the figures in the drama of the third republic. *Polish Sociological Review, 4,* 427–448.

Argyris, C., Schon, D.A. (1975). *Theory in Practice: Increasing Professional Effectiveness.* Jossey Bass.

Armstrong, J. S. (1983). The ombudsman: Learner responsibility in management education, or ventures into forbidden research. *Interfaces, 13* (2), 26–38.

Armstrong, S., Pagell, R., Campanario, J., & Ord, K. (2003). The ombudsman: Reaping benefits from management research: Lessons from the forecasting principles project. *Linthicum, 33* (6), 91.

Aufrecht, S. E., & Brelsford, G. (1983). The administrative impact of the Alaskan ombudsman. In G. E. Caiden (ed.), *International handbook of the ombudsman: County surveys.* Westport, CT: Greenwood.

Austrian Times Online News — English Newspaper. (17 February 2010). *Vienna Archdiocese has child abuse ombudsman.* Retrieved February 27, 2010 from http://www.austriantimes.at/news/General_News/2010-0217/20729/

Baker, A. (2002). Access vs. process in employment discrimination: Why ADR suits the US but not the UK. *The Industrial Law Journal, 31* (2), 113.

Bauer, F. (2000). The practice of one ombudsman. *Negotiation Journal, 16* (1), 59.

Binham, L. B. (2005). Employment dispute resolution: The case for mediation. *Conflict Resolution Quarterly, 22* (1), 145.

Birchard, K. (2001). Irish ombudsman finds medical records "atrocious." *The Lancet, 358,* 48.

Bonner, P.G. (2001). Institutional attitudes in context: A comment on Rawlings' "engaged elites — citizen action and institutional attitudes in commission enforcement." *European Law Journal, 7* (1), 114–119.

Brewer, B. (2007). Citizen or customer? Complaints handling in the public sector. *International Review of Administrative Sciences, 739.*

British and Irish Ombudsman Association (2009). Guide to principles of good governance.

Cadeddu, S. (2004). The proceedings of the European ombudsman. *Law and contemporary problems, 68* (1), 161.

Caiden, G. E. (Ed.). (1983). *International handbook of the ombudsman: Evolution and present function.* Westport, CT: Greenwood.

Caiden, G. E.; MacDermot, N.; Sandler, A. "The Institution of the Ombudsman." In Caiden, G. E. (Ed). *International Handbook of the Ombudsman.*

Canadian Franchise Association. (2010). *An ombudsman is....* Retrieved February 28, 2010, from http://www.cfa.ca/About_Us/Ombudsman.

Capozzola, J. (1968). An American ombudsman: Problems and prospects. *Political Quarterly,* 21, 289–301.

Carnegie Council. The Voice for Ethics in International Affairs. (April 11, 2008). *Michael Getler.* Retrieved April 19, 2010, from http://www.cceia.org/people/data/michael_getler.

Carson, S. (1986). People with gripes can find more ombudsmen. *Montreal Gazette,* p. F-1.

CBC/Radio-Canada. *Media accountability.* Retrieved April 19, 2010, from http://www.cbc.radio-canada.ca/accountability/ombudsman.shtml.

Clark, K. E. (1985). Improve employee relations with a corporate ombudsman. *Personnel Journal, 64* (9), 12–13.

Clausen, A. W. (1980). Listening and responding to employees' concerns. *Harvard Business Review.*

Cline, A. (2008). Ethics and ethos: Writing an effective newspaper ombudsman position. *Journal of Mass Media Ethics, 23* (2), 79.

Coca-Cola Bottling Company. (2007). *Ombuds office: A safe place to talk.* [Brochure].

Cole, D. (1983). (Ed.) *Conflict resolution technology.* Cleveland: Organization Development Institute.

Colorado State University. (n.d.) *Faculty advising manual.* Retrieved from http://www.casa.cocostate.edu/advising/faculty_advising_manual/chapter4/resolution.

Colvin, A.J.S. (2004). The relationship between employee involvement and workplace dispute resolution. *Relations Industrielles, 59* (4), 681.

Complaints are us! (2010). *Complaints are us! "We make things right again."* Retrieved April 18, 2010, from http:/complaintsareus.ca/.

Cominelli, L. (2001). The European Union ombudsman: First empirical observations. *Sociologia del Diritto, 28* (1), 91–118.

Corporate Ombudsman Association

Corte, G. D., & Mestres, S. G. (2002.) Social justice, legitimacy and legality: Civil society before the defender of the people in Argentina. *Revista Mexicana de Sociologia 62*(4), 69–90.

Council of Long Term Care Insurance Ombudsmen Cape Town, SA. (n.d.) Retrieved May 15, 2009, from http://www.ombud.co.za/res/pdf/codeofethics.pdf.

Cowan, J. (2001). The role of the ombudsman in the risk management process. *British Journal of Clinical Governance, 6* (3), 221.

Cox, C. (2009). Long-term care administrators' perceptions of the ombudsman program in the state of Missouri. *Journal of Elder Abuse & Neglect, 2* (1), 74.

Crean, F. (January 19, 2009). The Toronto ombudsman. *Annual report of the ombudsman.* (April 6, 2009-December 31, 2009.) Retrieved March 2, 2010, from http://www..toronto.ca/leg docs/mmis/2010cc/bgrd/cc45.5.pdf.

Cutchin, D.A., & Williams, J.O. (1984). Assessing managerial behavior in public management students. Paper presented at the annual conference of the American Society for Public Administration, Denver, CO.

Dalen, A., & Deuze, M. (2006). Readers' advocates or newspapers' ambassadors? Newspaper ombudsmen in the Netherlands. *European Journal of Communication, 21* (4), 457.

Daft, R. L. (1983). *Organization theory and design.* St. Paul, MN: West.

Danet B. (1978). Toward a method to evaluate the ombudsman role. *Administration and Society, 10* (3), 335–370.

Davis, L. E.; Cherns, A. B. (Eds.) (1975). *The Quality of Working Life.* N.Y.: Free Press.

Daus, M. W. (1997). Mediating disability employment discrimination claims. *Dispute Resolution Journal, 52* (1), 16.

Deal, T. E.; Kennedy, A. A. (1982). *Corporate cultures: The rites and rituals of corporate life.* Reading, MA: Addison-Wesley

De George, R.T. (February 19, 2005). *A history of business ethics.* Markkula Center for Applied Ethics, Santa Clara University. Retrieved May 14, 2010, from http://www.scu.edu/ethics/practicing/focusareas/business/conference/presentations/business-ethics-history.html.

DeShazer, S. H., & Cohen, J. (1998). Mediating employment disputes under the disabilities act. *Dispute Resolution Journal, 53* (1), 28.

Dodson, M., & Jackson, D. (2004). Horizontal accountability in transitional democracies: The human rights ombudsman in El Salvador and Guatemala. *Latin American Politics and Society, 46* (4), 1–27.

Dossetor, J. B. Report of the ombudsman-ethicist, 2002. *Canadian Medical Association Journal, 169* (7), 674.

Drucker, P. (1973). *Management.* New York: Harper & Row.

Dvorkin, J.A. (January 20, 2004). *Why an ethics guide for public radio?* NPR. Retrieved 16 November 2009 from http://www.npr.org/yourturn.ombudsman/2004/040121.

Dyer, C. (2009). Patients can now sue and complain about NHS at the same time. *British Medical Journal (International Edition), 338* (7698), 792.

Dyer, C. Ensuring harmony in the workplace. *Human Resource Management International Digest, 14* (3), 40.

Energias de Portugal (EDP) (2009). *Ethics ombudsman.* Retrieved 16 November 2009 from http://www.edp.pt/en/aedp/provedordeetica/Pages/ProvedorEtica.aspx.

Estes, C., Zulman, D., Goldberg, S., & Ogawa, D. (2004). State long term care ombudsman programs: Factors associated with perceived effectiveness. *The Gerontologist, 44* (1), 104.

Ewing, D.W. (1977). What business thinks about employee rights. *Harvard Business Review, 55*(5).

Ewing, D. W. (1983). *Do it my way or you're fired! Employee rights and the changing role of management prerogatives.* New York: Wiley, 1983.

Farrand, J. (2001). An academic ombudsman. *Journal of Financial Regulation and Compliance, 9* (1), 11.

Fazzi, C. (2004). Employers share lessons on ADR. *Dispute Resolution Journal, 57*(4), 88.

Fazzi, C. (2004). Lessons in ADR from corporate America. *Dispute Resolution Journal, 58* (4), 86.

Featherstone, M. (2001). *The obscure politics of conspiracy theory.* Oxford, UK: Blackwell.

Filinson, R. (2001). Evaluation of the impact of a volunteer ombudsman program: The Rhode Island experience. *Journal of Elder Abuse & Neglect, 13* (4), 1.

Filley, A., & Grimes, A. (1967). The bases of power in decision processes. *Proceedings of the Annual Meeting of the Academy of Management,* 133–160.

Filley, A. C., House, R., & Kerr, S. (1976). *Managerial process and organizational behavior.* Glenview, IL: Scott Foresman.

Foegen, J. H. (1972). Ombudsman as complement to the grievance procedures. *Labor Law Journal, 23,* 289–294.

Freeman, I. C. (2000). Uneasy allies: Nursing home regulators and consumer advocates. *Journal of Aging & Social Policy, 11* (2–3), 127.

Friedery, R. (2006). The European ombudsman as a forum for dispute settlement. *Allam-es Jogtudomany, 47* (2), 291–316.

Gadlin, H. The Ombudsman: What's in a Name? *Negotiation Journal.* January 2000, *16.* (1) 37–48.

Gellhorn, W. (1966). *Ombudsmen and others: Citizen protectors in nine counties.* Cambridge, MA: Harvard University Press.

Getlin, J. (2000). Ombudsman. *Columbia Journalism Review, 38* (6). 51.

Gilad, S. (2008). Accountability or expectations management? The role of the ombudsman in financial regulation. *Law & Policy, 30* (2), 227.

Gilad, S. (2008). Exchange without capture: The UK financial ombudsman services's struggle for accepted domain. *Public Administration, 86* (4), 907–924.

Gilad, S. (2009). Juggling conflicting demands: The case of the UK financial ombudsman service. *Journal of Public Administration Research and Theory, 19* (3), 661.

Godfrey, D. (2005). Radical plan for investment trust regulation. *Journal of Financial Regulation and Compliance, 13* (2), 121.

Government of Quebec. *An act respecting health services and social services,* R.S.Q. Chapter 42, updated May 1, 2010, articles 29–59.

Green, K., Armstrong, J., Kirkpatrick, S., Koehler, J., Tetlock, P. (2007). The ombudsman: Value of expertise for forecasting decisions in conflicts/comment: combating common sense and meeting practitioner needs/comment: Experts who don't know they don't know/comment: Factors promoting forecasting accuracy among experts: Some multimethod convergence, interfaces. *Linthicum, 37* (3), 287.

Grodnitzky, A. S. (Spring 1994). Federal courts enforce alternative dispute resolution agreements. *Employment Relations Today, 21* (2), 251.

Groger, L. (2004). Doing good for the aged: Volunteers in an ombudsman program. *Contemporary Sociology, 33* (2), 175.

Gwyn, W.B. (1976). Obstacles within the office of economic opportunity to the elevation of experimental ombudsmen. *Public Administration* 54, 177.

Harrisburg Patriot News 1986.

Harrison, T., & Doerfel, M. (2006). Competitive and cooperative conflict communication climates: The influence of ombuds processes on trust and commitment to the organization. *International Journal of Conflict Management, 17* (2), 129.

Harrison, T., & Morrill, C. (2004). Ombuds processes and disputant reconciliation. *Journal of Applied Communication Research, 32* (4), 318.

Hayford, S. L. (2000). Alternative dispute resolution. *Business Horizons, 43* (1), 2.

Hawes, C., & Kimbell, A. (2008). Elder abuse in assisted living and residential care: Examining the performance of licensure agencies, long term car ombudsmen and applications. *The Gerontologist, 48,* 153.

Hellriegel, D., & Slocum, J.W. (2009–2010). *Organizational behavior.* 13th Ed. Mason, OH: Southwestern Cengage.

Hertogh, M. (2001). Coercion, cooperation, and control: Understanding the policy impact of administrative courts and the ombudsman in the Netherlands. *Law and Policy, 23,* Part 1, 47–68.

Hill, L. B. (1982). The citizen participation-representation roles of American ombudsmen. *Administration and Society, 13* (4), 405–433.

Hill, L. B. (1983). The self-perceptions of ombudsmen: A comparative survey. In G. E. Caiden

(Ed.), *International handbook of the ombudsman: Evolution and present function.* Westport, CT: Greenwood.

Hill, L. B. (2002). The ombudsman revisited: Thirty years of Hawaiian experience. *Public Administration Review,* January/February 2002, 6.2, (1), 24–41.

Hill, P. (1971). *Towards a new philosophy of management.* New York: Barnes & Noble.

Hirschhorn, L.; Krantz, J. (1982) "Unconscious planning in a natural work group: A case study in process consultation." *Human Relations* 35(10), 805–844.

Hoenig, J. K. (1993). Mediation in sexual harassment: Balancing the sensitivities. Dispute *Resolution Journal, 48* (4), 51.

Hoey, J., & Todkill, A. M. (14 May 2002). Complaints and conundrums: An ombudsman-ethicist for CMAJ. *Canadian Medical Association.Journal, 166* (10), 1281.

Hoffman, D., & Stallworth, L. (2008). Leveling the playing field for workplace neutrals: A proposal for achieving racial and ethnic diversity. *Dispute Resolution Journal, 63* (1), 37.

Hoffmann, F., & Megret, F. (2005). Fostering human rights accountability: An ombudsperson for the United Nations? *Global Governance, 11* (1), 43–63.

Hoffman, S. (1996). Mandatory arbitration: Alternative dispute resolution or coercive dispute suppression? *Berkeley Journal of Employment and Labor Law, 17* (1), 131.

Hogan, N. S. (1980). *Humanizing health care: Task of the patient representative.* Oradell, NJ: Medical Economics.

Hunt, Sara S. (1989). Working through ethical dilemmas in daily ombudsman practice, 1989. National Coalition for Nursing Home Reform.

Hyson, S., (2009a). *Specialty ombudsman offices: The new breed of structural heretics.* Paper prepared for presentation at the Annual Meeting of the Canadian Political Science Association, Carleton University, Ottawa, 27 May 2009, 1–14.

Hyson, S. (2009b). The ombudsman research project: The provincial and territorial ombuds-offices in Canada. In S. Hyson (Ed.), *Provincial and Territorial Ombudsman Offices in Canada.* (pp. 3–26). Toronto, Buffalo, London: University of Toronto Press.

International Ombudsman Association (2007). *Code of Ethics.* http://www.ombudsassociation. org/standards/Code_Ethics_v1–07.pdf.

International Ombudsman Association. (2009a). *Standards of Practice.* Retrieved from http:// www.ombudsassociation.org/standards/ioa.

International Ombudsman Association. (2009b). *Best practices, a supplement to IOA's standards of practice.* http://www.ombudsassociation.org/standards/IOA_Best_Practices_Version3_ 101309.pdf.

Jessar, K. (2005). The ombud's perspective: A critical analysis of the ABA 2004 ombudsman standards. *Dispute Resolution Journal, 60* (3), 56.

Jogerst, G., Daly, J., & Hartz, A. (2005). Ombudsman program characteristics related to nursing home abuse reporting. *Journal of Gerontological Social Work, 46* (1), 85.

Jurkowitz, M. (2005). Keeping government onside. *Organisation for economic cooperation development. The OECD Observer, 24,* 61.

Kassing, J. W., & Armstrong, T. A. (2002). Someone's going to hear about this. *Management Communication Quarterly: McQ, 16* (1), 39.

Kast, F. E., & Rosenzweig, J. E. (1985). *Organization and Management: A Systems and Contingency Approach.* New York: McGraw-Hill.

Keith, P. (2006). Nursing home administrators' attribution of antifacility bias to ombudsman programs. *Journal of Applied Gerontology, 25* (2), 120.

Keith, P. M. (2000) Correlates of primary orientations of volunteer ombudsmen in nursing facilities. *Journal of Aging Studies, 14* (4), 373.

Keith, P. M. (2001). Correlates of reported complaints by volunteers in an ombudsman program in nursing facilities. *Journal of Elder Abuse & Neglect, 13* (3), 43.

Keith, P. M. (2001). Role orientations, attributions to nursing facility personnel, and unresolved complaints of volunteers in an ombudsman program. *Journal of Gerontological Social Work, 351* (5).

Keith, P. M. (2005). Correlates of change in perceptions of nursing facilities among volunteers. *Journal of Applied Gerontology, 24,* 125.

Keith, P. M. (2005). Nursing home administrators' views of volunteers' work in an ombudsman program. *Journal of Aging Studies, 19* (4), 513.

Keith, P. M., & Schafer, R. B. (2002). Expected and actual difficulties of volunteer resident advocates in an ombudsman program. *Journal of Applied Gerontology, 21* (4), 421.

Kiechel, W. (January 6, 1986.) No word from on high. *Fortune,* 125–126.

Kirkham, R. (2003). Why ombudsmen are important: Helping long-term patients. *The Journal of Social Welfare & Family Law, 25* (3), 267.

Kirkham, R. (2004). The latest from the UK ombudsmen. *The Journal of Social Welfare & Family Law, 26* (4), 417.

Kirkham, R. (2004). Ombudsman's section. *The Journal of Social Welfare & Family Law, 26* (1), 89–98.

Kirkham, R. (2004). Prevention is better than litigation: The importance of good administration. *The Journal of Social Welfare & Family Law, 26* (3), 301.

Kirkham, R. (2004). When is it appropriate to use the ombudsman? *The Journal of Social Welfare & Family Law, 26* (2), 181.

Kirkham, R. (2004). A year in the life of the parliamentary ombudsman. *The Journal of Social Welfare & Family Law, 26* (1), 89.

Kirkham, R. (2005). A complainant's view of the local government ombudsman. *The Journal of Social Welfare & Family Law, 27* (3/4), 383.

Kirkham, R. (2005). The ombudsmen of Northern Ireland, Scotland and Wales. *The Journal of Social Welfare & Family Law, 27* (1), 79.

Kirkham, R. (2006). Finally, reform is on its way. *The Journal of Social Welfare & Family Law, 28* (1), 81.

Kirkham, R. (2006). A review of the public sector ombudsmen. *The Journal of Social Welfare & Family Law, 28* (3), 347.

Kirkham, R. (2008). Explaining the lack of enforcement power possessed by the ombudsman. *The Journal of Social Welfare & Family Law, 30* (3), 253.

Kirkham, R. (2008). Human rights and the ombudsmen. *The Journal of Social Welfare & Family Law, 30* (1), 75.

Kirkham, R. (2008). Quiet moves toward proportionate dispute resolution: The law commission's consultation paper on administrative redress. *The Journal of Social Welfare & Family Law, 30* (2), 163.

Klaas, B. S., & DeNisi, A. S. (1989). Managerial reactions to employee dissent: The impact of grievance activity on performance ratings. *Academy of Management Journal, 32* (4), 705.

Laskov, H. (1985). The military ombudsman in Israel. In G. E. Caiden (ed.), *International handbook of the ombudsman: Evolution and present function.* Westport, CT: Greenwood.

LeBaron, M. (2008). *Watchdogs and wise ones in winter lands: The practice spectrum of Canadian ombudsman.* Paper presented at the 2008 Forum of Canadian Ombudsman (FCO) Liz Hoffman Ombudsperson Research Award Paper, 1–31.

Levine, G. (2004). Administrative justice and the ombudsman — concepts and codes in British Columbia and Ontario. *Canadian Journal of Administrative Law & Practice, 17* (3), 239.

Levine, G. J. (2009). Recapturing the spirit, enhancing the project: The ombudsman plan in twenty-first century Canada. In S. Hyson (Ed.), *Provincial and territorial ombudsman offices in Canada.* (pp. 292–307). Toronto, Buffalo, London: University of Toronto Press, 292–307.

Lilienthal, P. (2002). If you give your employees a voice, do you listen? *The Journal for Quality and Participation, 25* (3), 38.

Lippit, G. L. (1975). The trainer's role as an internal consultant. *Journal of European Training, 4* (5), 237–246.

Lipsky, D. B., & Avgar, A. C. (2005). Commentary: Research on employment dispute resolution: Toward a new paradigm. *Conflict Resolution Quarterly, 22* (1,2), 175.

Lo, C. W-H., & Wickins, R. J. (2002). Towards an accountable and quality public administration in Hong Kong: Redressing administrative grievances through the ombudsman. *International Journal of Public Administration, 25* (6), 737–72.

Lublin, J. S. (1987). In Britain, two women may lead but sexism rules. *Wall Street Journal,* March 13, 1987, p. 1.

MacMillan, J. (2008). "Whats in a name? Use of the term ombudsman." Commonwealth ombudsman website.

Magnette, P. (2003). Between parliamentary control and the rule of law: The political role of the ombudsman in the European Union. *Journal of European Public Policy, 10* (5), 677–94.

Marin, A. (2005). *DND/CF ombudsman—The way forward: A blueprint for an effective and credible DNC/CF ombudsman (Cont'd).* Retrieved March 26, 2009, from website of Canadian Department of National Defence/Defense nationale, http://www.ombudsman/mdn.ca/rep-rap/sr/sf-aa/rep-rap-05-eng.asp. 22 pages.

Marin, A. (September 12–15, 2006). *Innovate or perish.* Keynote address given to the twenty-seventh annual Conference of the United States Ombudsman Association. Ombudsman Ontario website, retrieved April 19, 2010 from http://www.ombudsman.on.ca/en/media/speeches/2006/innovate-or-perish.aspx.

Marin, A. (updated April 20, 2007). *Special reports: The way forward: A credible review and investigative process.* Retrieved May 14, 2010, from http://www.ombudsman.mdn.ca/rep rap/sr-rs/wf-aa/rep-rap-06-eng.asp.

Marin, A. (May 29, 2008). *Vital watchdog vs. paper tiger: What kind of ombudsman do you want to be?* Closing remarks to Association of Canadian College and University Ombudspersons, Halifax, Nova Scotia. Office of the Ombudsman of Ontario. Retrieved May 14 2010 from http://www.ombudsmanforum.ca/documents/speeches/marin_andre/uoa_2008-05-29_e.asp.

Marzick, A. M. (2007). The foster care ombudsman: Applying an international concept to help prevent institutional abuse of America's foster youth. *Family Court Review, 45* (3), 506.

Masi, Peter (2006). Forgoing ethics is not a wise choice for good leaders, effective governments, harmonious societies and prosperous nations in Melanesia: A perspective from PNG. Paper presented by ombudsman Peter Masi, OCPNG, on the occasion of the Savenaca Siwatibau Memorial Lecture Series, Port Vil, Vanuatu, 23 August. Retrieved April 28, 2010, from www.paclii.org/.

Mavris, C. I. (2001). The ombudsman institution in small states: The case of Cyprus. *Public Organization Review, 1* (2), 279.

McCabe, D. M. (1997). Alternative dispute resolution and employee voice in nonunion employment: An ethical analysis of organizational due process procedures and mechanisms — the case of the United States. *Journal of Business Ethics, 16* (3), 349.

McCabe, D. M., & Lewin, D. (1992). Employee voice: A human resource management perspective. *California Management Review, 34* (3), 112.

McConnell, J. S. (2004). News ombudsmen in North America. *Journalism and Mass Communication Quarterly, 81* (2), 456.

McDermott, P. E. (1995). Survey of 92 key companies: Using ADR to settle employment disputes. *Dispute Resolution Journal, 50* (1), 8.

McGillis, D. (Spring 1980). The quiet revolution in American dispute settlement. *Harvard Law School Bulletin,* 20–26.

McGillis, D. (1982). Minor Dispute Processing: A Review of Recent Developments." In R. Tomasic and M. Feeley, (Eds.) *Neighborhood Justice.* New York: Longman.

Meade, R. E. (2000). Resolving workplace disputes through mediation. *The CPA Journal, 70* (9), 60.

Mecanovic, I. (2000). Child's rights and their protection [Ombudsman for the protection of children's rights]. *Pravni Vjesnik, 16* (1–2), 7–28.

Merricks, W. (2007). The financial ombudsman service: Not just an alternative to court. *Journal of Financial Regulation and Compliance, 15* (2), 135.

Meyers, C. (2000). Creating an effective newspaper ombudsman position. *Journal of Mass Media Ethics, 15* (4), 248.

Meyers, J., Alpert, J. L., & Fleisher, B. D. (1983). *Models of consultation: Training in consultation.* Springfield, IL: Thomas.

Mintzberg, H. (1975). The manager's role: Folklore and fact. *Harvard Business Review.* July-August, 49–61.

Mitroff, I. (1983). *Stakeholders of the organizational mind.* San Francisco: Jossey-Bass.

Mollah, A. H., & Uddin, N. (2004). Ombudsman for Bangladesh: Theory and reality. *International Journal of Public Administration, 27* (111–12), 979–1002.

Montoro-Rodriguez, J., & Regensburger, A. (2004). Complaint reports from the long-term care ombudsman program in northeast Ohio: Improving the collection of data. *The Gerontologist, 44* (1), 158.

Morgan, G. (2006). *Images of Organization.* Thousand Oaks, CA.; Sage.

Morris, P. E. (2008). The financial ombudsman service and the hunt review: Continuing evolution in dispute resolution. *The Journal of Business Law, 8,* 785.

Munch, W. (2004). The ombudsman in the UN secretariat: A contribution to the modernization of personnel management in the United Nations. *Vereinte Nationen, 52* (4), 131–135.

Nabatchi, T., Bingham, L., & Good, D. (2007). Organizational justice and workplace mediation: A six-factor model. *International Journal of Conflict Management, 18* (2), 148.

Naisbitt, J. (1982). *Megatrends.* New York: Warner.

Naisbitt, J., & Aburdene, P. (1985). *Reinventing the corporation.* New York: Warner.

Nelson, W., Netting, E., Huber, R., & Borders, K. (2004). Factors affecting volunteer ombudsman effort and service duration: Comparing active and resigned volunteers. *Journal of Applied Gerontology, 23* (3), 309.

Nemeth, N., & Sanders, C. (2001). Meaningful discussion of performance missing. *Newspaper Research Journal, 22* (1), 52.

Netting, F. E., et al. (2000). Volunteer and paid ombudsmen investigating complaints in six states: A natural triaging. *Nonprofit and Voluntary Sector Quarterly, 29* (3), 419.

Netting, F. E., et al. (2002). Ombudsman standards. *Administrative Law Review, 54* (2), 535.

Netting, F. E., et al. (2002). Ombudsmen to help consumers regarding nursing home quality. *Health care financing review, 23* (4), 205.

Oklahoma Christian University (2008). *Ethics ombudsman.* Retrieved November 16, 2009, from http://www.oc.edu/ethics/.

Olson, F. C. (1984). How peer review works at control data. *Harvard Business Review.* November–December.

Ombudsman for Banking Services and Investments. (2008). *Our work.* Annual review 2008. Retrieved April 19, 2010, from http://www.obsi.ca/UI/AboutUs/OurWork.aspx.

Ontario Patient Representatives' Association. Retrieved April 19, 2010, from http://ontariopatientreps.ca/.

Organization Development Institute 1981.

Organization of News Ombudsmen. (April 19, 2010). *What is ONO?* Retrieved April 19, 2010, from http://www.newsombudsmen.org/what.htm.

Osorno Z., & Angel, M. (2003). The role of the ombudsman in democratic states. *Dereito: Revista Xuridica da Universidade de Santiago de Compostela, 12* (2) 121–9.

Owers, A. (2006). The protection of prisoners' rights in England and Wales. *European Journal on Criminal Policy and Research, 12* (2), 85.

Pardue, M. J. (2006). Public editor # 1: The collected columns (with reflections, reconsiderations, and even a few retractions) of the first ombudsman of the New York Times. *Newspaper Research Journal, 27* (4), 96.

Pegram, T. (2008). Accountability in hostile times: The case of the Peruvian human rights ombudsman. *Journal of Latin American Studies, 40* (1), 51.

Persson, D. I. (2004). Volunteer ombudsmen in the nursing home: Obstacles to retention. *Journal of Aging Studies, 18* (2), 205.

Peterman, N. The patient care ombudsman's new reality. *American Bankruptcy Institute Journal, 26* (6), 22.

Peters, A. (2003). Human rights commissions and ombudsman offices. *Common Market Law Review, 40* (5), 1303.

Peters, A. (2005). The European ombudsman and the European constitution. *Common Market Law Review, 42* (3), 69.

Peters, T. J., & Waterman, R. H. (1994). *In Search of Excellence.* New York: Harper and Row.

Plaisance, P. L. (2000). The concept of media accountability reconsidered. *Journal of Mass Media Ethics, 15* (4), 257.

Press Council of Ireland and Office of the Press Ombudsman. Retrieved April 9, 2010, from http://www.presscouncil.ie/.

Preston, N., Samford C., & Connors, C., in Peter Masi (2006), retrieved May 16, 2010, from http://www.paclii.org//cgi-bin/disp.pl./pg/OC/Speeches/Speech1.htm?query=peter masi ocpng 23 august 2006.

Pugh, S. (1978). The ombudsman: Jurisdiction, powers and practice. *Public Administration,* 56, 127–138.

Radice, S. (2008). Let's have more private sector ombudsmen. *The Ombudsman: the Newsletter of the British and Irish Ombudsman Association,* August 2008, *35.* Electronic version.

Ravich, R. (1975). Patient relations. *Hospitals,* 49, 107–109.

Ravich, R., & Rehr, H. (1974). Ombudsman program provides feedback. *Hospitals,* 48, 63–67.

Reb, J., et al. (2006). Different wrongs, different remedies? Reactions to organizational remedies after procedural and interactional injustice. *Personnel Psychology,* 59 (1), 31.

Redmond, A., Daigneault, M. & Williams, R. (June 2006). *Ombudsman to the rescue.* In Board Member. Retrieved May 14, 2010, from http:www.redmondwilliamsassoc.com.

Redmond, A., & Williams, R. (2003). *Benefits of an ombuds program to corporate governance.* Directors Monthly, National Association of Corporate Directors. Retrieved May 16, 2009, from http://www.redmondwilliamsassoc.com/articles/Benefits%20of%20an%20Ombuds %20Program%20to%20Corporate%20Governance-Board%20Dir.pdf.

Redmond, A., & Williams, R. (2004). Enter the watchmen: The critical role of an ombuds program in corporate governance. *Risk Management, 51* (9), 48–54.

Regis, C. (2004). Enhancing patients' confidence in access to health care: The Ontario or Quebec way? *Health Law Journal, 12,* 243.

The Removals Industry Ombudsman Scheme. (n.d.). Retrieved May 16, 2010, from http://www. removalsombudsman.org.uk/.

Reuss, H. S., & Anderson, S. V. (1966). The ombudsman: Tribune of the people. *Annals of the American Academy of Political and Social Science,* 363, 44–51.

Richey, B., et al. (2001). The effect of arbitration program characteristics on applicants' intentions toward potential employers. *Journal of Applied Psychology,* 86 (5), 1006.

Rief, L. C. (2004). *The ombudsman, good governance and the international human rights system.* Lieden, Boston: Martinus Nijhoff.

Rillier, E. (March, 1987). A man for all reasons. *The Bank's World,* 15–18.

Robbins, L., & Deane, W. B. (1986). The corporate ombudsman: A new approach to conflict management. *Negotiation Journal,* 2 (2), 195–205.

Ross, K. (1986). Providing staff a neutral ear. *Hartford Courant,* December 17, 1986, p. 6.

Rowat, D. C. (2002). Righting wrongs: The ombudsman in six continents. *Public Administration, 80* (4), 818.

Rowat, D. C. (2003). The new private-sector ombudsman. *Policy Options/Options Politiques,* (November 2003), 46–48.

Rowat, D. C. (2007). The American distortion of the ombudsman concept and its influence on Canada. *Canadian Public Administration/Administration publique du Canada, 50* (1), 42–52.

Rowe, M. P. (1987). The corporate ombudsman: An overview and analysis. *Negotiation Journal, 3* (2), 127–140.

Rowe, M. P., & Baker, M. (1984) Are you hearing enough employee concerns? *Harvard Business Review, 62* (3), 127–135.

Ruhl, K. (2007). The politics of human rights in the EU. *Espiral: Estudios sobre Estado y Sociedad, 14* (40), 39–62.

Sandford, J. W. (1985). A troubleshooter at Fairchild unit. *New York Times,* 32.

Schein, E. H. (1969). *Process consultation: Its role in organization development.* Reading, MA: Addison-Wesley.

Schein, E. H. (1985, 2004). *Organizational culture and leadership.* San Francisco: Jossey-Bass.

Scheirer, M. A. (1981). *Program implementation: The organizational context.* Beverely Hills, CA: Sage.

Seneviratne, M. (2000). The European ombudsman: The first term. *The Journal of Social Welfare & Family Law, 22* (3), 329.

Seneviratne, M . (2000). The local government ombudsman annual report 1998–99. *The Journal of Social Welfare & Family Law, 22* (2), 209.

Seneviratne, M . (2000). The parliamentary ombudsman's annual report 1998–99 (HC 572). *The Journal of Social Welfare & Family Law, 22* (1), 89.

Seneviratne, M. (2001). Homelessness and the local government ombudsman. *The Journal of Social Welfare & Family Law, 23* (3), 341–51.

Seneviratne, M. (2001). Ombudsman for children. *The Journal of Social Welfare & Family Law, 23* (2), 217.

Seneviratne, M . (2002). "Joining up" the Scottish ombudsmen. *The Journal of Social Welfare & Family Law, 24* (1), 89–98.

Seneviratne, M. (2002). Ombudsman's section. *The Journal of Social Welfare & Family Law, 24* (3), 335.

Seneviratne, M . (2002). Ombudsmen and police complaints. *The Journal of Social Welfare & Family Law, 24* (2), 195.

Seneviratne, M., & Cracknell, S. (2000). Local authorities, nuisance neighbours and the local government ombudsman. *The Journal of Social Welfare & Family Law, 22* (4), 451.

Senge, P. M. (1990). *The fifth discipline:The art and practice of the learning organization.* New York: Currency/Doubleday.

Serra, G. & Pinney, N. (2004). Casework, issues and voting in state legislative elections: A district analysis. *The Journal of Legislative Studies, 10* (4), 32–46.

Shelton, R. L. (2000). The institutional ombudsman: A university case study. *Negotiation Journal, 16* (1), 81.

Sherwyn, D. S., & Tracey, J. B. (2001). Mandatory arbitration of employment disputes: Implications for policy and practice. *Cornell Hotel and Restaurant Administration Quarterly, 42* (5), 60.

Sibbald, B. (2002). CMAJ appoints first ethicist/ombudsman. *Canadian Medical Association Journal, 166* (10), 1327.

Silver, I. (May-June 1967). The corporate ombudslnan. *Harvard Business Review,* 77–87.

Slate II, W. K. (1996). Violence in the workplace: Looking for ADR solutions. *Dispute Resolution Journal, 51* (1), 2.

Société des alcools du Québec. (August 2008). *Ombudsman, business relations and employees: In all fairness.* [Brochure].

Solomon, N. (2000). Deja vu at NPR. *The Humanist, 60* (3), 3.

Song, W., & Sala, V. D. (2008). Eurosceptics and Europhiles in accord: The creation of the European ombudsman as an institutional isomorphism. *Policy & Politics, 36* (4), 481–495.

Stallworth, L. E., & Malin, M. H. (1994). Workforce diversity. *Dispute Resolution Journal, 49* (2), 27.

Stallworth, L. E., & Stroh, L. K. (1996). Who is seeking to use ADR? Why do they choose to do so? *Dispute Resolution Journal, 51* (1), 30.

Stieber, C. (2000). 57 varieties: Has the ombudsman concept become diluted? *Negotiation Journal, 16* (1), 49.

Stoddart, J. (2006). Cherry picking among apples and oranges: Refocusing current debate about the merits of the ombuds-model under PIPEDA. *The Canadian Business Law Journal, 44* (1), 1.

Stopper, W. G. (2003). *Restoring trust: HR's role in corporate governance.* William G. Stopper (Ed). New York: Walker Group by The Human Resources Planning Society.

Stuhmcke, A. (2002). The rise of the Australian telecommunications industry ombudsman. *Telecommunications Policy, 26* (1), 69.

Stuhmcke, A. (2008). Changing relations between government and citizen: Administrative law and the work of the Australian Commonwealth ombudsman. *Australian Journal of Public Administration, 67* (3), 321.

Suksi, M. (2005). Case C-234/02 P, European ombudsman v. Frank Lamberts. *Common Market Law Review, 42* (6), 1765.

Sungurov, A. Y. (2002). From the experience of the development of the ombudsman institution in regions of Russia. *Polis: politicheskie issledovaniya, 12* (2), 147.

Tengilimoglu, D., & Kisa, A. (2005). Conflict management in public university hospitals in Turkey: A pilot study. *The Health Care Manager, 24* (1), 55.

Thacker, S. (2009). Good intentions gone astray: How the ABA standards affect ombudsmen. *Journal of the International Ombudsman Association, 2* (1), 65–88.

Thomas, D. (2001). Cross-order financial services and alternative dispute resolution in the European economic area. *Journal of Financial Regulation and Compliance 9* (2), 104.

Tosi, H.L. (2009). *Theories of organization.* Thousand Oaks, CA. Sage.

Trisler, S. (1984). Grievance procedures: Refining the open-door policy. *Employment Relations Today, 11* (3), 323.

Trist, E. (June 1981). *The Evolution of Sociotechnical Systems.* Toronto: Quality of Working Life Center.

Tsadiras, A. (2008). Unravelling Ariadnes' thread: The European ombudsman's investigative powers. *Common Market Law Review, 45* (3), 757.

Uggla, F. (2004). The ombudsman in Latin America. *Journal of Latin American Studies, 36* (3), 423–250. CSA Worldwide Political Science Abstracts.

Umstot D. D., Mitchell, T. R., & Bell, C. H. (October 1978). Goal setting and job enrichment: An integrated approach to job design. *Academy of Management Review,* 877

University of Hartford (n.d.). Office of the Ombudsman. Welcome to the Office of the Ombudsman. Retrieved May 16, 2010, from http://www.hartford.edu/ombudsman/.

Van Gramberg, B., & Teicher, J. (2006). Managing neutrality and impartiality in workplace conflict resolution: The dilemma of the HR manager. *Asia Pacific Journal of Human Resources, 44* (2), 197.

Van Roosbroek, S., & Van de Walle, S. (2008). The relationship between ombudsman, government, and citizens: A survey analysis. *Negotiation Journal, 24* (3).

Varuhas, J. (2009). Governmental rejections of ombudsman findings: What role for the courts? *The Modern Law Review, 72 (1),* 102.

Verkuil, P. R. (1975). The ombudsman and the limits of the adversary system. *Columbia Law Review, 75,* 845–861

Viitanen, K. (2009). Finland. *The Annals of the American Academy of Political and Social Science, 622,* 209–219.

Volhner, H. M., & Mills, D. (1966). (Eds.). *Professionalization.* Englewood Cliffs, NJ: Prentice-Hall.

Wagner, M. L. (2000). The organizational ombudsman as change agent. *Negotiation Journal, 16* (1), 99.

Watson, D. S., & Cooper, T. A. (2002). AORN creates new tools to improve member service, names long-time member as ombudsman. *Association of Operating Room Nurses/AORN Journal, 76* (5), 760.

Weber, M. (1947). *The theory of social and economic organizations,* trans. by A. M. Henderson and Talcott Parsons. Fairlawn, NJ: Oxford University Press.

Weiss, C. H. (1981). Use of social science research in organizations: The constraints repertoire theory. In H. D. Stein (Ed.), *Organization and the human services.* Philadelphia: Temple University Press.

Werner, W. B., Hardigree, C. E., & Okada, S. (2005). Phantom benefits: Reconsidering mandatory employment arbitration. *Cornell Hotel and Restaurant Administration Quarterly, 46* (3), 363.

Westin, A. F., & Salisbury, S. (Eds.). (1981). *Individual rights in the corporation.* New York: Pantheon.

Whitford, A. B., & Yates, J. (2002). Volunteerism and social capital in policy implementation: Evidence from the long-term care ombudsman program. *Journal of Aging & Social Policy, 14* (3–4), 61–73.

Wilburn, K. O. (1998). Employment disputes: Solving them out of court. *Management Review, 87* (3), 17.

Williams, J. (2004). Canadian financial services ombudsmen: The role of reputational persuasion. *Banking & Finance Law Review, 20 (1),* 41.

Williams, R.; Redmond, A. (2003). "Organizational Ombudsman Program: A Government

Trust Strategy." In W. Stopper (Ed.) *Restoring Trust: HR's Role in Corporate Governance.* N.Y.: The Walker Group.

Winterbauer, S. H. (1994). When things aren't what they seem: Labor issues in the nonunion workplace. *Employee Relations Law Journal, 20* (2), 189.

The World Bank (2010). The World Bank's ombuds services. Retrieved May 16, 2010, from http://web.worldbank.org/WBSITE/EXTERNAL/EXTABOUTUS/ORGANIZA TION/ORGUNITS/EXTCRS/EXTOMBUDSMAN/0,,contentMDK:20242799~menu PK:64166186~pagePK:64166161~piPK:64166140~theSitePK:468444,00.html.

Yokoi-Arai, M. (2004). A comparative analysis of the financial ombudsman systems in the UK and Japan. *Journal of International Banking Regulation, 5 (4),* 333.

Zack, A. M., & Duffy, M. T. (1996). ADR and employment discrimination. *Dispute Resolution Journal, 51* (4), 28.

Zecevic, R. (2006). Experiences of the ombudsmen in Sweden and Norway. *Medunarodni Problemi/International Problems, 58* (3), 306–25.

Zhang, X. (2006). Utilitarian institution and institutional welfare: An analysis of the ombudsman in HK. *Hangzhou Shifan Xueyuan Xuebao Shehui Kexue Ban/Journal of Hangzhou Teachers College (Social Sciences Edition), 28* (6), 52–56. CSA Worldwide Political Science Abstracts.

Ziegenfuss, J. T. (1980). Responding to people problems. *Business Horizons, 23* (2), 73–76.

Ziegenfuss, J. T. (1982). Do your managers think in organizational 3D? *Sloan Management Review, 24* (1), 55–59

Ziegenfuss, J. T. (1985a) *DRGs and hospital impact: An organizational systems analysis.* New York: McGraw-Hill.

Ziegenfuss, J.T. (1985b). Handling employee complaints. *Employee Services Management, 28* (4), 26–29.

Ziegenfuss, J. T. (1985c). *Patient/client/employee complaint programs: An organizational systems model.* Springfield, IL: Thomas.

Ziegenfuss, J. T. (1987). Corporate complaint programs make gains from gripes. *Personnel Journal, 66* (4), 40–42.

Ziegenfuss, J.T. (1988). *Organizaitonal Troubleshooters: Resolving Problems with Custormers and Employees.* San Francisco, CA.: Jossey Bass.

Ziegenfuss, J.T. (1993). *The Organizational Path to Health Care Quality.* Ann Arbor, MI.: Health Administrative Press.

Ziegenfuss, J.T. (April 1995). Corporate ombudsman at work in four fields: Health, banking, utilities and transportation. *National Productivity Review,* 97–109.

Ziegenfuss, J.T. (Summer 1998). The ombudsman's contribution to quality. *American Journal of Medical Quality, 13* (2).

Ziegenfuss, J.T. (February 1999). Patient representative and ombudsman programs: Organizational connections and unfinished work. Invited paper and presentation at Citizen Participation: A Challenge to Different Health Care Systems. Bonn, Germany.

Ziegenfuss, James T. (2002). *Organization and management problem solving: A systems and consulting approach.* Thousand Oaks, CA: Sage.

Ziegenfuss, J.T. (2006). *Strategic planning: cases, concepts and lessons.* 2nd ed. Lanham, MD: Rowman & Littlefield/University Press.

Ziegenfuss, James T. (2007). *Customer friendly: The organizational architecture of service.* Lanham, MD: Rowman & Littlefield/University Press.

Ziegenfuss, J. T., Charette, J., & Guenin, M. (1984). The patients' rights representative program: Design of an ombudsman service for mental patients. *Psychiatric Quarterly, 56* (1), 3–12.

Ziegenfuss, J.T., O'Rourke, P. (1995). Patient ombudsmen and total quality improvement: An examination of fit. *Joint Commission Journal on Quality Improvement, 21* (3), 133–142

Ziegenfuss, J. T., Robbins, L., & Rowe, M. (1987). *Corporate Ombudsmen: An Exploratory National Survey of Purposes and Activities.* Harrisburg, PA: Center for the Quality of Working Life, Pennsylvania State University, and Corporate Ombudsman Association.

Zimmerman, P. (2004). ADR and the workplace. *The CPA Journal, 74* (4), 14.

Index

Ackoff, R.L. 52, 85, 125
Addison 52
adjudication 24, 52–53, 59
age discrimination problem 9
Alderson, M. 38
Alpert, J.L. 56, 57
Alternative Dispute Resolution 13
American Airlines 53
American Electric Power 53
American Express 17, 38
American Hospital Association 143
analytical skills 184
Anheuser-Busch 36
Argyris, C. 54
Asahi Shimbun 39
authority: charismatic 86; hierarchy of 85; professional 79; rational/legal 89; traditional 88

Baker, M. 49, 50, 52, 53, 54, 68
Baylor University 33
behavior patterns 172
Bell, C.H. 59
Bell Laboratories 36, 68
Bill of Rights, AHA 143
Binham, L.B. 6
Blue Shield 68
Brewer, B. 7
The British and Irish Ombudsman Association 38, 143
Business Week 17

Caiden, G.E. 19, 48
Canadian Broadcasting Corporation/Radio Canada (RDI) 39, 40
Canadian Franchise Association 39
Carson, S. 20
cases: boss's home repair 157–158; chemical company 37–38; citizen's complaint 116–117; data fudging 22, 37, 101, 106–107;

discrimination 108–109; employee allegation of malfeasance 148–149; fired for refusing unethical practice 47; gas company customer 118; hospital housestaff ethical issues 130; hospital unit, nursing complaint 35–36; interdepartmental conflict 107–108; news media 40–41; patient care and diagnosis 154–155; patient ethical issue 150–153; patient treatment 20, 35–36, 115–116; personal problems: addiction and marriage 113–114; physical working conditions 111–112; prisoners 116; privacy violation 22; production sabotage 114; sabotage 26–27; salary dispute 112–113; sexual harassment 16, 110–111; sports activity 27–28, 179; suicide threat 26–27; supervisory conflict 109–110; travel denial (employee) 164–165; university student 33–34, 147–148; welfare recipient 117–118
centralization 78
Charette, J. 22
charismatic authority 86
cheating 28
Chemical Bank 17
Cherns, A.B. 180
City of Toronto 31
Cline, A. 39
Coca-Cola Bottling Company 38
coercive power 31
Colvin, A.J.S. 7
communication: benefits and outcomes of 80; open 13; as ombudsman function 48–50; ombudsman program and 80; purposes of 59
communication skills 183
competition, destructive 26–28
complaint(s): customer 12–13, 22, 114–115, 179–180; employee 11; identifying 25; investigation/intervention 25; monitoring

201